When Lawyers Write

When Lawyers Write

Richard H. Weisberg
Professor of Law
Benjamin N. Cardozo School of Law
Yeshiva University

Little, Brown and Company
Boston   Toronto

Library of Congress Catalog Card No. 86-082696
ISBN 0-316-92871-2

ALP

Published simultaneously in Canada by Little, Brown & Company (Canada) Limited

Printed in the United States of America

To my parents, Philip and Hazel Weisberg

Summary of Contents

I

Apologia and Introduction 1

II

Basic Skills for Busy Lawyers 49

III

Awareness of Audience Elaborated 85

IV

Organization 145

V

Writing in the Special Context of Law Practice 189

Contents

3

The Foundations of Effective Writing   31

II

Basic Skills for Busy Lawyers   49

4

Mastery of the Sentence: Keeping the Subject in Mind   51

Contents

5

The Vital Role of the Verb   61

6

Punctuation: Simple Rules about Commas and Other Helpful Pauses   71

III

Awareness of Audience Elaborated   85

7

Appropriateness: Recognizing the Spectrum of Your Writing   87

8

Losing Touch with Your Lay Reader   103

9

Universally Inappropriate Legal Writing Habits   111

16

Moving On Up: Learning to Edit Another's Writing

17

At the Top: Professional Responsibility and Taking Steps to Improve the Breed of Writing Lawyers

18

Special Tips for Various Kinds of Practice

19

Judicial Writing 253

APPENDIX

I

Twenty-three Rules of Legal Writing 265

APPENDIX

II

Testing What You Know: Some General Exercises on Legal Writing 269

Preface

I have attempted in what follows to place general writing questions in the specific context of legal writing and legal writing in the yet more precise context of the practitioner's workday. To that extent, although there are many works on writing, and even on writing for lawyers, I believe this book is unique.

The source of almost all of my examples is the work of some 1000 lawyers with whom I have consulted over a five-year period (1979-1984). Many were excellent writers, but few wrote flawlessly. Of the thousands of documents I reviewed during those years, approximately 350 serve as samples here; all have been changed sufficiently to make the actual sources unrecognizable (probably even to the original writer). But the authenticity of the practicing context for this writing will impress lawyers immediately and, I hope, challenge and stimulate them to reflect on their own skills.

Lessons or rules that might otherwise seem abstract appear here in the concrete atmosphere of daily practice, with all its pressures. Nonetheless, rules abound. Aside from specific rules of grammar, punctuation, verb-use, and so on, 23 basic rules of practitioner writing dot the book; these are set forth separately in Appendix I. There are also three charts, two dealing with varieties of appropriate tone and style (page 91) and the third with transition words to move from paragraph to paragraph (page 163).

The structure of the book is both simple and complex, straightforward and gyre-like. Of the five substantive parts, Part I places legal writing in its historical and contemporary setting; Parts II-IV deal with technical writing skills; and Part V situates the writing challenge to lawyers in various specialties and various career phases. (Exercises follow Parts II-IV and also appear in abundance in Appendix II. Suggestions about the exercises following Parts II-IV appear after the appendices. Likewise, many of the exercises in Appendix II have been analyzed elsewhere in the book.)

Few essential topics escape multiple treatment, however. Thus, on one level, writing problems are divided into five major areas. These are punctuation, grammar, syntax, word choice, and organization (see Chapter 3). These are in turn developed into subdivisions as follows: punctuation subsumes usage of commas, semicolons, parentheses, hyphens, and so on (Chapter 6); grammar treats noun and verb usage and agreement, etc. (Chapters 4 and 5, part of Chapter 9); syntax covers the placement of words within sentences and thus problems of dangling participles, prepositional misuse, confusion of tenses, that vs. which, and parallel structure difficulties (Chapters 9 and 10); word choice includes discussions of tone, jargon, usage, passivity (Chapters 7 and 8); and organization envelopes the concepts of document-wide as well as paragraph architectonics and planning (Part IV).

On another level, though, these same concerns are approached through analysis of particular kinds of legal writing: general correspondence, memoranda, contracts, conveyances, wills, briefs, and so on. Thus the recognized and more subtle "pet peeves" of legal writing are attacked from a number of directions. Discussions of loss of referent, impersonal and vague sentence structures, latinisms, or loss of organizational control highlight more than one technical or contextual chapter.

Verbosity, for another example, comes under attack in various sections of the book. Most noteworthy to the reader, perhaps, will be the treatment in Chapters 4 and 5. There I make the claim that the first cause of lawyerlike wordiness is poor *subject* (not verb!) choice. This claim runs against the grain of most recent analyses of our profession's wordy proclivities and allows the reader to see the effect of weak noun choice upon the verbs (§5.2) that follow. But I also treat verbosity in §8.1 (jargon), §§9.2 and 9.3 (various redundancies), and §§14.3 and 17.2 (boilerplate).

The structure thus allows the reader to emphasize at will either areas of difficulty or contextual kinds of writing, while it also adds system and spice to the analysis of pervasive writing difficulties. Use of both the Table of Contents and the Index will permit the reader to thumb through various treatments of any single topic. Thus the internal memorandum of law, for example, will be cited for extensive coverage in Chapters 3, 7, 11, and 15.

For the general reader seeking pragmatic guidelines, I recommend skimming the book consecutively but then turning to the chapter or subsection that covers a particular demand. These will change, of course, from situation to situation. The recent law school graduate who once stressed Chapter 15 may well wish to proceed to Chapter 16 and then Chapter 17 as his or her career advances. Lawyers who feel at home with punctuation may want to skip Chapter 6 in favor of tackling parallelism (Chapter 10) or tips on preparing outlines (Chapter 13). Judges should read Chapter 19.

At the heart of the book, however, is a single concept: *awareness of audience*. If lawyers, always thorough and often analytically brilliant, will simply recognize that writing always means writing *for* (another), their most pervasive stumbling blocks will all but crumble. Thus no reader should skip the audience-related chunks of the book, Chapters 3, 7, 8, 10, 11, and 14.

A single book cannot pretend to cover every facet of legal writing. Drafting, for example, while by no means ignored (§§7.2.4 and 18.1), raises extensive issues best covered in such specialized texts as those by Reed Dickerson and others. A helpful bibliography follows the appendices.

The perceptive reader will quickly note that I have chosen to use masculine nouns and pronouns in odd-numbered chapters and feminine equivalents in even-numbered chapters. This convention spares my reader the cumbersome devices proposed by writers these days to prove their goodwill. It also conveys the simple fact that, in writing talent as in every other professional domain, women and men excel equally.

Happy reading! Satisfying writing!

Richard H. Weisberg

April 1987

Acknowledgments

Many individuals and groups have helped me to understand the particular problems associated with legal writing and the often subtle ways in which those problems must be addressed. Among those groups are my "Law and Literature II" seminars at the Cardozo School of Law (1982-1985) and the many professional groups with which I have met through the years. Among those individuals, all of whom should receive credit for this book's merits and none of whom shares any blame for its weaknesses, I would mention the following: Alan Cooper, Eliane Dezon-Jones, Carl Felsenfeld, Leslie Gerwin, Hugh Murtagh, Diane Richards, Cheryl Weisberg, and Dana Wilson.

I thank these people warmly.

When Lawyers Write

I

Apologia and Introduction

1

In Defense of Traditional Legal Writing

> *Film Director:* Let's make sure that her voice is in sync with the film.
>
> *Film Producer:* Sync—shmink! Why don't you movie guys use ordinary words?
>
> *Film Director:* And if we did, would you understand us anyway?
>
> —Jerry Lewis, *The Errand Boy*

§1.1 THE PLACE OF TRADITION

"The demised premises"; "release, relinquish, and remit"; "thus revoking all wills by me heretofore made"; "in testimony whereof." Why would anyone write this way? The tendency, in a rootless age with small regard for the elderly (either corporeal or parchmental), is to answer: "No one would or should." Reform has descended on legal language, and those who strive solely for simplicity, plainness, or just novelty would wipe the slate clean. Banned forever from the reformer's lexicon are all latinisms, redundant verb clusters, syntactical inversions, and prepositional archaisms (the four cases above). With a francophile's zeal for linguistic purity (paradoxically directed in part against such gallicisms as "last will and testament," "null and void" or "*en ventre sa mere*"), some reformers strive unthinkingly to impoverish our legal language.

If I were not troubled by the way lawyers communicate, I would not have written this book. And if you were not dissatisfied by your own written work, or that of other lawyers in your midst, I could not have had it published. But let me state *ab initio* [!] a bias toward many forms of traditional legal language. None should be discarded in a knee-jerk reaction to linguistic reform, although each should be subject to a periodic critique. We owe much to those careful analysts of legal language who have published books in recent years: the David Mellinkoffs, Reed Dickersons, and Richard Wydicks who have loved the lawyer's peculiar verbal mannerisms enough to challenge them. It is time, nonetheless, to digest their offerings, to see where they have nourished us, and to integrate their contributions into a durable and sometimes vibrantly healthy corpus.

Does this mean that you will put my book down having learned little about the language you use everyday? I think not. Instead, you can anticipate learning much but also being left free to retain what is efficient and even esthetically pleasing in your technical vocabulary while undergoing a cure for what is unnecessary and counterproductive in the way you write. If you are a draftsman, I will try to sort the wheat from the chaff of that painstaking, time-honored legal art form. (Remember that Stendhal, the famous nineteenth century French novelist, remarked that the Code Napoleon was the most formally pleasing *literary* work he knew.)[1] If you are a litigator, I will permit you at least some of the formulaic language that you may (perhaps wrongly) assume the judge expects from you. If you do deals, I will offer you the cold comfort of leaving virtually untouched your sophisticated '30's-act documents while suggesting that your covering letters and general correspondence do not have to look so fancy (and often go

---

[1] *See, for example,* Stendhal's letter to Balzac (October 28-29, 1840), in which Stendhal reveals that he read at least three pages of the Code Civil every night while writing *The Charterhouse of Parma*. Stendhal says that this exercise was necessary in order to attain the proper tone in his own writing. 3 Stendhal: Correspondance 401 (H. Martineau ed. 1968), my translation.

unread when they do). If you are a managing attorney or senior lawyer vested with the awesome responsibility of supervising your department's form documents, I will assist you to cut verbiage (by as much as 60 percent) without sacrificing either meaning or professionalism.

There is no need to attack blindly all types of traditional legal language. The main point of this book (which you will see reiterated at least once per section)—that being aware of your audience almost guarantees effective legal writing—induces broadscale reform only in certain areas of the lawyer's work. In other professional situations reform should be more modest, for no efficiency is gained therein [!] by undercutting tradition and fixing what already works.

§1.2 THE INFLUENCE OF LAW SCHOOLS

Few adult pursuits depend as much or for as long upon educational achievement and influence as does the law. In effect, one year of training, as reflected in six or seven examinations, dictates entire careers. Those at the top of the fledgling group "make Law Review" and reap all the continuing career blandishments predictable thereafter. Yet, paradoxically, excellence in substantive performance as a novice may well yield diminished writing ability. As an alumnus of a fine law review, I recall the experience of reading this circular, handed out to all recruits:

ADVICE FROM EDITORS TO INCOMING STAFF MEMBERS

After a satisfactory outline has been completed, the actual writing of the note remains. Since the mechanics of writing will vary enormously with the scope and content of the note and with the style and approach of the author. It is important, however, that a note be in as tight as possible a condition when it is submitted to the editors for appraisal and revision, even though considerable alterations in wording and organization may result from the revision process. In part this is a matter of self-interest: Under current procedure, officers for the third-year are chosen on the basis of their work product as they have submitted it to the editors. But more importantly, the writer has the most intimate connection with the piece he has produced, and the ultimate quality will reflect his efforts more than that of anyone else. Thus, save a considerable amount of time before the deadline set for the final submission for your own revision; look at each passage of the note extra times for substantive content, logic, and persuasive style. Do not be satisfied with less than your best effort.

As a plea for careful writing and editing, this excerpt hardly inspires what it theoretically seeks. The fragmented second sentence and the ungrammatical fifth sentence are only part of the problem; we shall analyze the selection more fully later. (*See* pages 51, 56.) In fact, however, law review "style" generally proves to be as colorless, wordy, and even grammatically incorrect as the sample. After law school, those at the top of the class enter their often privileged apprenticeships without exposure to excellent writing or, worse, with the impulse to talented writing bred out of them.

For the rest of the class there is greater hope. Unindoctrinated into the bland, formulaic editing and writing of the law review, these students are more likely to retain any natural or acquired writing talent brought by them into professional school. Further, an uninterrupted three-year immersion into the case law may yield models that the relatively new institution of writing-by-committee all too often ignores. For as Robert A. Ferguson[2] has recently observed, there is a tradition in American culture of highly literate lawyers, who

> were part of a now-forgotten configuration of law and letters that dominated American literary aspirations from the Revolution until the fourth decade of the nineteenth century, a span of more than fifty years. Half of the important critics of the day trained for law, and attorneys controlled many of the important journals. *Belles lettres* societies furnished the major basis of cultural concern for post-

[2] R. A. Ferguson, Law & Letters in American Culture 5 (1984).

Revolutionary America; they depended heavily on the legal profession for their memberships. Lawyers also wrote many of the country's first important novels, plays, and poems. No other vocational group, not even the ministry, matched their contribution.

The tradition of linkage—the marriage of law and literature—is epitomized in law school training by exposure to brilliant appellate writing. While law review and even to some extent first-year "legal research and writing" courses usually seek a mediocre base of blandness, the casebooks inevitably supply the student with at least a few majestic examples of individual style. These judicial models will be invoked often in the pages that follow, for they stand as proofs of legal literacy in an age of social scientific jargon, computerese, and "plainness."

Law school, whether a happy or sad, highly successful or only average part of the lawyer's past, can evoke memories and models of fine professional writing. One of these deserves special attention and analysis at the beginning of our journey into legal language, for it marks the richest parameter of our often barren professional territory:

HYNES V. NEW YORK CENTRAL R. CO.
221 N.Y. 229
Court of Appeals of New York, 1921

CARDOZO, J. On July 8, 1916, Harvey Hynes, a lad of 16, swam with two companions from the Manhattan to the Bronx side of the Harlem River, or United States Ship Canal, a navigable stream. Along the Bronx side of the river was the right of way of the defendant, the New York Central Railroad, which operated its trains at that point by high-tension wires, strung on poles and crossarms. Projecting from the defendant's bulkhead above the waters of the river was a plank or springboard, from which boys of the neighborhood used to dive. One end of the board had been placed under a rock on the defendant's land, and nails had been driven at its point of contact with the bulkhead. Measured from this point of contact the length behind was 5 feet; the length in front 11. The bulkhead itself was about 3½ feet back of the pier line as located by the government. From this it follows that for 7½ feet the springboard was beyond the line of the defendant's property and above the public waterway. Its height measured from the stream was 3 feet at the bulkhead, and 5 feet at its outermost extremity. For more than five years swimmers had used it as a diving board without protest or obstruction.

On this day Hynes and his companions climbed on top of the bulkhead, intending to leap into the water. One of them made the plunge in safety. Hynes followed to the front of the springboard and stood poised for his dive. At that moment a crossarm with electric wires fell from the defendant's pole. The wires struck the diver, flung him from the shattered board, and plunged him to his death below. His mother, suing as administratrix, brings this action for her damages. Thus far the courts have held that Hynes at the end of the springboard above the public waters was a trespasser on the defendant's land. They have thought it immaterial that the board itself was a trespass, an encroachment on the public ways. They have thought it of no significance that Hynes would have met the same fate if he had been below the board and not above it. The board, they have said, was annexed to the defendant's bulkhead. By force of such annexation it was to be reckoned as a fixture and thus constructively, if not actually, an extension of the land. The defendant was under a duty to use reasonable care that bathers swimming or standing in the water should not be electrocuted by wires falling from its right of way. But to bathers diving from the springboard there was no duty, we are told, unless the injury was the product of mere willfulness or wantonness—no duty of active vigilance to safeguard the impending structure. Without wrong to them, crossarms might be left to rot; wires highly charged with electricity might sweep them from their stand and bury them in the adjacent waters. In climbing on the board, they became trespassers and outlaws. The conclusion is defended with much subtlety of reasoning, with much insistence upon its inevitableness as a merely logical deduction. A majority of the court are unable to accept it as the conclusion of the law.

We assume, without deciding, that the springboard was a fixture, a permanent improvement of the defendant's right of way. Much might be said in favor of another view. We do not press the inquiry, for we are persuaded that the rights of bathers do not depend upon these nice distinctions. Liability would not be doubtful, we are told, had the boy been diving from a pole, if the pole had been vertical. The diver in such a situation would have been separated from the defendant's freehold. Liability, it is said, has been escaped because the pole was horizontal. The plank when projected lengthwise was an extension of the soil. We are to concentrate our gaze on the private ownership of the board. We are to ignore the public ownership of the circumambient spaces of water and of air. Jumping from a boat or a barrel, the boy would have been a bather in the river. Jumping from the end of the springboard, he was no longer, it is said, a bather but a trespasser on a right of way.

Rights and duties in systems of living law are not built upon such quicksands. . . . The truth is that every act of Hynes from his first plunge into the river until the moment of his death was in the enjoyment of the public waters and under cover of the protection which his presence in those waters gave him. The use of the springboard was not an abandonment of his rights as bather. It was a mere byplay, an incident, subordinate and ancillary to the execution of his primary purpose, the enjoyment of the highway. The byplay, the incident, was not the cause of the disaster. Hynes would have gone to his death if he had been below the springboard or beside it. The wires were not stayed by the presence of the plank. They followed the boy in his fall and overwhelmed him in the waters.

. . . We think there was no moment when he was beyond the pale of the defendant's duty—the duty of care and vigilance in the storage of destructive forces. This case is a striking instance of the dangers of "a jurisprudence of conceptions" (Pound, Mechanical Jurisprudence, 8 Columbia Law Review 605, 608, 610), the extension of a maxim or a definition with relentless disregard of consequences to "a dryly logical extreme." The approximate and relative become the definite and absolute. Landowners are not bound to regulate their conduct in contemplation of the presence of trespassers intruding upon private structures. Landowners are bound to regulate their conduct in contemplation of the presence of travelers upon the adjacent public ways. There are times when there is little trouble in marking off the field of exemption and immunity from that of liability and duty. Here structures and ways are so united and commingled, superimposed upon each other, that the fields are brought together. In such circumstances, there is little help in pursuing general maxims to ultimate conclusions. They have been framed *alio intuitu*. They must be reformulated and readapted to meet exceptional conditions. . . .

[Action allowed.]

This opinion, read by almost all first-year law students, should stand in our imaginations as the exemplar for our own professional writing. Form and substance merge and a personalized style is made to serve a strictly legal function with grace, efficiency, and effectiveness. Let us test more carefully how this opinion accomplishes its goal and then keep this test in mind until we refer to it again in the last chapter of Part I.

Harvey Hynes is instantly personalized: a "lad of 16," he and his "companions" as well as other "boys of the neighborhood used to dive" from defendant's board into the "navigable stream" below. The Hynes narrative projects Cardozo's reader into the familiar world of innocent boyish fun; the imperfect tense with reference to the neighborhood boys reminds us that we all "used to" act this way, and the pluperfect—"for more than five years swimmers had used it as a diving board without protest or obstruction"—continues the stylistic implication that only the defendant railroad's behavior has interfered with a more idyllic past to which, if we do not find the railroad culpable, *we* may never again return.

"On this day," Cardozo continues, drawing our imaginations not only to a specific human being but now also to a specific moment in history. The judge reminds us that one of Harvey Hynes's companions has just plunged safely from the diving board. The scene is readied for the fatal moment. "Hynes followed to the front of the springboard and stood poised for his dive." We have before us not merely a lawsuit, a dry series of issues, but a living lad, about to be killed by electrical wires falling from the defendant's pole.

Twenty-five lines of vivid factual narrative now give way to Cardozo's equally creative description of the second implied enemy of Harvey Hynes, the courts below. As much as Harvey gains tangibility in the opinion, the courts and the law that they have used to deny liability become depersonalized. The pronoun "they" is superimposed on these opponents of Harvey Hynes: "They have thought it immaterial"; indeed, "they have said" that the legal technicalities override human realities. Furthermore, "they" have said this to "us"—the opinion's author and its reader have become allies. "But to bathers diving from the springboard, there was no duty, we are told"; "we are to ignore the public ownership of the water and of air." They use "much subtlety of reasoning" and logic, and they find against Hynes; *we* see the large picture, and the railroad must pay.

Cardozo's opening gambits in *Hynes* are not aberrational. They are but exceptional examples of what all appellate judges do: frame the facts and legal arguments in a manner supportive of the court's view. Rhetoric and style march along with legalisms. Precedents *contra* are denigrated through style: Form and language will assist the correct result not only to emerge but also to gain authority.

Hynes concludes with a series of visual images in harmony with the legal point being made. This was ever Cardozo's technique. Thus, starting in the middle of the opinion, the stylist matches metaphor to law in expressing why "the truth is" that this difficult case must go for the plaintiff: "Rights and duties in systems of living law are not built upon such quicksands." These lines cast our imaginations into a spatial sphere evocative of the boy's last moments on earth. The railroad's arguments, based on the "quicksands" of ancient property law concepts, are equated with the sad end of Hynes's life on the sands adjacent to the Harlem River. There begins a congruous stream of imagery, continuous until the end of the opinion, where, in its moving climax, the poet-judge seals his argument:

> Rules appropriate to spheres which are conceived of as separate and distinct cannot both be enforced when the spheres become concentric. There must then be readjustment or collision. . . . We think that considerations of analogy, of convenience, of policy, and of justice exclude him from the field of the defendant's immunity and exemption and place him in the field of liability and duty.

Just as the electric wires collided with Harvey Hynes, sending him into the spiral of his death, so the "spheres" of law supporting the railroad are sent to their demise by that simple, realistic justice with which they collide in this particular case. Harvey Hynes, excluded forever from "the field" of mature human development, at least can be posthumously situated by the poet-judge "in the field of [the defendant's] liability and duty." Justice and "the lad of 16" prevail, equally through style as through legal—indeed jurisprudential—logic.

11

The lesson for the busy practitioner or judge is to recall the potential for effective writing within his craft. Many forms of everyday legal writing, like the most striking selections from the casebooks, allow for the stamp of a personal style; all such efforts require a controlled combination of form and substance. The practitioner's remembrance of the best writings produced within his field, the very stuff of his law school experience, will inspire and assist the quest for an appropriate personal style of professional writing.

§1.3   THE NOTION OF "PROFESSIONALISM"

Lawyers know they speak a specialized language, and they assume that others will either ignore or ridicule it. They accept being satirized as a cost of their professional role even as they come to enjoy the use of their language within the professional group itself. In fact, as reflected in serious fiction or popular culture, the outsider's view of legal language is less one of ridicule than of suspicious respect. Lawyers seem to hold a monopoly on the mysterious incantations that unlock the door to power. This perception breeds both resentment and high fees. It is not without legitimacy, but it is right for the wrong reasons.

To understand the unique and valuable skill of the lawyer, we must stress the *first* half of the act of communication, that half that members of the laity universally demand from their lawyers and wholeheartedly respect when they find it. How the lawyer *listens*—how he sizes up all the angles of a situation, all the parties and their differing and often incoherent demands, their need for some overriding system—this is the first and most vital element of the way the lawyer communicates. What he then does with this ability to distinguish and detect, how he translates chaos into linguistic order, this strikes the laity as secretive, foreign, almost extraterrestrial.

Lawyers should be justly proud of that first, mediating capacity. But they have no similar professional investment in reducing their insights to unintelligible writings. Whether drafting a contract, writing a memorandum of law, or dictating a letter, the lawyer should no more confuse needless obfuscation with professionalism than should the nonlawyer confuse it with law.

Both sides of the communications coin are displayed in the following example from the cases (*In re Kimmel's Estate*, 278 Pa. 435, 123 A. 405 (Sup. Ct. 1924)). Note the lawyerlike ability to discern order where none else can, coupled with the tendency to produce a new form of disorder in the final written version.

THE PURPORTED HOLOGRAPHIC WILL:

Johnstown, Dec. 12.

The Kimmel Bro. and Family We are all as well as you can espec fore the time of the Year. . . . Boys, I wont agree with you about the open winter I think we are gone to have one of the hardest. Plenty of snow & Verry cold verry cold! . . . I will wright in my next letter if I come I have some very valuable papers I want you to keep fore me so if enny thing hapens all the sock money in the 3 Bank liberty lones Post office stamps and my home on Horner St goes to George Darl & Irvin Kepp this letter lock it up it may help you out. Earl sent after his Christmas Tree & Trimmings I sent them he is in the Post office in Phila working.

Will clost your Truly,
Father

THE COURT:

[T]he difficulty, in ascertaining the writer's intent, arises largely from the fact that he had little, if any, knowledge of either law, punctuation, or grammar. In the present case this is apparent from the paper itself; and in this light the language . . . must be construed. . . .

When resolved into plainer English, it is clear to us that all of the quotation, preceding the words "I have some very valuable papers," relate to the predicted bad weather, a doubt as to whether decedent will be able to go to Glencoe because of it, and a possible resolution of it in his next letter; the present one stating "we will see in the next letter if I come." This being so, the clause relating to the valuable papers begins a new subject of thought, and since the clearly dispositive gifts which follow are made dependent on no other contingency than "if enny thing happens," and death did happen suddenly on the same day, the paper, so far as respects those gifts, must be treated as testamentary.

It is difficult to understand how the decedent, probably expecting an early demise—as appears by the letter itself, and the fact of his sickness and inability to work, during the last three days of the first or second week preceding—could have possibly meant anything else than a testamentary gift, when he said "so if enny thing hapens [the property specified] goes to George Darl and Irvin"; and why, if this was not intended to be effective in and of itself, he should have sent it to two of the distributees named in it, telling them to "Kepp this letter lock it up it may help you out."

[Paper admitted as valid holographic will.]

I have used this opinion to exemplify "irony" to students in my Law and Literature class. With every apparent sense of professional competence, the court in *Kimmel* endeavors both to understand another speaker and then to convey its understanding through a new writing. The latter turns out to be, unwittingly, almost as incomprehensible as Mr. Kimmel's original statement. Such poignant irony, evoking the excerpt from *The Errand Boy* at the beginning of this chapter, deserves further analysis.

The second paragraph of the opinion begins with the court's claim to linguistic ascendancy over poor Mr. Kimmel: "When resolved into plainer English . . ."—but is the remainder of the opinion "plainer"? The very first sentence, consisting of 70 words, leaves its reader in the lurch. What, for example, is its subject? "All of the quotation"? Then how can we explain the verb "relate," which is in the plural? Did the court get confused by the subordinate phrase "preceding the words . . ." and forget that it had a singular subject on its hands? And then what of the pronoun "it," used twice before the semicolon? Did the decedent really link his trip to Glencoe to the first "it," namely the weather? If so, did "The present one"—this letter—really promise "a possible resolution of [the second] it" (still the weather?) "in his next letter"? It may be time to look back at poor Kimmel's original document simply to find out where all these references go. Kimmel, it turns out, is clearer than the court!

Recalling its original commitment to "plainer English," the

court suddenly throws up a semicolon (*see* Chapter 6). But the independent clause required after the semicolon does not materialize. Perhaps, as seems also true of the semicolon stuck into the virtually incomprehensible 119-word final sentence of the opinion, the court was simply substituting the handiest punctuation mark for true syntactical coherence.

The point here may be no more complex than that confident assertions of professional status do not alone produce competent work. When a lawyer's legitimate claim to superior listening and reading skills is "resolved into" an unreadable new document, the circle of linguistic aberration is closed. Kimmel's functional illiteracy has become the court's self-parodic enigma.

The lawyer's sense of professionalism correctly subsumes his skills as a communicator. No one, at least in a professional context, listens better and discerns meanings more accurately. What I will consistently call "awareness of audience" pervades the lawyer's role as mediator, advocate, counsellor. Why does it not follow through into the act of writing, which so often terminates and defines the case forever? Perhaps, like Jerry Lewis's film director, the lawyer scorns his audience and despairs of ever being understood. Or is it that professional pride actually motivates the lawyer to be incomprehensible? Or is it the absence of the required, technical skills of writing? The next chapters explore these and other factors affecting the present climate in the world of legal writing.

2

Why the Need for Change

§2.1 INEFFECTIVENESS

Suppose you were a carpenter. Your collection of tools includes a Phillips screwdriver, which you use every day. But for a while you have noticed that the tool is inconsistent. It only occasionally performs its function. As often as not the work needs to be redone, or the finished product is not quite right. Perhaps the cross on the head of the screwdriver is dulled and no longer quite fits the screws.

So it is with the tool of legal writing. Its function is to assist the lawyer in a variety of tasks; frequently, the tool is not in good working order and it inhibits her, causing extra work or failing to bring about the desired result altogether. If a tool does not satisfy its only reason for being, if it does not get you where you need to be, it must be fixed or cast aside. You would only retain it if there were no alternative. The tool of language, however, is infinitely variable.

As Chapter 1 indicated, traditional legal writing is a "prized" tool or rather a series of tools. In many contexts, the tools need only minor repair. Language being what it is, an imperfect medium of communication, the system has not done badly over the centuries. But when a tool does not get the job done (and where change is readily possible), that tool should not be applied to a task just because it has always been done that way.

Take the word "therein," which is used only by lawyers these days (I call such words "lawyerisms") and a tool I myself employed in a sentence toward the end of §1.1. (Try reconstructing that sentence without using "therein." The variations you come up with may not seem like improvements.) It turns out that this tool ("therein") was effective in the context. But let us look at several other documented cases in which practitioners have used it ineffectively.

First, the lawyer who writes to a client, requesting her to sign and return an enclosure:

☐ Please execute the hereinenclosed at the place indicated therein and return to the undersigned.

In this case, there is no assurance that the writer will achieve her ends; the lawyerism, one of four in the brief phrase cited, is simply ineffective. The tools "execute," "therein," "hereinenclosed," and "undersigned" may work for certain tasks the lawyer performs (*see* §7.3). Here they not only risk alienating the nonlawyer who is the intended recipient of the letter but also discouraging her from performing the needed tasks of signing and returning the enclosure.

The next case proves that, even when used by lawyers to communicate exclusively with each other, the tool "therein" can produce an ineffective result. This excerpt is from an affirmation in opposition to a motion:

☐ It is clear from reading the texts of the statute that plaintiffs first must satisfy all of the requirements of Section 901, including each of the five subdivisions therein, and then plaintiffs must convince this Court that this action is an appropriate one under Section 902. Plaintiffs thusly have the burden of establishing that this action can and should be maintained as a class action.

Here the writer seems fairly compelled to use the word "therein"— so much so that she needlessly structures her first sentence around it. (Rather than applying our Phillips screwdriver to the appropriate task, she is shaping the task to abide the Phillips. But you cannot effectively drive a nail into a wall with a screwdriver!) The already long and murky sentence finally breaks down under the sheer weight not only of the word "therein" but of the entirely useless seven-word phrase it culminates. When the barbarism "thusly" encumbers the very next sentence, the judicial (and judicious) reader may be forgiven a loss of attention and comprehension even before she reaches the redundant "can and should" nearer the end of the paragraph.

The paragraph might be rewritten like this:

■ It is clear from reading the statute that plaintiffs must (1) satisfy all of the requirements of section 901 and (2) convince the court that this action is appropriate under section 902. Plaintiffs therefore have the burden of establishing that this action should be a class action.

Simpler though it might be to apply, the rule here is not completely to rid our professional language of these kinds of usages. ("Thusly" is an exception and shall never darken our door again.) Rather it is, using a standard of effectiveness, to fit the usage to the task at hand. As Part III herein [!] will illustrate, too much legal writing fails the test for effectiveness.

§2.2 INEFFICIENCY

Assuming (as we never should) an ideal reader, one who will finally uncover our meaning no matter how long it takes her to reread our words, we should still move to eliminate inefficiencies in our written work. The *average* legal document is 25-33 percent too long. If style and elegance appear anachronistic, certainly cost effectiveness and efficiency are all the rage: Time, money, eyesight, and paper mean as much to lawyers these days as they do to business people and conservationists. Another example of the misuse of "therein" exemplifies the inefficiency of certain linguistic tools, even when they may be ultimately understandable. In the example below, "therein" appears with four other "lawyerisms" in a covering letter to a mixed group of in-house lawyers and nonlegal executives:

> ☐ Enclosed herewith, please find five (5) drafts each of the Investment Agreements and the above-captioned bond offerings. Please also find therein certain amended language. Please address all comments to the undersigned.

This passage, despite its relatively sophisticated intended audience, runs a risk of not accomplishing its aim. Indeed, the enclosure itself, with no covering letter at all, contains most of the information. (*See* page 93.) Yet lawyers pen such blurbs every day, perhaps on the assumption that they are constrained by an unwritten code of professional behavior to waste their own and their audience's time with pompous verbosity. No efficiency is served in this passage by the lawyerisms "herewith," "thereto," "undersigned," or our old friend "therein." On the contrary, these words, multiplied by thousands, cost lawyers, their secretaries, and their audiences many hours over the length of a career.

A straightforward covering letter would have been more efficient and more effective:

> ■ I would appreciate receiving your comments on this amended version of the Investment Agreements and bond offerings [(five drafts of each are enclosed)].

Note that the bracketed language is necessary only to "perfect the files" (i.e., the letter, when filed, will provide a record that five drafts were sent) because the presence of five drafts is obvious to the recipient.

Having worked with senior attorneys to cut the verbiage from in-house form documents, I have seen the delighted smiles of lawyers who are creating efficiency through language. But in this, as in virtually every category of legal writing, most of the cutting remains to be done. When enlightened senior attorneys may not be around, the novice will have to find the courage to remove the fat from the form. (Caveat: The eyebrows of adversaries and of courts are far less likely to be raised than those of in-house old-timers, so tread softly if you are junior; forge ahead if you are first among equals or a sole practitioner. *See* Chapter 17.)

In the interest of efficiency, hundreds of form documents such as the following must be revised:

☐ The undersigned, an attorney admitted to practice in the courts of this state, associated with Jane R. Doe, the attorney of record in this action for XYZ Corporation, affirms under the penalties of perjury, and pursuant to Section 007 of the Code of Civil Procedure, that the following facts are true.

Previously hereto discussions were had between this office and that of the plaintiff in order to reconcile the differences before resorting to the Court for help. These discussions proved to be fruitless.

Wherefore your affiant prays that defendant's motion be granted in all respects.

Try revising this with efficiency in mind before you read my shortened version below.

■ As an associate of the attorney of record in this action for defendant XYZ Corporation, I affirm [under oath] that plaintiff and this office have been unable to reconcile our differences before resorting to the Court. I therefore ask that defendant's motion be granted.

Penalties flow automatically—and without need for laborious citation to statute—from false allegations made by attorneys to courts. Also, the two words in brackets, which already replace 22 words in the original, are probably themselves unnecessary.

There is a need for change.

§2.3 STATUTORY REFORM

Even if lawyers were to remain, as a profession, unconvinced of a need for change in their writing, many state legislatures have taken the initiative. Professional attention to simplified language is now mandated for a wide variety of transactions in which a relatively unsophisticated consumer may be assumed.

The fruit of both popular disenchantment (*see* §2.4) and internal reformers, these expansive plain English laws are now in effect in 7 states.[1] New York and New Jersey were among the first to move forward, New York's statute becoming effective on November 1, 1978, the New Jersey's on October 16, 1980. Although neither provision practices what it preaches, they are worth citing at length:

NEW YORK GENERAL OBLIGATIONS LAW

Sec. 5-702. **Requirements for Use of Plain Language in Consumer Transactions**

a. Every written agreement entered into after November first, nineteen hundred seventy-eight, for the lease of space to be occupied for residential purposes, or to which a consumer is a party and the money, property or service which is the subject of the transaction is primarily for personal, family or household purposes must be:

1. Written in a clear and coherent manner using words with common and every day meanings;
2. Appropriately divided and captioned by its various sections.

Any creditor, seller or lessor who fails to comply with this subdivision shall be liable to a consumer who is a party to a written agreement governed by this subdivision in an amount equal to any actual damages sustained plus a penalty of fifty dollars. The total class action penalty against any such creditor, seller or lessor shall not exceed ten thousand dollars in any class

---

[1] Connecticut, Hawaii, Maine, Minnesota, New Jersey, New York, and West Virginia.

action or series of class actions arising out of the use by a creditor, seller or lessor of an agreement which fails to comply with this subdivision. No action under this subdivision may be brought after both parties to the agreement have fully performed their obligation under such agreement, nor shall any creditor, seller or lessor who attempts in good faith to comply with this subdivision be liable for such penalties. This subdivision shall not apply to agreements involving amounts in excess of fifty thousand dollars nor prohibit the use of words or phrases or forms of agreement required by state or federal law, rule or regulation or by a governmental instrumentality.

b. A violation of the provisions of subdivision a of this section shall not render any such agreement void or voidable nor shall it constitute:

1. A defense to an action or proceeding to enforce such agreement; or

2. A defense to any action or proceeding for breach of such agreement.

c. In addition to the above, whenever the attorney general finds that there has been a violation of this section, he may proceed as provided in subdivision twelve of section sixty-three of the executive law.

NEW JERSEY STAT. ANN.

56:12-2. Contracts to be Written in Simple, Clear, Understandable and Easily Readable Way

A consumer contract entered into on or after the effective date of this amendatory and supplementary act shall be written in a simple, clear, understandable and easily readable way. In determining whether a consumer contract has been written in a simple, clear, understandable and easily readable way as a whole, a court or the Attorney General take into consideration the guidelines set forth in section 10 of this act. Use of technical terms or words of art shall not in and of itself be a violation of this act. . . .

58:12-10. Guidelines

a. To insure that a consumer contract shall be simple, clear, understandable and easily readable, the following are examples of guidelines that a court or the Attorney General consider in determining whether a consumer contract as a whole complies with this act:

1. Cross references that are confusing;
2. Sentences that are of greater length than necessary;
3. Sentences that contain double negatives and exceptions to exceptions;
4. Sentences and sections that are in a confusing or illogical order;
5. The use of words with obsolete meanings or words that differ in their legal meaning from their common ordinary meaning;
6. Frequent use of Old English and Middle English words and Latin and French phrases.

b. The following are examples of guidelines that a court or the Attorney General may consider in determinating whether the consumer contract as a whole complies with this act:

1. Sections shall be logically divided and captioned;
2. A table of contents or alphabetical index shall be used for all contracts with more than 3,000 words;
3. Conditions and exceptions to the main promise of the agreement shall be given equal prominence with the main promise, and shall be in at least 10 point type.

Response among lawyers to the plain English statutes has been good (perhaps because litigation under them has not been threateningly widespread). I (among others) have worked in-house with lawyers to simplify consumer documents and have yet to see any show of professional resentment against the legislation. Even so, an early New York commentator[1] spoke of attorneys only "grudgingly" accepting the law and flagged the observation that postlegislation "sentences are coherent, words are nontechnical, but the finished products in many instances are insulting to children in nursery school." Time has shown, however, that effective reform of consumer documents need not mean using an extreme of simplemindedness to replace the convoluted "party-of-the-first-part"

---

[1] *See* Allister, Plain Language: An Approach to the Problem, 52 N.Y. St. B.J. 382-388 (1980).

phrases so rightly condemned in the past. Lawyer and consumer alike have come to appreciate shorter forms, simpler English, and better communication.

§2.4 RELATIONSHIP WITH THE LAITY

There are two schools of thought about legal language's effect upon the public and specifically upon clients. Apologists claim members of the laity expect to be mystified and would be upset to pay someone who sounds just like themselves; reformers stress the nonlawyer's ridicule of the way lawyers speak, the increasing difficulty of juries in understanding legal instructions from the bench, the needless alienation of the client's commonsense approach to speech.

These arguments and the tensions from which they spring are not new. At least since Dickens, the common law's speech has been satirized roundly in each generation. Mr. Jaggers, Dickens's foremost fictional lawyer (in *Great Expectations*) "cross-examine[s] his very wine when he ha[s] nothing else in hand" and studiously avoids using the first person pronoun in even the most spontaneous of situations. And Faulkner's perennial lawyer-hero, Gavin Stevens, self-confessedly talks too much and too obscurely. Yet these two lawyer figures, and many others in serious and popular literature, often succeed precisely *because* of their odd way of speaking. Clients seek out Mr. Jaggers, and he is a stronghold of the bar; Gavin Stevens is surely the leading lawyer in Faulkner's Yoknopatawpha County.[2] (*See* §9 of the Bibliography.)

So the paradox of lay suspicion as to legal language goes unresolved. But in our present generation, the scales seem to be tipping against professional obfuscation and toward reform. People's tolerance for legalism is sharply reduced: "say what you mean" has

[2]*See* Weisberg, The Quest for Silence: Faulkner's Lawyer in a Comparative Setting, 4 Miss. C.L.R. 193-212 (1984).

begun to replace "sound like a lawyer," both in interprofessional and in lawyer-client dealings. Reasons abound for this shift, including both the ignorant tendency to blame lawyers for everything from "big government" to rising insurance costs and the more benign general trend to be "honest" and "up front" when communicating. Whichever reformist approach we heed, there is surely no justification for stilted, patronizing, or incomprehensible communication from an attorney to a nonlawyer.

We have already seen how ineffective legalese is when imposed on clients in ordinary correspondence. (*See* §2.1.) At the very least, lawyers must train themselves to write plainly to their clients and to organize such letters and memos to reflect a nonlawyer's expectations and tolerance for complexity. (*See* Chapters 8-10.) But lack of awareness of the lay audience can carry far greater costs than a client's temporary annoyance or inconvenience. Consider the following consent form, penned in consultation by doctors and their lawyers and designed to elicit consent from potential participants in an experimental course of medical study (all mistakes are in the original):

☐ CONSENT TO PARTICIPATE IN A RESEARCH PROJECT

Project Title: Controlled Study of the Efficacy of Adenine Arabinoside for the Treatment of Vericella Zoster Infections in Immunocompromised Patients

[I]

You (your proxy) are invited to participate (enroll you) in a therapeutic study of vericella zoster virus infections, conducted by the National Institutes of Health. It is important that you read and understand the following general principles which apply to all participants in our studies: a) participation is entirely voluntary; b) personal benefit may not accrue from participating in the study, although knowledge may be gained that will benefit others; c) withdrawal from the study may be accomplished at any time without jeopardy or prejudice.

[II]

The nature of the study, the risks, inconveniences, discomforts and other pertinent information about the study are discussed below. Please feel free to ask any questions you may have of those discussing the project with you.

[III]

You have been selected because you have a viral infection which could, but rarely have serious consequences. Because of your underlying illness this infection can spread to vital organs (one out of ten to one out of twenty patients), such as the lung and cause serious illness or even death (one out of fifty).

[IV]

An experimental drug, vidarabine (adenine arabinoside, Ara-A), is being evaluated as a therapeutic agent for this virus infection, in an on-going collaborative study. This study is doubleblind and placebo controlled such that patients will receive either the drug or a placebo, without knowing which, for a period of five days and observed an additional nine days.

[V]

The risks of receiving this medication (Ara-A) particularly in combination with the medications necessary to control your underlying disease itself, and/or the effects of the virus infection itself may produce toxic effects which include depression of whiteblood cells (can lead to infection) and platelets (can lead to bleeding) production. In addition, a few instances of jitteriness and tremors have occurred in patients with kidney or liver disease. These risks have been explained to you and, moreover, they will be monitored during the study. You have been informed that no other established therapy is available for this illness. Thus, no other formal therapy will be denied to you.

[VI]

The potential benefits of receiving this drug is faster resolution of the disease with, perhaps, the prevention of serious disease. This possibility can only be established by studies of the sort proposed.

[VII]

You will be hospitalized to receive medication. During this time, we will take blood and urine specimens to assess potential toxicity. You will be followed after discharge on several occasions to be sure that the infection has resolved. The blood tests that will be performed will be done on blood drawn with a needle from a vein in your arm. A maximum of 6 tablespoons of blood will be collected during any six week period. As you know blood drawing may be associated with local pain and skin discoloration and rarely fainting in those so predisposed.

[VIII]

Information regarding your illness including laboratory data will be entirely confidential. Your identity will not be disclosed but your response to treatment in the study may be included with that of the other patients in the reports to the medical literature.

[IX]

The Clinical Center will provide short-term medical care for any physical injury resulting from your participation research. Neither the Clinical Center nor the Federal Government will provide financial compensation or long-term medical treatment for such injuries.

[X]

I have been given the opportunity to discuss pertinent aspects of the research study, to ask questions and hereby consent to participation in the project outlined above. I have been assured that I may voluntarily withdraw from this study at any time.

The need for change in the way lawyers write emerges poignantly here, even though the sample clearly attempts to be plain. Somewhere along the way its authors picked up some rules on simplifying English, but they never learned the reason for the rules: Always keep your audience in mind. Here, as so often in legal writing, the express purpose and intended reader of the document were forgotten. The passage deserves a detailed analysis.

Examples of audience-avoidance pervade the document. In Paragraph I, the "general principles" defy easy understanding largely because they are written impersonally, that is, with abstract nouns rather than human beings as subjects. (*See* Chapter 4.) The final phrase, "without jeopardy or prejudice," is legalistic and unhelpful to the potential patient.

Paragraph II is clearer, although marred in its first sentence by a parallelism problem masked, uncomfortably, as a grammatical error. (I will revise this sentence on page 34.) The opening of Paragraph III is equally flawed. (Can you detect the error?) Little improvement is to be found in the paragraph's confusing second sentence. Here vital information is conveyed as to several material risks of the procedure, but the participant must work hard to assimilate the data.

Paragraph IV begins obliquely and probably mimics older boilerplate. The authors have lost sight of what they are attempting to do: inform the nonprofessional potential participant. Faulty parallelism creates an ambiguity in the overly long opening to Paragraph V, but the latter ends quite plainly. Aside from the grammatical error beginning Paragraph VI (can you spot it?) and the perennial parallelism problem in the closing seven words of Paragraph VII, the trend toward true communication continues through the end of Paragraph VIII.

Paragraph IX is the clincher. Which risks are uncovered here, and which remain hidden? What does "your participation research" mean? Who will have to pay for "long-term medical treatment"? How is the latter different from "short-term medical care"? Is "medical care" the same as "financial compensation"? Is this paragraph saying something like "If our treatment makes you sick, we'll care for you at our expense for a week, after which we'll neither care for you nor pay for care provided by others"?

Change is needed in the way lawyers write for nonprofessionals, as this purportedly reform-influenced document shows, not because nonlawyers are simplistic or prejudiced against attorneys. Change is needed to serve the ends of simple justice and of a legal system accessible to those who pay for it.

3

The Foundations of Effective Writing

§3.1 A COMMAND OF BASIC WRITING SKILLS

For generations, lawyers paid no particular attention to postgraduate or remedial instruction in basic English. As I discussed in Chapter 1, lawyers were in the forefront of American literate culture. And that culture could be counted on, in terms of its educational system, to reach reading, 'rithmetic, and writing. Whatever problems younger lawyers had with the latter skill could be dealt with in the small, apprentice-oriented practice typical of this nation's first century and a half.

Times have changed. Lawyers cannot count on elementary, secondary, college, or even legal education to instill adequately the basics of writing. Furthermore, the link between law and letters is no longer strong, so the individual attorney has no cultural incentive to hone his linguistic skills. Finally, the old apprenticeship system of promoting good writing within the firm or department has grown obsolete. Senior attorneys may not be good writers themselves or they may be poor editors or they may lack the time or the desire to cure the writing deficiencies of their juniors. Juniors are all too likely to respond with debilitating fear to overtures from seniors about writing, wrongly (but understandably) equating such criticism with an attack on their legal skills generally. (*See* Chapter 16.)

Yet lawyers have as much right to demand literacy from their fellows, and the laity has as much interest in good legal writing, as at any time in the past. Despite this, I have found that a basic grasp of English is lacking in fully 40 percent of the lawyers with whom I have dealt as a writing consultant. Putting aside for the moment their capacity to structure and organize, lawyers fail themselves, each other, and the laity by violating the tenets of punctuation, grammar, syntax, and word choice. Brief examples of all four breaches follow, with corrections—all taken from actual documents I have seen.

§3.1.1 Punctuation

The misplacement or omission of a mark of punctuation can change the meaning of a sentence. Compare with their revised versions the incorrectly punctuated sentences that follow.

☐ The Company's involvement if any, in the design of other items is not relevant.

■ The Company's involvement, if any, . . .

☐ There as in the case at bar, it was the executive type of secretary, a "Gal Friday" who was served.

■ There, as in the case at bar, it was the executive type of secretary, a "Gal Friday," who was served.

☐ This would increase her exposure to harm and Company X would be liable for her injury.

■ This would increase her exposure to harm, and Company X . . .

☐ That is "commodities," is defined as tangible personal property of like grade and quality.

■ That is, "commodities" is defined as . . .

☐ X believes that the vast majority of the non-Swedish fasteners entered at New York, but will not be certain until it receives further information from Y.

■ X believes that the vast majority of the non-Swedish fasteners entered at New York but will not . . .

☐ X may risk liability, however it continues to produce widgets nonetheless.

■ X may risk liability; however, it continues to . . .

§3.1.2 Grammar

Unfair as it may seem, a simple, unconscious grammatical error can lead the reader to question the writer's skill on other levels. Look at the following examples.

☐ The city and county of Los Angeles has adopted a Realty Transfer Tax.

■ The city and county of Los Angeles have adopted . . .

☐ After weighing all of the evidence, we find that the reasonableness of licensees' and staff's expressions of risk are not materially affected by the interveners' criticisms.

■ . . . the reasonableness of licensees' and staff's expressions of risk is not materially affected . . .

☐ Since the mechanics of writing will vary enormously with the scope and content of the note and with the style and approach of the authors. (*See* page 5.)

■ The mechanics of writing . . .

☐ Any claims to income-producing property that a party makes in such an action must be based on their marriage rather than anything related to the property.

■ Any claims to income-producing property that a party makes . . . must be based on his [the] marriage . . .

☐ The language of the release can be interpreted in two ways; the first is clearly the most dispositive of this issue.

■ . . . the more dispositive of this issue.

☐ A spouse who receives alimony or other payments that are includible in his gross income under Section 71 may deduct that portion of the attorneys' fees of the divorce.

■ . . . that portion of the attorneys' fees for the divorce.

☐ This memorandum ends with making arguments very similar to X's.

■ This memorandum ends by making arguments similar . . .

☐ Borrowing from the reasoning in the cases, and applying the time-worn canons of construction, it appears that the interpretation accorded the predecessor of Section 6511 has been accepted by Congress.

■ Borrowing from the reasoning in the cases, and applying the time-worn canons of construction, I conclude that the interpretation . . .

§3.1.3 Syntax

Syntax is the part of grammar that involves the relations among words: the placement of words within a sentence.

☐ The nature of the study, the risks, inconveniences, discomforts and other pertinent information about the study are discussed below. (See page 27.)

■ The nature of the study—the risks, inconveniences, and discomforts involved—as well as other pertinent information about it are discussed below.

☐ Moreover, since 1984 when issue was joined, plaintiff showed no desire to diligently prosecute this action.

■ Moreover, since 1984 when issue was joined, plaintiff showed no desire to prosecute this action diligently.

☐ You have been selected because you have a viral infection which could, but rarely have serious consequences. (*See* page 27.)

■ You have been selected because you have a viral infection that could, but rarely does, have serious consequences.

☐ There have in addition been various attempts to codify the official interpretation exception.

■ There also have been various attempts . . .

☐ As security for funds advanced pursuant to the Agreement, X plans to take an assignment, as agent for the participating banks of the money outstanding from time to time in various collateral accounts into which the U.S. Government is to make the proceeds of the Construction Contract available.

■ As agent for the participating banks, X plans to secure funds advanced pursuant to the Agreement by taking an assignment of the money periodically outstanding in accounts made open by the U.S. Government to the proceeds of the Construction Contract.

§3.1.4 Word Choice

Word choice includes spelling, redundancy, jargon, and so on. Mistakes of this kind are probably the easiest to catch and correct.

☐ As to potential liability of X, it is apparant that similar factors should receive consideration.

■ . . . it is apparent that similar factors should receive consideration.

☐ In a case where a transfer of realty by a liquidating corporation to its stockholders is concerned, no such attempt will be made.

■ In a case involving a transfer of realty by a liquidating corporation to its stockholders, no such . . .

☐ The proposed statutory amendments would appear to make it likely that reliance on an OCC rule would constitute a valid defense.

■ The proposed statutory amendments indicate that reliance . . .

☐ As you requested this morning, I will summarize here those aspects of Indiana law that cause some concern in light of our lack of knowledge about X and the origin of the gold involved.

■ This letter provides the requested summary of aspects of Indiana law rendered problematical by our lack of knowledge of both X and the origin of the gold involved.

☐ The statute which I am analyzing may be compared with the Restatement formulation.

■ The statute [that] I am analyzing may be . . .

☐ In a similar vain, plaintiff's counsel has failed to show he is qualified.

■ In a similar vein . . .

☐ *Questions Presented.* 1. Is a guarantee, blank as to amount, void and unenforceable? 2. Is a guaranty, blank as to amount, voided if the blank is filled in by one not expressly authorized to do so?

■ [guarantee or guaranty?]

☐ Defendant's failure to oppose the motion was inadvertant.

■ Defendant's failure to oppose the motion was inadvertent.

These representative sentences indicate how much work needs to be done on the basics. All were written by active lawyers and some by otherwise competent writers. The effect on the audience of such sentences is jarring, however, and can sharply diminish the reader's receptivity to the points being made. (I once reviewed a brief to the highest court in the state, replete with punctuation, grammar, and spelling errors. The author, an experienced litigator, could not understand why he had been losing lately on what seemed to him winning legal arguments. Over time, improved writing improved his track record.)

Part II of this book provides elaboration upon, and extensive strategies for, improving basic skills in English. If a reader (as is likely) has found anything of himself in this chapter's examples, that is the place to turn. First, however, I advise him to complete Part I. In the following pages I offer—even for the lawyer who has mastered basic English skills—three preliminary rules necessary to excellent legal writing. (Further rules will follow throughout this book.)

§3.2 SUFFICIENT PLANNING OF A PROJECT

§3.2.1 Apportionment of Research vs. Writing

Q. Why did you bury your memo's key fact on page 12? And why is your best legal argument strewn out over several disconnected paragraphs?

A. Well I only had between midnight and 8 A.M., when it was due on the partner's desk, to write the thing. I guess some of it got mixed up.

Q. How long did you spend researching it?

A. Three full weeks.

This dialogue comes from real life, not whole cloth. Lawyers habitually research and research and then leave themselves no time to bring order out of chaos at the writing stage. But on what basis will that diligent research be judged? On the excellence of the researcher's library skills? Will the reader excuse sloppiness in the written product, which alone survives those three weeks of professional energy?

RULE 1.   Never apportion less than 25 percent of a project to the piece of writing that culminates it. (*See also* Rule 20.)

§3.2.2   Organizing before Writing

Organization is so crucial a stage in all writing projects that I devote all of Part IV to it. Suffice here to set forth a rule:

RULE 2.   Never leap into prose.

Lawyers often see anything in prose as binding precedent, even their own first drafts. It is therefore virtuous to delay, by whatever method, the move from research to expository writing. The precious gap between data gathering and prose analysis can be filled by an outline, an assortment of subject-indexed cards, a colored-pencil system of setting off the various subjects researched, or any other method the individual writer finds helpful. But the gap must be created. However busy the lawyer, he will not succeed professionally unless he gives himself some opportunity to organize prior to writing.

§3.3   WRITING FOR OTHER LAWYERS

§3.3.1   Thoroughness

The most sought-after virtue of legal writing that is intended for fellow lawyers is thoroughness. Indeed, effective writing often seems directly competitive with thorough writing, and the average lawyer (if he deems himself faced with the choice) will favor the latter. If this leads him to throw in the kitchen sink, should we commend him even if the rest of the document is overwhelmed and its overall structure defeated?

Anyone who has edited legal documents knows the case of the memorandum with the buried fact or argument without which the rest of the memo makes little sense. Or the brief that cites every section of a statute and every case decided under it, often before the writer has made his own argument clear. (For an elaboration of both these situations, *see* Chapters 11 and 15.) Neither offends the thoroughness model; neither represents good writing. The lawyer who receives such a memorandum or the judge who reads such a brief may insist on thoroughness, but like any reader of analytical writing he expects information to be framed with a clear indication of what is important and what is only background or secondary.

The fact is that thoroughness can and should coexist with effective legal writing. If a lawyer loses ten points out of ten for omitting relevant data, he loses nine out of ten for forcing his reader to provide the organizational scheme that lends order to the data provided. Thus almost the same amount of care must be devoted to the effective expression of information as was given to its exhaustive compilation.

My argument stops short of equating law with other fields in which the manner of expression is either identical to (literary art) or more important than (propaganda, advertising) the substance of the communication. Lawyers writing for lawyers *should* respond to the clear demand of that audience for completeness. I argue only that completeness is merely a necessary, not a sufficient, characteristic of good lawyer-to-lawyer writing. Sensitivity must be shown—almost to the same degree as when writing for a nonlawyer—to the audience's attention span, ability to separate the wheat from the chaff, knowledge of the specific subject matter treated, and so on.

Yes, lawyers expect thoroughness from each other. But they also demand and deserve an effective presentation of data. It is the author's responsibility, not the reader's, to create order out of chaos. And thoroughness alone cannot provide an ordering system. The writer is master of his reader's fate and should create, for the sake of both, a well-planned document.

§3.3.2   A Fully Attentive Assumed Reader

The complement of thoroughness is attention span. Just as the legal reader expects thoroughness from his lawyer-writer, the latter tends to assume an audience fully attentive to his every word. (Some lawyers go so far as to expect complete attentiveness even when they are writing for clients and other nonlawyers, as discussed in Chapter 8.) The expectation of a fully attentive legal reader relies upon one's colleagues' willingness at least to read something carefully and from cover to cover.

To some extent, this collegial assumption is well founded. Certainly a contract, deed or will, and probably a trust indenture, securities prospectus, or judicial opinion, will be read exhaustively by an attorney if it relates somehow to his client's needs. Lawyers are paid for this attentiveness to detail—paid, indeed, for being the scrupulous readers so lacking in other parts of contemporary American society. But should the assumption of a fully attentive reader be extended to other common situations? Are lawyers, for example, more likely than the laity to read general correspondence, from greeting to signature, with consistent care? Will a partner or senior associate in a law firm peruse minutely every paragraph of an internal memorandum of law? Should the author of a law journal article assume a captivated professional reader?

Clearly the *aim* of the writing largely determines the response of its reader. The writer cannot rely in every situation upon a fully attentive reception. It is the writer's job to make sure of his reception or at least to maximize the chances that his main thoughts will penetrate, even if secondary or tertiary ones do not.

Thus, even though *as readers* we lawyers must try to conform to the expectations of our colleagues and to read all documents as attentively as possible, *as writers* we must never assume more than a human response to our words. Throughout this book, I shall continuously emphasize the strategies designed to keep readers on our wavelength, to preserve their attention, and to enhance our effectiveness as professional writers.

§3.3.3 A Professional Tone

I have indicated so far in this chapter that both the thoroughness model for writing and the expectation of a fully attentive audience should be balanced against other virtues and realities that are present when lawyers write. Less clear are the factors tending to mitigate against the use of professional tone in lawyer-to-lawyer writing. Lawyers, unlike ordinary mortals, feel comfortable with the stilted speech, impersonal constructions, lawyeristic jargon, and latinisms that have defined our peculiar language for years. All of these violate elementary stylistic principles (just test them against Strunk and White's latest table of contents[1]) and all contribute to the special tone we associate with legal writing. This tone can be utilized wonderfully as well as dismally. An exceptional example follows.

One will find this same suggestion of sure and calm conviction in some of the judgments of Lord Mansfield. The slave Somerset captured on the coast of Africa, is sold in bondage in Virginia, and brought to England by his master. The case comes before Mansfield on the return to the writ of habeas corpus: "The state of slavery is of such a nature that it is incapable of being introduced on any reasons, moral or political, but only positive law, which preserved its force long after the reasons, occasions, and time itself from whence it was created, are erased from memory. It is so odious that nothing can be suffered to support it, but positive law. . . . I care not for the supposed dicta of judges, however eminent, if they be contrary to all principle. The dicta cited were probably misunderstood, and at all events they are to be disregarded. Villainage, when it did exist in this country, differed in many particulars from West India slavery. The lord never could have thrown his villain, whether regardant or in gross, into chains, sent him to the West Indies, and sold him there to work in a mine or in a cane field. At any rate villainage has ceased in England, and it cannot be revived. The air of England has long been too pure for a slave, and every man is free who breathes it. Every man who comes into England is entitled to the protection of English law, whatever oppression he may heretofore have suffered, and whatever may be the color of his skin. 'Quamvis ille niger, quamvis tu candidus esses.' Let the negro be discharged." It

[1] W. Strunk, Jr., and E. B. White, The Elements of Style (3d ed. 1979).

41

is thus men speak when they are conscious of their power. One does not need to justify oneself if one is the mouthpiece of divinity. The style will fit the mood.[2]

This selection is from Cardozo's classic essay on judicial style, "Law and Literature." There he makes the argument that style and tonal quality are as important for appellate opinions as is substantive logic. He exemplifies one kind of stylistic approach with the internal quotation from a judgment by Lord Mansfield. We will recognize in both these giants not a rebellion against lawyerlike tone but instead a capitalization upon it for maximum effect. Knowing that their audience (immediate and ultimate) is almost exclusively one of fellow lawyers, Cardozo and Mansfield do not hesitate to use all of the familiar tonal props of legal communication:

1. impersonal construction ("One will find");
2. term of art ("on the return to the writ");
3. archaism ("from whence");
4. mildly redundant noun cluster ("reasons, occasions, and time itself");
5. mildly verbose transition ("at all events");
6. latinism (*"Quamvis ille . . ."*).

In fact, not untypically of legal writers renowned or not, Cardozo and his mentor Mansfield deliberately adopt a lawyerlike tone the better to drop the key and memorable phrase on their readers. Mansfield's "The air of England has long been too pure for a slave, and every man is free who breathes it," and Cardozo's "The style will fit the mood" emerge from the peculiar pattern of the setting to remain with us forcefully.

So, in the following considerably more typical and everyday setting, lawyer-to-lawyer writing employs a familiar tone to convey a strong message:

---

[2] Benjamin N. Cardozo, Law and Literature, in Selected Writings of Benjamin N. Cardozo 343-344 (M. Hall ed. 1947) (cited elsewhere as Selected Writings).

John Smith, Esq.
X, Y, & Z
Anywhere

Dear John:

Further to our conversation this afternoon, I enclose for your information copies of the following:

(1) form agreement establishing a Corporate Card System (CCS) that provides for individual billing to employee cardmembers and a waiver of liability to the corporation for certain charges on employee cards; and

(2) form agreement establishing a CCS that provides for central billing to the corporation and no waiver of liability for employee changes.

Each form agreement also includes as an exhibit thereto the membership rules for employee cardmembers.

As we discussed, I would like you to prepare and courier to me early next week draft Card Application Agreements for Agency Cards and for Employee Cards. Please keep in mind that I have never reviewed these form agreements, and I reserve judgment as to whether they will be much help in preparing additional Card Program materials.

Yours sincerely,

William Jones, Esq.

The tone is eminently lawyerlike and thus open to the kinds of criticism directed by reformers against legal language. (For my reaction to the word "thereto" in the middle of the letter, see Chapter 1.) Indeed, William Jones was assuming a "fully attentive reader," as most lawyers do when writing to each other, for the opening gambit of the letter is surely *not* an attention grabber. It merely recapitulates what both sides already know. Yet, to achieve several ends, lawyers typically save the meat of their letters for subsequent paragraphs. (Again, this is never a good strategy when writing to nonlawyers.) First, tone is established and thoroughness guaranteed. Everything the correspondent (and the files) needs to know as background is provided and the traditional exhaustive description of the enclosure then follows. (I call these paradigms of legal tone in the correspondence setting the "recapitulation" and "attachment" conventions; *see* page 93.) Only then does Jones tell Smith the real reason for the letter. He conveys in the process a demand for further work, a stipulated mode of getting that work to him, and a vital tone of skepticism as to the value of that work for certain additional purposes.

Tone, like thoroughness and full attentiveness, is part of the lawyer-to-lawyer writing process. But each expectation must be balanced against other factors and periodically criticized as potentially leading to inefficiency. Should Jones have placed his last, and only substantive, paragraph at the beginning? Or would he thereby have lost ground, not as yet having established the professional tone of the letter and sacrificing the freedom to be fairly blunt? These questions must be left for the moment to be taken up again fully in Chapter 7, but they indicate both the subtlety and the necessity for reflection imposed upon the profession when lawyers write.

§3.4 THE MAJOR PATH TO EFFECTIVE WRITING: AWARENESS OF AUDIENCE

§3.4.1 Purpose: Why Am I Writing This Document?

Part I closes fittingly on the book's major theme, awareness of audience as the path to good legal writing. If the lawyer constantly posits, during the act of writing, the actual and potential readers of his document, many of the usual legal writing flaws will disappear. The first and simplest step along this path involves a surefooted knowledge on the writer's part of the reason or reasons for the document he is creating. Prior to this evaluation, no word should be written. After it, many seemingly peculiar decisions may be excused. The key is author awareness of the aims of the document: all else will follow.

To begin with a few basic comments, I note that the purposes of general correspondence are never those of a drafted contract;

that the author of an internal memorandum of law has different aims than those of an external memo writer or of an appellate advocate. Furthermore, each letter has its own unique bundle of aims (even each opinion letter!); each memorandum carries with it a unique set of problems and assumptions; each judicial opinion its own peculiar challenges and tone.

Consider some of the writings already presented in Part I. Contrast for example Cardozo's decision in *Hynes* (page 7) with the court's in *Kimmel's Estate* (page 13). Although we are dealing here with two widely varying judicial competencies and styles, the real difference between the opinions rests with Cardozo's constant awareness, and the *Kimmel* court's eventual loss, of *purpose*. Of course, both were satisfying the immediate aim of rendering a decision, just as every legal writer fulfills a rudimentary purpose simply by completing the manuscript at hand. But an effective document requires more: the grasp by its author of *all* his major goals in writing it. Thus Cardozo, in depicting Harvey Hynes's tragic death, knew that he was grappling with a substantive tort-property law that ran against the plaintiff's interest. His aim, having deemed the case meritorious, was not only to rattle off a judgment but to move his audience to accept the decision despite the thorny legalisms in opposition to the holding. Each sentence, probably each word, was crafted with this primary goal in mind.

Not so successful, the court in *Kimmel* lost sight of at least one of its own stated goals: to put in plain English the testamentary scheme of the functionally illiterate holograph writer. As the court retreated further and further into linguistic confusion, its sentences grew larger and larger, until finally the reader had to go back to the holograph itself to regrasp the legal issues.

The irony of *Kimmel* is often mimicked in everyday legal writing as lawyers violate, contradict, and forget the very aims they have set for a document. These aims may not be easily articulated. For example, the successful letter writer, William Jones, Esq. (page 43), not only was requesting information from his correspondent; he also wished to set a certain tone with John Smith, Esq., to recapitulate their past relationship on the transaction, and to describe fully the documents enclosed. Jones grasped each of these goals *before* he began writing the letter, never lost sight of them, organized the whole with his goals in mind, and wrote an effective (if peculiarly "lawyer-like") letter. This leads me to the third rule the attentive reader will recall I promised a few pages ago:

RULE 3. Articulate your document's aims before you write it.

§3.4.2 Audience: Immediate and Longer Term

If the awareness of a document's aims stands as a prerequisite for the document's effectiveness, conjuring its lifelong audience is even more vital. Most lawyers manage to visualize the immediate audience for their document: a client, a judge, a senior associate or partner, an administrator, judicial colleagues, fellow academic specialists, and so on. As we have begun to recognize, even this foreground vision often blurs when lawyers write, particularly if their audience is the laity. (*See* §2.4.) What lies in the background may never gain focus.

Yet the single factor that distinguishes the act of writing from all other professional pursuits is that the *end product lasts forever*. Beyond the immediate reader for every legal document exists an infinity of potential readers. For a contract or will, for example, there may eventually be a court, and this background most lawyers do grasp; less obvious is the inevitable risk of multiple audiences for other kinds of documents. How many young lawyers draft a memorandum, for example, as though it will be read only by the senior attorney who specifically requested it? How much basic information is thus left out (or buried) on the assumption that the senior colleague "knew about it anyway"? But even if the senior attorney recalls the information, what will be the reaction of another lawyer, later called into the matter, who rightly relies on the memo to be thorough? Or of yet another, years later, who takes the memo from the files when a similar case comes into the firm? Or of the personnel committee, when they eventually review the writer's full professional record and amass everything he has ever written? (For hints to the young memo writer, *see* Chapter 15.)

Every legal writer must try to conjure the unknown reader

who may eventually turn to his document. Judges must be reminded of the academic critic reading opinions decades later and of the fact that the opinion bears the judge's name in perpetuity and not that of a clerk. (*See* Chapter 19.) Draftsmen, always cognizant of the threat of an eventual judicial audience, must also envision colleagues inside and outside their department who may use the drafter's language as "boilerplate" and thus must always hone their language to a trim minimum shorn of redundancy, verbosity, and obscurantism. (*See* Chapter 7; §18.1.)

The needs of the immediate audience, always paramount, may be difficult enough to grasp. This book never strays far from the goal of assisting legal writers to keep that audience always in mind. The specter of the longer term reader obviously requires even more attentiveness and imaginative understanding. Attorneys do not learn this in law school, but it is fundamental to their professional success. Part III will return to these themes.

First, however, we proceed to helpful hints for lawyers about the basics of English. Without mastery of the sentence and its components, no amount of sensitivity concerning the audience will cure inept professional writing.

II

Basic Skills for Busy Lawyers

4

Mastery of the Sentence: Keeping the Subject in Mind

§4.1 WHO OR WHAT IS PERFORMING THE ACTION?

Noun and verb marry to form a good sentence. Although the verb choice seems especially to bog lawyers down, noun choice often causes a bad marriage, too. If every sentence begins with "It" or "There," then most of the potential spouses line up as "is," "seems," "may," or "can"—not a very attractive list.

> **RULE 4.** **Choose the real, not the passive, subject of your sentence.**

Lawyers have the freedom to *name* enjoyed by all other writers. If the lawyer-writer knows who (or what) is performing the sentence's action, she should ordinarily make that person (or thing) the subject of the sentence. Lawyers often disobey this deceptively simple rule. Thus: "In a 1976 amendment to the Federal Energy Administration Act, additional remedies were added." (Since the amendment added the remedies, why did the writer avoid making it the subject?) Or "After a satisfactory outline has been completed, the actual writing of the note remains" (see page 5). (Why have inanimate objects become subjects, instead of the really active force, "you," implied in the sentence?)

51

Many lawyers suffer from a fear of naming. The result is a peculiar kind of sentence in which the noun shows up late, if at all:

> ☐ Borrowing from the reasoning in the cases, and applying the time-worn canons of construction, it may be concluded that the interpretation accorded the predecessor of section 6511 has been accepted by Congress.

This sentence typifies faulty writing due to noun aversion. It exemplifies a pervasive way in which lawyers demonstrate their fear of naming—by turning verbs into nouns. The result is a poor choice of subject and a weak sentence. The question *who* is doing the concluding is put off as long as possible and then answered by the impersonal "it"; even Congress as an active force disappears into yet a second passive construction as the sentence ends.

Sometimes lawyers need to fudge. Usually, however, they can and should specifically name the subject that is the active force in their sentence. Thus:

> ■ *I* conclude, having read the cases and applied the canons of construction, that *Congress* has accepted the interpretation accorded the predecessor of Section 6511.

Many lawyers, in their unwillingness to name the real subject, will take a verb and, by adding *-ing*, create an inappropriate subject. Thus:

> ☐ Applying the firm commitment rule to the plan affects the participant's beneficial ownership.

The effect of substituting such words (which are called *gerunds*) for real subjects is to diminish the force of the sentence. Compare, "The firm commitment rule affects the participant's beneficial ownership." Fewer words, and a truer subject, produce a better sentence.

Or consider the supervisor who wished to advise a colleague to adopt a different legal argument. "Stating the case that way is not a helpful approach," she writes. The verb "state," once turned into a noun-subject, depersonalizes and weakens the sentence. Furthermore, it virtually compels the writer to use the weak verb "is." What has been gained, aside from twice as many words, over "Please state the case differently"?

Along with *-ing*, lawyers often retreat to words ending in *-tion;* the result is the same. Here is an example of that habit taken to an extreme:

> ☐ The ultimate termination of this litigation would be materially advanced by correction, at this stage, of the deprivation of due process resulting from denial to X of access to information at issue.

Any sentence with five *-tion* words is a bad sentence. The subject, "termination," sets the weak trend, for it avoids the central thought, namely that "the court should allow X access to the information, hence curing the deprivation of due process and hastening the end of this litigation."

RULE 5.   Do not avoid your true subject by lengthening a verb into a noun.

§4.2   KEEP THE SUBJECT CONSTANTLY IN MIND

Once the subject has been named, the sentence is off to a good start. But then the writer must never lose sight of that subject. Consider this phrase from the *Kimmel* decision (page 13):

> ☐ When resolved into plainer English, it is clear to us that all of the quotation, preceding the words "I have some very valuable papers," relate to the predicted bad weather . . .

Like many legal writers, the court starts moving through subordinate clauses and impersonal constructions until finally naming the subject, "quotation." But then the court errs again by forgetting what it had named. As happens fairly often, an intervening noun ("words") confuses the writer, and by the time he arrives at the verb ("relate"), the court makes the verb agree with "words" instead of the sentence's true subject.

Failure to keep the subject in mind often leads to grammatical error and syntactical confusion. Sometimes a writer can lose concentration and fall into the *Kimmel* trap from word to word:

☐ The city and county of Los Angeles has adopted a Realty Transfer Tax.

But more frequently the lapse takes place in the course of a long sentence, in which intervening nouns confuse the writer into forgetting the number (or gender) of the true subject:

☐ The equitable standards applied by the federal courts in most circuits in determining a motion for relief made under this third provision of clause (5) has been strict—nothing less than a clear showing of grievous wrong.

The lesson for the legal writer is simple and forms the next rule.

RULE 6. Having named the true subject of your sentence, keep him, her, it, or them constantly in mind until the sentence is over or a new subject has been named.

§4.3   FEATURE THE SUBJECT; DO NOT BURY IT

No one has definitively tracked the thought patterns that lead to the written sentence, but common sense tells us that the subject of the sentence must be close to uppermost in the thinker's mind. While in some forms of creative or philosophical writing symbols and abstract nouns may predominate, in legal writing the sentence's true subject is usually a person (meaning also a corporate or legislative entity) or a tangible thing. So for lawyers, as much as other expository writers, people and things usually begin the process of turning a thought into a sentence.

If we instead (as we usually must) analyze from the finished product, we should not have to work our way back to the original thought that inspired the sentence. Too often, in legal writing, the reader must recapture the author's thought through an act of reconstruction; as we see in the following example, this sometimes happens even when the writer takes pains to identify her subject explicitly:

> ☐ The subject of this appeal is from an order of the court below affirming an order of the trial court that confirmed a report of the Social Referee upholding as valid the service of process upon defendant.

If the writer had deleted the preposition "from," she might have had a grammatical sentence, but her subject would be just as difficult to find. Rule 4 commanded us to choose the real subject, and had this writer done so, her reader might have been spared the search. Instead, the sentence runs on and on, throwing false subjects at the reader and attaching needless words to those subjects.

> False subject 1: "subject"; extra words: "The subject of"
> False subject 2: "appeal"; extra words: "this appeal is from"
> False subjects 3, 4, 5: "order," "order," "report"; extra words: everything from "affirming" to "Referee"

But what is the real subject of this sentence? The answer leads us, as is not uncommon, to the end of the written utterance. What starts as first in the lawyer's mind somehow winds up last on the page. Suppose the writer had kept that vital subject in mind, making it the star of the sentence, instead of a bit player?

> ■ Defendant appeals an order of the court below [. . .] upholding as valid against it the service of process.

55

I have placed the ellipsis in brackets because the sentence as re-written with its "star" as subject probably needs no additional verbiage. (Whether the intervening decisions need reiteration is a secondary issue.) By featuring the active subject, the writer strongly enhances her sentence.

> RULE 7. Do not bury the subject, but place it as close to the beginning of the sentence as possible.

§4.4 PRONOUNS

Pronouns are small words that lawyers, more than most writers, need badly. The cardinal sins of repetition and wordiness are mitigated by the effective use of pronouns; if the writer correctly locates and controls the real subject of the sentence, pronouns can take over and guide the reader safely and efficiently through the most complex of thoughts. Thus pronoun usage belongs in this part of our analysis, linked as it is to the quest for strong subjects.

The most common pronouns are "it," "he," "she," "I," "we," "you," "they," and "who." Pronouns can be used in place of the nouns in a sentence, but only if the pronoun's antecedent (the noun to which the pronoun refers) can be clearly identified. For example, in the sentence "Ellen took Julie to lunch because she wanted to discuss the case" it is not clear whether "she" refers to Ellen or Julie. In a situation such as this, you must say "Ellen took Julie to lunch because Ellen [or Julie] wanted to discuss the case." Of course, you could say "Ellen took Tom to lunch because she wanted to discuss the case" because there is no doubt about whom the pronoun refers to. When there is any chance of the pronoun's antecedent being unclear, however, you are better off to repeat the noun.

Lawyers need to use pronouns, but, as we first saw in the Law Review editor's pamphlet (§1.2), often misuse these small words:

☐ But more importantly, the writer has the most intimate connection with the piece he has produced, and the ultimate quality will reflect his efforts more than that of anyone else.

Here, the pronoun "that" is erroneously linked to a plural antecedent.

Sometimes the nature of the sentence—the nouns used in it— make it hard to use pronouns effectively (as in the sentence above with two potential "shes"). Placing other nouns that a pronoun could refer to between a pronoun and its antecedent can also be confusing to the reader.

☐ Steve took the book off the shelf, picked up his coffee, and sat down to read it.

In this sentence the reader will realize that Steve is reading his book and not his coffee, but there is a moment's confusion because "it" could refer to either. In general, place the pronoun as close to its antecedent as possible or, again, repeat the noun.

Aside from the necessity of linking pronouns to clearly defined antecedents, there must be special attention in legal writing to correct agreement of pronoun and verb. "Each," "none," "neither," and "either" can be difficult, as in this sample:

☐ Y manufactures fasteners at its [correct usage] facilities in Utah. None of the fasteners sold by Z are [incorrect] manufactured by Y. Each of its [unclear usage at this point] fasteners are [incorrect] stamped with the identifying mark "Y."

"Each" (like "someone," "everybody," "nobody") always takes a singular verb; "none" also takes the singular when, as here, it serves as a pronoun meaning no one or not one. "Neither" and "either" can also be confusing, for example, "Neither the Fourth Circuit nor the Ninth Circuit recognize(s?) that rule." Since both subjects are singular, the verb should be singular, "recognizes." If both subjects were plural, then the verb would be plural: "Either the bearings or the pins were defective." Usually, the hard case is when one subject is plural and one is singular. Then the verb should agree with the subject that is closest to it: "Neither she nor *they like* that holding." But, "Neither they nor *she likes* that holding."

Again, the lawyer's tendency to long sentences increases the risk of pronoun misuse. Thus, "Each of the foreign manufacturers serving the trade from which Y purchases raw materials *have their* own distinctive trademark" confused the writer, who lost control of her singular subject "each" and made the italicized errors. The same error can mar the seemingly easier pronoun "all," which usually takes a plural verb. Hence, "Article 240 does not expressly provide for the situation where all but one of the co-executors *refuses* or *fails* to qualify or act." Again, the errors appear in italics.

Lawyers can and do rely on pronouns to reduce verbiage and to keep sentences manageable. But the effective use of pronouns presupposes a firm grasp on the subjects to which they refer. Thus each of the rules offered so far in this chapter come(s?) once again to center stage.

§4.5 THE REST OF THE SENTENCE FOLLOWS

Some analysts of legal writing have suggested that its major fault is poor verb choice. Weak verbs constitute, without a doubt, a stumbling block to effective writing, and I treat that problem in the next chapter. However, once the lawyer *seizes and uses* the true subject of her thought, strong verbs will follow as the night the day. In the following example of passive verb use, we can detect the writer's original error, which was one of incorrect *noun* choice:

☐ Moreover, in specific relation to Rule 16-a-6, not only is it required that an insider report the acquisition of a put, call, or straddle (Sec. Exch. Act Rel. No. 9499), but it is also provided that the reporting of the *exercise* of an option is not excused from reporting requirements.

This 49-word sentence includes three repetitions of the verb "is" and can surely be criticized for blandness in that regard. Closer analysis reveals that both its verbosity and its weak verbs derive from a failure to seize the true subject. Fudging with the twice-used impersonal "it," the writer also tried the suffixes *-tion* and *-ing*, forming the weak nouns (see Rule 5) "acquisition" and "reporting." The latter is then repeated as an adjective. Neither "it" nor these remaining nouns track the writer's true thought patterns. What is the real subject? The SEC rulings of course, one of which is cited almost as an afterthought in the cumbersome sentence's midstream parenthetical. Suppose the writer had moved effectively from thought to subject? Here is a possible outcome:

■ In relation to Rule 16-a-6, the Commission requires that an insider report not only the acquisition of a put, call, or straddle (Sec. Exch. Act. Rel. No. 9499) but also the *exercise* of an option.

The real subject, once seized, virtually dictates a strong verb ("requires," instead of "is") and, with a minimum of additional fine tuning, converts an overweight blob into a slim (35-word) powerhouse of information.

Colorful and precise verbs always please a reader more than bland and impersonal ones. However, with little time to pick and choose verbs, and perhaps little training in the act of writing, the legal writer can achieve strength through the more simple identification of her subject matter.

We all remember the comparisons made in elementary school such as "The dog ate the cat" with "the cat was eaten by the dog." For the professional writer, involved in seemingly more complex thoughts, the sixth-grade model stands the test of time. Compare "The Commission requires" with "It is required by the Commission," and the final sentence analyzed in this section comes again into focus, as does much of the needless bland wordiness so frequently found when lawyers write.

5

The Vital Role of the Verb

§5.1 MAKING IT ACTIVE

An active verb has two characteristics, one negative and one positive. To be "active," a verb must:

1. not be derived from the infinitive "to be";
2. link the subject to an object or to another appropriate part of speech.

To reinvigorate the active verbal juices flowing through even the most seasoned legal writer, he must periodically recite five simple sentences.

1. "I love the law."
2. "The law needs good writers."
3. "Good writers seek brevity."
4. "Brevity thrives where strong verbs abound."
5. "I love strong verbs."

"Love" is a strong verb. So is any verb that in appropriate situations ties together the subject of a sentence with the object it is affecting. For example, "John loves Mary" ties together John and Mary through a verb describing as strongly as possible John's action in her regard. Similarly, in a more legalistic mode, "The Price-Anderson waiver of defenses clause benefits the claimants in this action" is a good, active sentence. The verb, "benefits," links the subject to the object. Yet the lawyer who wrote the original sentence chose to invert the structure, placing the object first, the subject last, and a weak verb form in between:

☐ Claimants in this action would be benefitted by the Price-Anderson waiver of defenses clause.

Why do lawyers frequently invert the subject and object? The best answer, short of psychoanalytic expertise, emphasizes the profession's proclivity toward passive verb forms. These forms, in turn, reflect on the level of syntax the lawyers' ingrained cautiousness. Once "to be," in any of its forms, creeps in, passivity and its progeny raise their heads. Yet overuse of this verb often produces obfuscation and ambiguity rather than professional prudence.

The careful reader has noted, on the other hand, the use of "is" or "are" several times in this chapter alone. "To be" is a necessary verb—and not only for Hamlet. There is no reason to avoid it *unless* it replaces a preferable, stronger verb. The writer, once attuned to the pitfalls of passivity, will become sensitized to this preference. In the following sentences, passivity creates not only the unavoidable concomitant of wordiness but also other problems:

☐ *Weak:* This report is required to include a forecast of nuclear power demands for the next five years.

■ *Strong:* This report must include [or did the writer mean, "The Commission requires this report in order to ascertain"] a forecast of nuclear power demands . . .

☐ *Weak and grammatically incomplete:* To confirm our earlier telephone conversations, without further research it is impossible to determine whether the proposed merger of the various companies will constitute an assignment of the tenant's interest.

■ *Strong:* As I indicated to you, I cannot say at the present whether the proposed merger of the various companies constitutes . . .

Not all strong verbs directly link subject to object. Of the five sentences I recommended for recitation at the beginning of this chapter, for example, the fourth did not use a linking (or *transitive*) verb. Yet "Brevity thrives where strong verbs abound" surely constitutes a strong sentence epitomized by a lusty, descriptive verb. Many strong verbs are not directly followed by an object but instead by one of the following parts of speech:

1. *Preposition plus indirect object*: "Mr. X's attorney spoke *to him* yesterday."
2. *Adverb:* "Ms. Y argues *well.*"
3. *No part at all:* "Brevity thrives where strong verbs *abound.*" (In this sentence, a classical *intransitive* verb proves that strong verbs can end a thought, too.)

The language redounds with vividly descriptive words of action. When the legal writer finds such a verb and uses it to link his subject directly to an object, the sentence is almost inevitably strong. But the writer need not avoid nonlinking constructions as long as the verb choice remains as strong as possible.

RULE 8. Use forms of the verb "to be" (e.g., is, are, be (+ verb), was, were, etc.) only if other verbs will not work better.

§5.2 TAKING THE VERB OUT OF VERBOSITY

Lawyers craft verbose sentences for many reasons peculiar to their training and their professional traditions. But an essential factor contributing to legal wordiness is verb choice. And the key transgressor, as I have already stated, is the verb "to be." Just as "The cat was eaten by the dog" increases the verbiage over "The dog ate the cat," many a legal sentence takes on extra baggage solely because of its writer's undue reliance on "to be": There follow some egregious, but documented, examples:

☐ Your petitioner is also desirous of obtaining an intermediate order.

■ Petitioner also seeks an intermediate order.

☐ Further, in a 1976 amendment to the FEAA, additional remedies were added.

■ A 1976 FEAA amendment provided additional remedies.

☐ The duty of payment of the *droit de succession* is upon the beneficiaries.

■ The beneficiaries must pay the *droit de succession*.

☐ In Title 12 of the U.S. Code, there are approximately nine sections using the words "in concert with"; in none of them is there an interpretation of that phrase.

■ I have found nine sections of Title 12 of the U.S. Code using the words "in concert with," but none interpreting that phrase.

☐ In a case where a transfer of realty by a liquidating corporation to its stockholders is concerned, no attempt to project value will be made.

■ In a case involving a transfer of realty by a liquidating corporation, X will not attempt to project value.

By minimizing "to be" usage, the lawyer automatically sharpens and tightens his written work product.

§5.3 INFINITIVES

The basic form of the verb is the infinitive: "to speak," "to do," "to be," "to sue," and so on. The infinitive is required after certain verbs, such as "need," "try," "want," and "hope." ("I need to see you," "I try to do well," "I hope to be home at five.") It can also be a helpful tool for pulling together complex sentences through parallel use of several infinitives. ("I hope to see you soon at your office and to clear up a variety of pending matters.")

Lawyers may not always know what an infinitive is, but by and large they use that verbal form adequately. (*See* §10.2, however, for further discussion of infinitives as a tool for parallel control of lengthy sentences.) The one area I wish to emphasize at this point is the use and abuse of *split* infinitives. These whipping boys of traditional grammarians occur whenever a word or phrase intervenes between the component parts of the infinitive. Thus, "I want to really do well on that exam," or "He intends to, somehow or another, find an answer," are both split infinitives.

Although most authorities counsel against it, many reformers of legal language paradoxically condone split infinitive usage. They see nothing wrong with sandwiching the verb form around single adverbs or even multiple, prepositional phrases ("There is no need to at this time move forward on the project"). My instincts here are conservative:

RULE 9.   Avoid split infinitives.

I have two arguments in support of Rule 9. First, as the exemplary sentences will shortly indicate, split infinitives can be graceless and unnecessary. Second, the lawyer who splits his infinitives risks raising the eyebrow of a reader who may recall no other writing rule besides the one in question. Since the integral infinitive usually looks and reads better, and since splitting it may be costly, the lawyer should respect the traditional rule.

In the following sentences, split infinitives glare out at the reader, potentially disaffecting or even confusing him:

☐ We should, however, urge that the guideline be amended so as to explicitly state the variations.

☐ If the Court deems further factual development necessary on the commerce clause claim, for example, it may still be able to finally determine the preemption claim.

☐ Incredibly, there has been no showing that the plaintiff has the finances to vigorously pursue this action. Yet, in order to adequately and fairly represent her class, she must sustain this burden.

Later in the same brief from which the last, double-fisted split infinitive is derived, the hapless writer continues:

☐ No discovery has been conducted to date to amass evidence to support the instant application on behalf of the class, and to more importantly assist this Court in reaching its determination.

To not always split or never to split, that is the question. Experience shows me that split infinitives often raise hackles, are usually clumsy, and sometimes go hand in glove with other writing difficulties. Lawyers should keep that little word "to" glued to the other half of the verbal form. Language modifying the infinitive can almost always be placed either before or after the infinitive, although admittedly that choice must be made with care:

☐ *Wrong:* There were additional safety features available to further reduce risk.

■ *Right:* . . . to reduce risk further.

■ *Not as Good:* . . . further to reduce risk.

§5.4   SUBJUNCTIVES AND CONDITIONALS

Difficult even for expert writers, the subjunctive and conditional forms of the verb often stymie lawyers. In the following example, the memo writer correctly employs the standard subjunctive mode:

■ If any real property were subject to the power of attorney, it is very probable that a New York court would apply the law of the situs of the real property.

What image is conjured in the reader's mind by the fifth word of this sentence? If you sense that the writer is conveying skepticism about the power's application to "any real property," you are on his wavelength. The word "were," as in the phrase "If I were King," when used in such a setting provides a powerful tool for conveying the unreality of the proposition expressed. This is called the subjunctive mode of expression, and it is available for all verbs as a mechanism to place the action of the sentence strongly in doubt, or more rarely, to express supplication, as in "If the court please."

The subjunctive mode does not require an "if" clause, although its uncertainty usually implies one. Thus, "Were I to get angry . . ." strongly hints at the missing "if." But the subjunctive can also be conveyed with the helping (or *auxiliary*) verb "should,"

■ Should he go, you will accompany him.

■ Should the situation develop, our side will benefit.

The subjunctive must be distinguished from the conditional. Although the latter also, of course, expresses uncertainty, the degree of uncertainty is usually less and the outcome of the situation clearly predictable if the contingency occurs. The first author could have written for example:

■ If any real property was subject to the power . . . a New York court would apply . . .

The change from "were" to "was" in the fifth word moves the usage from subjunctive to conditional and makes the contingency more likely and less speculative; thus, Prince Charles:

■ If I was King, you would be grand vizier.

The conditional tense is used all the time by legal writers to convey potential outcomes of realistic but contingent situations. The key here is to master easy rules of corresponding tense use as between the contingency ("if") clause and the outcome ("then") clause.

	If	*Then*
Present	If the court is reasonable	plaintiff will prevail (future)[1]
Past	If the court was reasonable	plaintiff would prevail (conditional)
Pluperfect	If the court had been reasonable	plaintiff would have prevailed (conditional past)
Subjunctive (present)	If the court be reasonable (compare: If the court please	plaintiff will prevail (future) plaintiff will offer into evidence)
Subjunctive (past)	If the court were reliable	plaintiff would stand a chance

[1] Note, however, that a present tense if clause may, occasionally, take a present tense then clause but only if the if clause has the meaning "when": "If a claim is timely filed, the statute of limitations is avoided"; or "If a manufacturer, who has not registered pursuant to §4222(a) of the Code, makes a sale for further manufacture under §4221(a)(1), the manufacturer remains liable for the manufacturer's excise tax."

"If-then" constructions, as we have seen, may stand either in the subjunctive or the conditional. Since the latter deals more directly with realistic contingencies, it suffices for almost all legal writing. But the subjunctive remains available for effective gradations of mood and nuance:

■ If defendant's argument be [were] even remotely acceptable in this jurisdiction, settled law will [would] fall by the wayside.

§5.5   WHEN TO TACK ON *-ING* OR *-ED*

The previous chapter encouraged strong noun choices and hence advised against using *-ing* words as nouns. Lawyers all too often enter the path of verbosity by transforming verbs into nouns (*gerunds*) and then into subjects (e.g., "state" into "stating" into "stating the position accurately is the aim of this memo"), but nothing should prevent them from using *-ing* words that remain, in fact, verbs. Such words are called *participles,* more specifically, present participles. Verbs followed by the ending *-ed* are called past participles.

Lawyers can use participles in all the ways other writers do, and they have even more need to do so. Participles provide both stylistic variation and syntactical control over long sentences. Lawyers take such help where they can find it.

Stylistic variation. Let us take four common verbs in legal parlance, find their participial variation, and demonstrate their potential for a more colorful style.

Basic verb	Present/Past participle	Variation potential
allege	alleging/alleged	Alleged as true, defendants' contentions are inaccurate. (Compare the stodgier: Defendant makes these allegations, but they are inaccurate.)
stipulate	stipulating/ stipulated	Stipulating certain facts, plaintiff goes on to assert that others are for jury determination. (Compare: Plaintiff, who stipulates certain facts, goes on . . .)
revoke	revoking/revoked	Revoking all wills that I have made previously, I execute this present one . . . (Compare: I revoke all prior wills and execute this present one . . .)
issue	issuing/issued	Issued on the settlement date, these securities bear a valuation determined thereafter. (Compare: These securities, which were issued on the settlement date, bear . . .)

Whichever variation one may prefer, the very presence of stylistic choice enhances the craft of legal writing. But choice implies responsibility, and the duty owed a participle is not to leave it dangling. Chapter 9 treats this risk in detail; suffice for the moment to look at our four exemplary sentences above. In each case, the phrase including the participle was *immediately* followed by the precise subject performing the participial action. If the writer keeps the subject in mind and names him, her, or it quickly, and in close proximity to the participle, dangling participles will be avoided.

☐ *Wrong:* Walking toward the bench, the argument arose.

■ *Right:* Walking toward the bench, the two lawyers began to argue.

6

Punctuation: Simple Rules about Commas and Other Helpful Pauses

§6.1 FOUR SIMPLE COMMA RULES

Use a comma to separate a series of words, phrases, or clauses. This most basic kind of comma use rarely confuses lawyers. It assists them, in fact, through such typical lawyerisms as "release, relinquish and remit," "convey, deliver and assign," and "incompetent, irrelevant and immaterial." Yet even the rudimentary has its perils. The attentive reader may have already noticed one. Am I counseling, she may have asked, that a comma be placed before the conjunction at the end of the series, as in the full sentence beginning "It assists them. . . ," or that no comma precede the conjunction, as in the various quoted phrases within that sentence? (A *conjunction* is that little word that pulls together longer parts of the sentence—such words as "and," "or," and others we will cover later in this chapter.) Experts differ on the question, but the majority advise using the final comma to avoid all ambiguity, and I tend to agree. Many common sentences demonstrate the risks of not inserting the final comma.

☐ My favorite mixtures of colors are red and blue, green, violet and mauve and purple and magenta.

Here I have wrongly omitted the comma before the final compound noun, "purple and magenta," and the resulting ambiguity is thrust needlessly on the reader. In order to help the audience to align and distinguish the elements in the series, the comma is added.

> ☐ Assuming that the Board of A has the authority to declare a stock split, there are certain steps the Board must consider in order to distribute the shares of stock in accordance with Ohio law, A's Articles of Incorporation and Code of Regulations and NASD rules.

In this sentence's series, consisting of a mixture of single and compound elements, the deletion of the final comma was erroneous. The element "and NASD rules" must be set off clearly from the preceding dual attribute of A's corporate requirements in order to nip audience confusion in the bud.

Better, therefore, to include commas before all final "ands," "buts," and so on, to satisfy the twofold aim of consistency and ambiguity avoidance. (As a starting exercise, the reader should return to the first paragraph of this section and repunctuate it.)

Rarely, ambiguities arise in a series consisting of only *two* elements. In the usual case, no comma is needed here (e.g. "She will choose X or Y"; "He requires A and B") but sometimes—and there is no grammatical rule for this—a comma is used simply to indicate a pause. Note the outcome in this familiar friend (*see* page 58):

> ☐ Article 240 does not expressly provide for the situation where all but one of the coexecutors refuse or fail to qualify or act.

The last seven words of this sentence create enough possible meanings to keep a logician busy for part of a day. By omitting commas, the writer forces her audience to play that role. As the sentence reads, both "refuse" and "fail" seem in apposition to "qualify or act." But can anyone "refuse . . . to qualify"? Here, untypically, a comma is needed before the conjunction "or" to cure the ambiguity and set apart what amounts to a two-element series.

Use a comma to set off subordinate material. As I noted in the last two chapters, subject, verb, and object form the heart of most sentences. If the writer keeps these elements always in mind, she will also recognize which part of her sentence plays a subordinate role. Such elements are usually set off by commas. In the following example, the lawyer does this inconsistently:

☐ Subsequently, four months before the bankruptcy, the plaintiff dropped the foreclosure action. Upon bankruptcy, the trustee in bankruptcy alleged in response to the plaintiff's petition that the deed of trust was preferential and fraudulent as to creditors.

The first sentence is perfect. The introductory word ("Subsequently") is set off, as is the descriptive phrase (four months . . .), from the core subject, verb, and object ("plaintiff," "dropped," "foreclosure action"). The second sentence begins well; the introductory phrase is set off by a comma. But then, while (properly) departing from the syntax of the first sentence, the writer loses control of punctuation. Instead of a straightforward subject, verb, and object, the writer varies with subject, verb, adverbial phrase, and direct object clause ("trustee," "alleged," "in response" . . . , "that the deed . . ."). The subordinate language, "in response to the plaintiff's petition," should have been set off by commas. Writers must remember to use a comma in *two* places when the subordinate material comes in the middle of a sentence, as it does above and also in the following example.

■ The company, contrary to the literal dictates of the judicial order, is unable by itself to perform the remaining work.

Often, legal writers throw a single comma in, forgetting or hastily omitting the second. The result can be worse than a complete omission:

☐ We believe that since the Authority is planning to conduct systematic experiments, the legislature should defer to the results of such study.

☐ Filling in blanks on an incomplete, but executed guarantee does not constitute an alteration.

☐ Each owns the policies as separate, not community property.

In all but the last of these three sentences, set-off commas were not absolutely required; however, once the writer chose to put one in, the second had to follow. Sometimes the writer *must* set-off in order to avoid ambiguity, as in the sentence, "At the close of Plaintiff's case, Defendant moved this Court pursuant to Rule 50(a) of the Federal Rules of Civil Procedure for a directed verdict." Correctly setting off the introductory phrase, the writer failed to set off further the phrase "pursuant to . . . Procedure." Commas before and after that phrase cure the mild ambiguity that otherwise results (i.e., do the last four words relate to the Rules or to the motion specifically—undoubtedly the latter).

Use a comma to separate two grammatically complete thoughts (independent clauses) within the same sentence. This rule, one of the easiest to master, causes lawyers no end of trouble, as does its analogue, which I will treat next. The trick is to recognize one of the conjunctions and then to see how it pulls thoughts (rather than elements in a series, as in the first rule) together. Such conjunctions are called *coordinating,* and include "and," "but," "or," "nor," "for," "yet," and "so." The following sentence serves as a paradigm:

☐ No policy has been articulated by the courts for this proscription but prudence in bank operations seems to be a primary aim of the National Bank Act.

First, where is the coordinating conjunction, the word that ties together the two independent clauses in the same sentence? (Note that it is *not* the word "for," which here acts as a preposition; contrast, "I cannot go, for the firm is holding its weekly luncheon then," in which "for" *is* a coordinating conjunction.) Here, "but" ties the thoughts together. The rest of the exercise as to comma usage is simple: if the words following the coordinating conjunction form a grammatically complete sentence, with a new subject, a comma *must precede the conjunction.*

Both the application of and the explanation for the rule are illustrated by the paradigm sentence. There, the lawyer failed to use a comma, and the reader of the sentence experienced a needless sense of temporary confusion. She then had to re-read the sentence, providing the pause mentally where the writer should have included it as a physical mark.

Do not use a comma when any part of the thought following the coordinating conjunction needs to relate back to the earlier thought to make it grammatically complete. This variation on the third rule is deceptively simple to apply. It requires, again, only the location of the coordinating conjunction and the analysis for grammatical completeness of the words following the conjunction. Compare the following pairs of sentences.

- The court exercised its discretion and granted summary judgment.

- The court exercised its discretion, and *it* granted summary judgment.

- The contract looks attractive to buyer but fails to respond to seller's needs.

- The contract looks attractive to buyer, but *the deal* fails to respond to seller's needs.

- I found Torts easy yet Contracts hard.

- I found Torts easy, yet Contracts was hard.

In the first sentence of all three pairs, the conjunction is followed by a grammatically incomplete thought. The language after the conjunction thus needs to relate back to a subject ("court," "contract") or a subject-verb ("I found") to achieve completeness. No pause is desired before the conjunction in these sentences. No comma should be used. But the converse is true of each of the second sentences in the three pairs.

If the lawyer can master these four rules, she will use commas effectively in most situations calling for them. Of course, I have not covered all the rules for this vitally important punctuation tool.

Some I will deal with later (e.g., use after parentheses, *see* §6.3; use in non-restrictive clauses, *see* §10.1). In the main, however, these four rules will carry the day, and I urge the reader to drill them further with the review exercises at the end of Part II. First, however, we will look at other, less widely utilized punctuation marks.

§6.2 THE SEMICOLON

The semicolon is far less important than the comma, and it is possible to live without it; however, it offers stylistic nuance and flair to the lawyer's syntactical arsenal. The trick, again, is to flash the punctuation mark accurately and to maximum effect on the reader.

A decade or so ago, a fellow named William Myatt published a slim volume called *Stalking the Wild Semicolon.* Although in fact he devotes only one of his 44 pages to the topic, part of his wisdom is worth quoting here:

> Semicolons are handy gadgets for use when you feel that two or more parts of a sentence are too different to be tied together by a comma and too alike to be separated by a period. But beware because semicolons are cute and fun to make. People have been known to become infatuated with semicolons. Overindulgence in semicolons can lead to dizziness, shortness of breath, hairy palms and government intervention.

Extending Myatt's image just a bit, I can confirm that lawyers, too, like to play with semicolons. The result can be pleasurable but not always for reader as well as writer. Fairly typical of the confused approach to semicolons are the two next examples, both from the same memorandum of law:

☐ The facts did not present the court with a situation where a seller of commodities was discriminating in price to its purchasers of the same commodity; the evil that the RPA is designed to prohibit.

☐ The court remanded the case for a trial on the merits, however, no subsequent case history appeared.

In the first sample the writer inserts a semicolon where none belongs; in the second, she omits one where it is virtually mandated (before "however").

Perhaps the most fundamental requirement of semicolon usage is that the words following the semicolon must form a grammatically complete sentence. This instantly eliminates the first usage above. A comma would have sufficed. But note that, even if the writer had followed the semicolon with "this is the evil that the RPA . . . ," thus forming a complete sentence, the semicolon would have been inappropriate. The two sides of the full sentence are not sufficiently connected to each other to justify the usage.

On the other hand, the second sentence cries out for a semicolon preceding the word "however" (one of the favorite magnet words attached to this particular mark). The two halves are closely connected—so much so that the coordinating conjunction "but" might have joined them. (*Quaere:* should the comma be retained in the sentence as rewritten to replace "however" with "but"?) Since the writer chose the word "however," and since the latter is *not* a coordinating conjunction, the sentence as written is in fact a run-on. The semicolon was required here, a less attractive alternative being a period after "merits" and a new second sentence.

Semicolons blend already closely yoked ingredients into an elegant, unified product. They do best when linking pithy elements ("The statute of limitations is three years; this action is therefore barred.") and begin to weaken badly when one or both sides go on too long:

☐ The statute does deal with the powers of an administrator under certain circumstances; however, inasmuch as it does not directly concern itself with independent administration of an estate, it does not mention the effect of these circumstances upon the independent status of the administrators.

A period would have been preferable here, as it would in almost all cases of length before or after the proposed semicolon.

The flexibility enjoyed by the user of semicolons distinguishes that mark from the comma and, as we have seen, highlights the stylistic advantage of using the mark well. But in one area familiar to lawyers, the semicolon plays an important technical role, namely as a divider among parts of complex series elements:

■ This view of the reviewing court's role in the regulatory process has several connotations: the EPA is held to a strict standard of articulating the basis of its decision, *Kennecott Copper Corp. v. EPA, supra;* it may be directed to supply additional information to the court, *Natural Resources Defense Council v. EPA,* 478 F.2d 875 (C.A. 1 1973); it may be ordered to certify a complete "record of expert views and opinions, the technological data and other relevant material, including the state hearings, on which the Administrator himself acted." *Appalachian Power Co. v. EPA,* 477 F.2d 875 (C.A.4 1973).

In this series, consisting of fairly typical legal citation and annotation, the semicolon assists the reader to terminate points along the writer's analytical spectrum.

Note that such a series often begins with a colon, as above. Note also that each part of the series should recommence a parallel syntactical structure ("the EPA is held . . . , "it may be directed . . . , "it may be ordered . . ."). If this pattern is followed, the reader will keep her way throughout the longest of annotated string citations. The semicolon can be used to separate items in a series any time the items themselves contain commas. The three color-sets at the beginning of this chapter, for instance, could have been separated by semicolons.

Not so successful was the following sample:

☐ Finally, it seems that the most likely scenario in which the Florida statute would apply to invalidate some or all of the power would be in the case of a Florida forum; Florida land; and a Florida choice of laws rule.

Here the writer exemplifies what William Myatt would call an "infatuation" for semicolons. The series was too short to justify the usage, and commas would have sufficed.

§6.3 HYPHENS, DASHES, BRACKETS, AND PARENTHESES

These four marks cause lawyers few problems. Hyphens bother writers only when used to break words at the end of a line; with the advent of word processing, the problem disappears *en passant*. For those Neanderthals (like myself) who still type an occasional manuscript on old-fashioned machines built more than three months ago, the word-divider is an occasional necessity. In general, words should be divided only at the end of a syllable ("there-at," not "the-reat"); if you are in doubt, check a dictionary.

Dashes divide a thought from the rest of the sentence. When typing, use double hyphens (which in print would be dashes)—as opposed to commas or parentheses—only for special emphasis. Remember to use hyphens before and after the emphasized material, which need not be in the form of a complete sentence.

Brackets should serve only one function, to mark off, *within quotations,* language that is the writer's and not the quoted source's. Such language ordinarily is inserted to permit the reader to gain a sense of the quotation's context, as follows:

■ In the British [naval] statute, 22 Geo. 2 ch. 33 [1749, repealed 1860], many allusions are made to the office of the lord high admiral, who's [*sic*] review powers were considerable.

Parentheses separate from the body of a sentence language that relates to the main thought but is not central to it. The rest of the sentence, apart from the parentheses, should be a grammatically complete entity without relying on the parenthetical language. This extends to the sentence's punctuation, which should appear *outside* the parenthesis:

■ The contractor is in a position to perform the remaining interference work (Exhibit A), such as it is, without economic hardship (see the letter dated 22 July in Exhibit B).

Parentheses, then, are different from commas (although commas sometimes serve the same function) and from dashes, both of which ordinarily set off language somewhat more central to the main idea.

The nuances are fine, and the writer has some latitude in deciding among commas, dashes, or parentheses. For example, the following sentence could be punctuated variously:

☐ Defendant's argument never overly persuasive failed to convince the court.

The writer's choice depends on the emphasis she wishes to give to the phrase "never overly persuasive." The greatest emphasis takes dashes; the normal emphasis, commas; and the least, parentheses. Context and goal determine the punctuation.

Lawyers also employ parentheses (and sometimes brackets) in citation form determined by sources and authorities unique to the venue or situation in which the lawyers are writing. This usage falls outside the scope of this book.

Review Exercises
for Part II*

■ **Punctuate correctly the following sentences. (No parentheses are called for.)**

1. In *X v. Y* a "creeping tender offer" case the company whose shares were purchased was incorporated in Delaware however that was the state's only contact with the transaction in question.

2. Z argued that as a practical matter both the conditional sale financing and the chattel lease financing achieved the same net result and that both transactions were regularly entered into as a part of its finance business.

3. The Commission decided that the benefits of normalization exceed the detriments and it issued the order with changes recommended by staff.

4. Plaintiff had his car towed from the scene of the accident to a repair shop but he never had the car repaired.

5. With respect to the litigation pending between X Corp. and Y Corp. X Corp. has projected that if X Corp's motion to stay litigation were granted and an arbitrable award were rendered in Germany it could not subsequently enforce the award in the federal district courts of the United States since the arbitration agreement is invalid under German law.

*See page 289 for suggestions about these exercises.

■ **Revise the following sentences. (Stress noun and verb choice.)**

1. It would appear based on Section 875, then, that to determine whether the Company was engaged in trade or business in the U.S., if it were a foreign corporation, we would have to determine whether its subsidiary is engaged in such trade or business.

2. The alleged purposes of this business and union combination and conspiracy were to engage in a systematic campaign of unlawful and tortious interference with plaintiff's business in the metropolitan area, including acts of business and physical pressure, intimidation, coercion, obstruction of the plaintiff and the tenants in connection with the move into the building, and acts to unlawfully eliminate plaintiff as a competitor in the metropolitan area.

3. The source of my information and belief are my law office records, which I believe to be true.

4. In my conversation with X, I was told that if the Company does not take Y back, a full-time person will be hired.

5. Completion of payment milestones dependent upon Y's performance shall be evidenced by a performance demonstration witnessed and accepted by X. Completion of all other milestones shall be evidenced by submission of certification or documentation by Y.

■ **Choose the best word or phrase.**

1. Neither the Administrator nor his deputies _____ the regulation.
   a. understand
   b. understands
   c. would appear to understand

2. Each of the proposed statutory provisions _____ the requisite protections.
   a. omit
   b. omits
   c. may not be said to include

3. In order to complete an inter vivos gift, it is necessary _____ dominion and control.

    a. to clearly relinquish
    b. to clearly and without ambiguity relinquish
    c. clearly to relinquish
4. Pleased with the development of the litigation, _____ .
    a. the case brought new business to the attorney.
    b. the attorney accepted new business brought in by the case.
    c. it allowed the attorney to increase his business.
5. Putting aside the decision's precedential value, _____ as between the parties.
    a. it is fair
    b. fairness prevails
    c. I find it fair

■ **Eliminate verbiage in these sentences by changing the subject, the verb, or both.**

1. The appropriate standard by which the existence of a *prima facie* case may be measured in a discharge case is modelled on the test articulated in *McDonnell Douglas v. Green.*

2. A witness will be provided by X to testify as to cost breakdown for the bills which had previously been provided to both defendants by X.

3. The payroll office will make provision for the distribution of pay checks.

4. Registration of claims will be accepted at the offices of Smith and Smith.

5. Finding the exception to the hearsay rule is the only means by which plaintiff can hope to have that evidence admitted.

III

Awareness of Audience Elaborated

7

Appropriateness: Recognizing the Spectrum of Your Writing

§7.1 DEGREES OF DIRECTNESS, INFORMALITY, AND SIMPLICITY

Legal writing tends to be unnecessarily monolithic. The part of professional expression that is constrained by form comes to overwhelm the residue, which might otherwise allow for greater liberality of expression. As we have seen, lawyers needlessly alienate and confuse certain audiences by adopting stylistic postures fitting only for other audiences.

Section 3.4 introduced the notion that all good writing begins with awareness of audience. But even if that hurdle be leapt, the aim of the document must be juxtaposed to the needs of the identified reader or readers. Thus the first step of literally imagining the document's probable readers will lead nowhere if the image is not broadened to encompass a living, needful, responsive, three-dimensional "other" on the receiving end of the process. And even such a fully humanized document will be unsuccessful if the writer's goals remain vaguely defined or inadequately conveyed.

Lawyers write either for each other or for the laity, a simple enough observation that is rarely recalled in the heat of producing a document. Instead, nonprofessionals fall victim to violations of their legitimate expectations as lay readers, and instead of directness, informality, and simplicity, they receive the following.

87

§7.1.1   Lawyer-to-Nonlawyer

1. *Indirectness:*

   ☐ From the point of view of expediency, a settlement is advised.

2. *Formality:*

   ☐ Please acknowledge receipt of the above by signing the enclosed copy of this letter and returning the same to the undersigned.

3. *Complexity:*

   ☐ Vincristine, actinomycin D, and adriamycin may cause ulceration of the skin at the site of injection, if they are inadvertently injected into the tissues instead of directly into a vein.

   You may participate in studies relating to use of laminar-air-flow facilities, bone marrow fusion, and total intravenous nutrition while being treated for your tumor. The use of these modalities will be selected in each case by a controlled randomization. Should it become apparent during the period of treatment that one of the alternatives in each case is superior to the other, you will be treated in the manner which is proven to be superior.

RULE 10.   Avoid all lawyerisms and jargon when writing to nonlawyers.

Lawyer-to-laity writing should be fully humanized. Jargon has no place in such communications. The risks of directness are fewer than with fellow practitioners and far outweighed by the benefits of comprehension. Informality, analogously, yields responsiveness without sacrificing respect. Complexity may temporarily dazzle, but it, too, eventually pales beside the information-gathering potential of the simple touch.

The aims of all three writers in the examples above were foiled, not facilitated, by the stilted language chosen. But suppose their audience had been fellow lawyers? Is it always true that lawyer-to-lawyer writing benefits from higher levels of indirectness, formality, and complexity? The next examples of intra-professional writing prove that "sounding like a lawyer," even here, has its limitations.

§7.1.2 Lawyer-to-Lawyer

1. *Indirectness* (from a memorandum sent to a senior associate in house):

☐ The application of the Act in this case may violate due process because Hicksville may lack sufficient contacts with this transaction such that the maintenance of this action would exceed the court's personal jurisdiction over the defendants.

2. *Formality* (from a motion for summary judgment, a letter, and an internal memorandum):

☐ In the aforementioned matter, the basis of the motion is that defendant, as owner of the premises and plaintiff's customer thereat, is liable for payment of said bill.

☐ Attached hereto are exhibits A and B, hereinafter referred to as "A" and "B."

☐ The John Doe Company, heretofore known as The Doe Store, is obligated under said contract to perform such services as listed in Schedule I, annexed hereto.

3. *Complexity* (from an internal memorandum):

☐ The ability of a foreclosing mortgagee to avoid joining a lessee in a foreclosure proceeding or to obtain leave to discontinue as against the lessee, right up to the time of sale, with the result that the lessee may remain in undisturbed possession after such sale, allows a mortgagee to agree to the "non-disturbance" clause often sought by lessees and contained in many leases.

These passages indicate the extremes of needless obfuscation when lawyers write for each other. If we stepped back and read these as a Blackstone or a Marshall or a Cardozo might, we would wonder what was amiss in this great old profession.

In all of the lawyer-to-lawyer examples, the writer failed to discriminate a *spectrum* of appropriate styles. Putting the audience sensitivity needed in lawyer-to-laity writing together with spectrum awareness required intra-professionally, we arrive at the position illustrated in Charts 1 and 2 on the following page.

§7.2 TAILORING TONE TO THE CASE AT HAND

Not having mastered the spectrum of audiences and goals basic to effective communication, many legal writers fail to adopt an appropriate tone. Or more accurately, they find a single tone and stick to it no matter how varied the range of professional writing. Less frequently, lawyers attempting to expand their tonal range lose sight of their audience and experiment in the wrong medium. The trick, of course, is to meld the goal of the document with awareness of audience and in the process to achieve tonal appropriateness.

§7.2.1   General Correspondence

Along the usual spectrum of professional writing, general correspondence is the freest category. Apart from technical letters, which include opinion letters or specialist-to-specialist correspondence involving specific points of law, letters dictated at one's office

CHART 1
The Spectrum When At Least One Nonlawyer Will Read Document
Scale varies from least (−) to most (XXX) within category.

	Letters	*Internal memo*	*External memo*	*Consent form, etc.*	*Consumer contract*	*Judicial opinions*	*Contracts, wills, other technical writings*
Directness of exposition	XXX	XXX	XXX—if all on writer's "team"; or varies	XXX	XXX	XXX*	XXX
Informality of tone	XXX	varies with audience	varies with audience	XX	XX	X	X
Simplicity of language (avoidance of technical language)	XXX	XXX	XXX	XXX	XXX	XX	−

*An exception, brought to my attention by participants in programs I have conducted for judges, involves the lower court judge who dislikes the appellate rule but is bound to apply it.

CHART 2
The Spectrum When Only Lawyers Will Read Document
Scale varies from least (−) to most (XXX) within category.

	Letters	*Internal memo*	*External memo*	*Litigation related*	*Non-consumer contracts*	*Corporate and technical writings*
Directness of exposition	varies with aim of letter	XXX	XXX—if all on writer's "team" only	XXX	XXX	XXX
Informality of tone	XX	varies with audience	varies with audience	—	X	X
Simplicity of language	XX	XX (less if only fellow specialists are the likely readers, but see §7.3.2)	XX	XX	−	−

are not that different from those penned at home. Here the writer can accurately envision the primary audience and, even while considering the possibility of eventual additional readers, suit the tone to the correspondent.

In other contexts we have seen several examples of good and bad letters, both to fellow lawyers and to nonlawyers. (See, e.g., excerpts at pages 18, 20, 43, 88.) The bad letters to nonlawyers were always ascribable to stilted tone; Rule 10 (page 88) was not yet mastered, and the reader was bombarded with the "hereinbefores," "aboves," and "thereats" so offensive to nonlawyers and so retrograde to the letter's true aims.

Can lawyers envision a human audience and write humanely? The following letter proves the potential existence and power of tonally appropriate general correspondence.

May 6, 1979

Dear Mr. X:

This letter is to give you some information about the closing of your apartment, which should take place shortly. I will contact Y, Inc. to arrange for a closing date and time shortly after your meeting with the board of directors of the cooperative, which is scheduled for May 6.

At the closing you will need a check for $392,750.00, which is the balance due at closing. This amount should be paid by a bank check or your personal certified check and paid to the order of X.

Please bring several blank personal checks with you to pay for the maintenance adjustment and any other small amounts that will have to be paid at closing.

If you have not already done so, please have your insurance broker obtain an insurance binder for the apartment. The effective date of the policy should be the date of the closing. Also, before you come to the closing, you should inspect the apartment for any missing or damaged items and to see that the apartment is "broom-clean."

If you have any questions, do not hesitate to contact me. I look forward to meeting you very soon.

Very truly yours,

George Mitchell, Esq.

Attorney George Mitchell, by returning to basics, has achieved the proper tone. Combining document goal with awareness of audience, he excells at his profession by following his humane instincts as a writer. Lawyer-to-laity correspondence calls for little more than this.

Letters to fellow lawyers are different. As we have seen (pages 43, 91), some traditional indirectness may be appropriate, although there is rarely an excuse in letters for formalism and stilted speech (page 89). Indeed, the main tonal difference in letter writing to lawyers (as opposed to nonlawyers) derives from the ensconced ways of *beginning* intra-professional correspondence. While I will reiterate the structural effects of these conventions in Chapter 11, they are worth identifying here because they clearly affect tone.

In writing to a nonlawyer, as George Mitchell recognized, attorneys ordinarily should be direct in tone. This means, more often than not, getting to the point of the letter fairly rapidly. On the other hand, letters to lawyers often delay the main point in deference to the following conventional opening gambits.

1. *The attachment mannerism:*

   ☐ Attached please find a copy of a regulation effective in December 1982, concerning two topics: the cash accounting for capital maintenance notes and requirements for cash reserves for deposit accounts.

2. *The recapitulation mannerism:*

   ☐ This letter confirms our telephone discussion that we need your department's approval for two new savings certifications offered by our industrial loan company in X. They are the Custom Design Certificate and the Savings Account Certificate. Two samples of each are included.

3. *The social mannerism:*

   ☐ It was a pleasure to meet with you, Pat, Bob, and Alice at your office last Wednesday at 2 P.M.

Tonally, these mannerisms are professional and quite appropriate. They add little to the status quo, but they do keep everyone's files straight. They should not be used in letters to nonlawyers, who expect to find out rapidly the reasons for the letter rather than the situation's general history.

§7.2.2 The Memorandum of Law

The memorandum of law designed only for internal circulation has more in common with general correspondence than with less subjective kinds of legal writing, such as drafting. The lawyer should strive for tonal directness, since the aim of these memos is direct communication of information. Of course, greater leeway is permitted in the use of technical language because the presumed audience consists of other lawyers. But the tone can be far less stilted, and the style far more personal, than in documents that risk eventual perusal by potentially adversarial readers.

Most lawyers, at least in my experience with hundreds of them, fail to capitalize on the appropriate, direct memorandum tone. Few lapses in awareness of audience are as glaring or as costly as the blindness, particularly among younger lawyers, to the memorandum's implicitly liberating nature.

Not that the internal memorandum lacks formal, or structural, constraints (*see* page 154 and §15.3). Tone and style come alive, however, if the lawyer is prepared to translate technical knowledge into direct information. And direct information, not legalistic fudging, is what the audience wants.

Consider this typical opening:

☐ You have asked me to consider the implications of Section 16(a), specifically Rule 16a-b promulgated thereunder, on Section 16(b) liability. Reference is made to memoranda submitted on March 12 and March 26, 1986, wherein other aspects of Section 16(b) liability were discussed. The facts, questions presented, and discussions in the above-mentioned memoranda are incorporated herein by reference.

The first six words (although themselves stylized) are direct enough, but the rest of the paragraph falls off rapidly into caricature. The writer seems to have felt that since he was analyzing a statute he needed to write like a legislative committee instead of an individual lawyer. Meanwhile, his reader is forced to wade through the absurdly unnecessary series, "thereunder," "wherein," "above-mentioned," and "incorporated by reference" to get to the paragraph's message. Considering how slim that (recapitulated) message is, the lawyerisms conveying it seem especially grotesque.

Or, consider the following attempts to transmit more substantive learning to an in-house superior:

☐ That statute, in essence, provides that every agreement, promise, or undertaking is void unless it, or some note or memorandum thereof, is in writing and subscribed by the party to be charged therewith . . .

☐ Buyers employed agents to find suppliers of commodities and to effect purchases thereof. Sellers of said commodities had been paying brokerage fees to persons in similar positions . . .

☐ All of the purchases by the defendants of XYZ shares took place outside of Center City and therefore, it has been suggested, it would offend due process to allow Center City to regulate those transactions.

In all three samples, the writer simply forgot that his audience needed direct information, not obfuscation or formalism more appropriate to some adversarial contexts. In the first, the writer needlessly tracks convoluted statutory language although the promise ("in essence") was to provide a clearer *paraphrase*. In the second, the words "to effect purchases thereof" force the reader to translate his colleague's memo into understandable English, and the lawyerism "said" (as an adjective) would be more appropriate to a real estate conveyance; in the third, the phrase "it has been suggested" is downright bizarre, since it hides *from a colleague* the source of the suggestion.

RULE 11.   When writing for colleagues in house, convey information with the utmost directness and avoid a needlessly complex or impersonal tone.

This rule, perhaps more than most, may seem to need fine-tuning in light of the writer's sense of immediate audience and specific context. There may be some senior lawyers who demand stilted speech in their memos. Usually, however, this "demand" is a figment of the memo writer's imagination. Most lawyers want a straightforward exposition of already complex legal and factual material; they do *not* want yet another piece of legalese to deconstruct. Above all, the rule speaks to *directness,* not necessarily simplicity or jargon avoidance. The latter is a separate question, treated in §7.3.2.

Informality does have its limits and should not be confused with directness. The tone, even though direct, must be professional. Colloquialisms, arguably appropriate in some letters, may not sit well in a memo:

☐ X and Y agreed to contribute 100 percent of the cost of acquiring, owning, and maintaining the property, till the fifth semiannual mortgage payment was to become due.

"Till" is tonally jarring in this context.

§7.2.3   Litigation Related Documents

Somewhat more constrained is the litigator. *Somewhat.* Through the years I have begun to see that, apart from statutory constraints on some adversarial documents (e.g., affidavits, pleadings), the litigator enjoys considerable stylistic freedom. In fact, judges are more inclined to resent stilted and verbose documents—particularly briefs and supporting memoranda—than to respect blind allegiance to formalistic language. I treat this at greater length in Part V in dealing with reform of boilerplate.

Nonetheless, adversary documents require, from the perspective of awareness of audience, a more consistently formal and respectful tone than do the other genres so far considered. Thus, much as the following prose (from a brief to an appeals court) may strike us as refreshing, it is not appropriate to the context:

☐ If the Board really and truly believes that the level of inflation will drop to 6.19 percent in 1980, then it is out of step with the consensus of economic prognosticators. . . .
  Now let's look at what the experts are projecting. . . .

§7.2.4 Legal Instruments

Traditionally, the technical skill of "drafting" legal instruments (contracts, wills, conveyances, etc.) liberated the lawyer-writer to be his most disciplined and professional self. Writing primarily against the threat of eventual judicial interpretation and scrutiny, the draftsman would bring to bear all his technical skills and would care little for the informal mechanisms of direct communication. Drafting was legal writing at its most rigorous and poetic.

To a large extent, the extreme and challenging constraints of drafting remain unchanged by time and reform (*see* §7.3.2; Chapter 18). However, the immediate audience of most documents, as we noted early in Part I, has come more into focus recently. The fact that a consumer contract not only protects one side from eventual litigation but also *explains* to the other the terms of the arrangement now may require the draftsman to consider more simple and direct language. The securities lawyer may need to tailor some of his drafting to lay requirements of comprehension and full disclosure.

In general, however, this end of the legal writing spectrum brings with it a unique set of technical constraints. Fittingly, drafting has thus been analyzed in volume-length studies such as Reed Dickerson's. I do not ignore it here; I emphasize it to remind lawyers that most of what they do stands in contradistinction to drafting and that legalistic mannerisms and technical speech, appropriate to drafting, have little value elsewhere.

§7.3 APPROPRIATE USES OF JARGON

§7.3.1 Three Reasons Why Jargon Survives

Some reformers would sweep the slate clean of all arcane and strange-sounding words used uniquely by lawyers. My emphasis, however, is on audience, goals, and appropriateness. The same language to which we objected as bizarre in the context of a letter or memorandum may be entirely felicitious (and indeed irreplaceable) in the context of drafting, judicial opinions, and specialist-to-specialist legal speech. Thus to the "knight-on-white-charger" variety of reformer who asks "Why use that lawyerism when an ordinary word or words suffice?," I would reply: "Why replace them if they work?" But "work," as this book has defined the verb, always means "acts appropriately for the intended audience, given the goals of the document itself." The dispute in its fullness concerns the language specialist more than the average practitioner and is better left for resolution elsewhere. I will try only to instill in the legal writer a desire to use his professional language, *with all its quirks,* as effectively as possible in all circumstances.

Three examples from the law of wills serve to focus our discussion. Let us begin with the phrase "Last Will and Testament." As Professor Mellinkoff observes, the phrase is redundant and typifies noun clusters combining synonymous English and law French usages. Let us follow up with the weird adjectival form of the word "said" ("the *said* parties") used that way only by lawyers. And, finally, we will analyze the phrase "per stirpes." All three of these usages displease purists. Yet, for three somewhat disparate reasons, all three continue to be appropriate in the testamentary context.

The titular phrase "Last Will and Testament" survives, in my opinion, for *esthetic* reasons. As Pascal said hundreds of years ago, "The heart has reasons which reason cannot grasp," and in this regard lawyers, too, have a heart. The bald word "Will," fully equal to the descriptive task, lacks the panache of the original; moreover, the redundancy seems almost appropriate in a setting deliberately designed *by the law itself* to stress solemnity and formalism. If the testamentary requirements of attestation, execution, and probate sometimes seem primarily to serve form more than substance, what could be more fitting than a title that acts similarly?

"Said," used as an adjective, survives for a quite different reason: *utility*. Try as he might, the draftsman cannot always replace "plain English" for legal jargon. In some cases, as it turns out, lawyerisms have survived for pragmatic reasons. The adjective "said" is one of those cases. Although "this" or a pronoun sometimes comes close to the mark, neither lends the precision that "said" offers:

■ I give, devise, and bequeath [!] to my wife, Jane Doe, all the rest, residue, and remainder[!] of my estate, wheresoever situate [!]. In the event that my said wife [this wife?] [she?] [my wife?] shall not survive me, I give the said remainder to the X Home for the Aged.

"Said" provides unambiguous explicitness to the draftsman. "This wife" is simply unclear; "she" is better, but only because of the pronoun's absolute proximity to the referent, a disadvantageous choice when (as frequently happens) the reference to Jane Doe must be repeated further down in this and even subsequent paragraphs, where the word "she" is far less clear; and "my wife" might later be construed to mean someone other than Jane Doe, someone else who at some time played that role in the Testator's life.

"Said" is bizarre, but it is irreplaceable not only to the drafter of wills but to other technical lawyers as well. Odd but replaceable, the redundant word clusters and the archaic "wheresoever situate" (all demarcated by a bracketed exclamation point above) have also managed so far to survive reform. Again, I would ascribe their longevity to aesthetics rather than utility.

But what of the phrase "per stirpes," symbolic here of the hundreds of Latin and law French words still used everyday by fully modernized American lawyers whose penchant for foreign languages probably extends no further? Like "said," some of these words are hard to replace efficiently. (*"En ventre sa mere,"* another testamentary phrase, may be terrible French and otherwise meaningless, but to put it into understandable English would not be worth the effort.) But "per stirpes" has two viable English counterparts, recognized by all practitioners: "by the stocks" and "by representation." The survival of this latinate jargon is for a third, discrete reason: *inertia*. And jargon that lasts solely because of inertia should be eliminated from the lexicon.

RULE 12. When writing exclusively for fellow specialists or when drafting, use jargon if it is pleasing to you *and* your audience or if it cannot be improved by ordinary English; do not, however, use jargon reflexively or out of habit alone.

§7.3.2 Defining the Jargon-Receptive Audience

A key part of Rule 12, particularly the esthetic component of the rule, involves, once again, awareness of audience. I hope I have firmly established that jargon has no place in communications with the laity. The days of dazzle and mystification are at an end, as nonlawyers have become more sophisticated and less tolerant of obfuscation for its own sake. But does jargon pose any risk of disenchanting the fellow practitioner?

A generation or so ago, *Plain Words* (an excellent British text on bureaucratic writing) said this about "expert-to-expert writing":

> "Really there are times", writes Mr. G. M. Young sadly, "when I feel that civilisation will come to an end because no one will understand what anybody else is saying."
>
> Official writing plays a comparatively small part in building this new Tower of Babel. But it cannot escape all blame. When officials are accused of writing jargon, what is generally meant is that they affect a pompous and flabby verbosity. That is not what I mean. What I have in mind is that technical terms are used—especially conventional phrases invented by a Government department—which are understood inside the department but are unintelligible to outsiders. That is true jargon. A circular from the headquarters of a department to its regional officers begins:
>
> > The physical progressing of building cases should be confined to . . .
>
> Nobody could say what meaning this was intended to convey

unless he held the key. It is not English, except in the sense that the words are English words. They are a group of symbols used in conventional senses known only to the parties to the convention. It may be said that no harm is done, because the instruction is not meant to be read by anyone unfamiliar with the departmental jargon. But using jargon is a dangerous habit; it is easy to forget that the public do not understand it, and to slip into the use of it in explaining things to them. If that is done, those seeking enlightenment will find themselves plunged in even deeper obscurity.[1]

Although some lay reformers now feel less constrained than before, painting their simplifying mission with a broad brush extending to technical writing, I concur with this passage. For the legal writer thinking through his use of jargon in the expert-to-expert setting, awareness of audience and then control over subject matter must replace a knee-jerk use of bizarre (if professionally recognized) language. The threshold question involves envisioning the expert audience that is most likely to peruse the document. For the advocate, this can mean familiarizing himself with the various judicial styles to which he must appeal: If a judge abjures jargon in his own style, there is good reason to avoid it when briefing his court. Even if the judge's written (or oral) style looks arcane, the litigator cannot be certain that jargon will be *received* favorably by the court. Similarly the lawyer writing for a given administrator or agency must try to glean the stylistic requirements (if any) and proclivities of those entities before assuming audience receptivity to jargon.

Trial and error often must occur before the writer gets to know the reader's competencies and taste. The best hint, implicit in Rule 12, is to try jargon-reduced documents until it is proven that the audience requires otherwise. (But note: This hint decidedly does not apply to situations in which there is a remote chance that litigation will arise when plain speech replaces timeworn jargon. See §17.2 on in-house reform of boilerplate, however, to recognize how much discretion the supervising attorney enjoys to simplify documents without arousing in-house or judicial controversy.)

[1] E. A. Gowers, The Complete Plain Words 78 (1954).

As *Plain Words* indicates, once awareness of audience has revealed a jargon-sympathetic expert reader, the writer nonetheless retains full responsibility for clear-headed language that accurately reflects the document's goals. Jargon, far from adequately replacing lucidity, *requires* it constantly.

8

Losing Touch with Your Lay Reader

§8.1 JARGON: HEREIN OF SOUNDING LIKE A LAWYER AT THE WRONG TIME

If I seem to stress lawyer-to-laity communication to the point of doctrine, it is because the profession suffers needlessly from its failings in this area. The costs to the lawyer range from bad public relations to wasted time, the former because our world is now less tolerant of professional mystification, the latter because when readers cannot decipher language, requests and advice must be repeated, and inefficiencies ensue.

The charts at page 91 called on the legal writer to tailor her speech when the likely audience included at least one nonlawyer. Increasing sensitivity to readership permits, of course, finer gradations in tone; some nonlawyers (perhaps "clients" within the lawyer's corporation, perhaps external business people) may be more sophisticated than others. Indeed, some lay specialists may tolerate (and appreciate) jargon while some nonspecialist lawyers may not. As a general rule, however, even the most specialized nonlawyer finds jargon disequilibrating at worst, humorous at best.

To seal the point, I reproduce here a letter from Jane Doe, Corporation A's lawyer, to a nonlawyer executive of Corporation

Z, providing him with certain information and asking him to do certain things:

May 14, 1985

Mr. Jones, Vice President
Z Corporation

Re: Power Line Easement
Center City, North Dakota

Dear Mr. Jones:

In connection with the above captioned transaction, I enclose herewith a copy of a Power Line Easement ("Easement"), fully executed and acknowledged by A ("A").

Pursuant to your request, the original copy of the Easement was forwarded directly to the Valley Public Service District in North Dakota. As we discussed on the telephone, the proposed form was redrafted in order to more clearly set out the property description for the Easement. The proper form of acknowledgement was also added.

In reviewing and executing this Easement, we have noted that B Power Company ("B") has not assumed any liability for any damage that may result in connection with the Easement. We have assumed that it was Z's choice not to require B to indemnify A for such damage.

Section 19 of the lease dated as of June 3, 1956 between A, as lessor, and Z, as lessee (the "Lease"), provides that Z will fully indemnify A for all liabilities, claims, and costs arising from any injury or damage to any person or property occurring on or about the service station property, any use, non-use, or condition of the property or any failure of Z to comply with the terms of the Lease. It is our understanding that, notwithstanding the absence of an assumption of liability by B under the Easement, Z's obligation to indemnify A in accordance with Section 19 of the Lease will in no way be limited, restricted, or otherwise modified either in respect of the property included in or affected by the easement or in respect to any other portion of the above caption service station property.

I have also enclosed herewith the original copy of a survey for the above-captioned service station and a copy of my cover letter to Mr. Frank Smith of the Valley Public Service District.

Please acknowledge receipt of the above by signing the enclosed copy of this letter and returning the same to the undersigned.

Very truly yours,

Jane Doe, Esq.

JD/ad
Enc.

Receipt Acknowledged
this   day of May 1985

By _____

As noted periodically, awareness of audience dictates the success or failure of each professional document, and awareness of audience requires interweaving the *aims* of the document with the *needs* of the immediate and potential reader or readers. In the case of a letter to a lay reader, awareness of audience calls for the elimination of all jargon. Reading from start to finish here, the following words disappear from Jane Doe's letter, replaced by the parenthetical simplification:

the above captioned (this)
herewith (   )
Pursuant to your request (As you asked)
the above captioned (this)
herewith (   )
the above captioned (this)
Please acknowledge receipt of the above (?)
and returning the same to the undersigned (returning it to
    me)

As the jargon falls away, ambiguities as well as awkwardness are revealed. In the last paragraph, a key request has been buried under jargon. What exactly is lawyer Doe asking executive Jones to do?

Furthermore, the substantively central fourth paragraph, while lacking in standard legal jargon, can hardly guarantee lay understanding of the 1956 lease. Jargon, in this sense, is the lawyerlike proclivity to paraphrase a preexisting document into greater confusion than the original. Annoying even to fellow lawyers (*see* §7.2.2), this strain of jargon must utterly mystify lay readers. Let us attempt a clear restatement of the first sentence of that paragraph, placing in brackets the awareness of audience technique exemplified:

■ Please keep in mind [transition to related, but new, subject] the June 3, 1956, lease between A as lessor and Z as lessee [short sentences for clarity]. This lease [no special term of art—"lease"—required in a letter] provides that Z will fully indemnify A for all liability of any kind arising from the use of the service station property or from Z's failure to comply with the lease. [If Jane Doe needed to give Mr. Jones the fuller description, she should have quoted *directly* from the lease; probably she did not intend the legalistic description that finally came out.]

The long paragraph's second sentence ("It is our understanding . . ."), which must have been central to the writer's purpose, is buried structurally (*see* §8.2) and incomprehensible linguistically. Consisting of a triple negative ("notwithstanding the absence . . . will in no way be limited"), the sentence also epitomizes legal jargon in two other ways. First, it mystifies the lay reader through an inapposite redundant verb cluster, "in no way be limited, restricted, or otherwise modified"; then, it mixes prepositions through the unidiomatic, "either in respect *of* the property included . . . or in respect *to* any other portion . . . .".

Had Jane Doe thought through the importance of this sentence and the nature of her reader, she might have placed the sentence earlier (*see* §8.2) and come up with more suitable language. For example:

■ Although [Since?] B has not assumed liability under the Easement, we believe that Z's Section 19 obligation under the lease remains fully in effect and that neither the Easement itself nor other aspects of the service station property affect that obligation.

§8.2 PRESENTATION VS. THOROUGHNESS: A NEEDLESS STRUGGLE

We have not yet done with Ms. Doe's letter. Jargon marks it off as unsuccessful, but so does another basic error of lawyer-to-laity writing: burying the key thoughts.

RULE 13. A lawyer need not sacrifice thoroughness to achieve an effective written presentation.

As with tone, complexity of presentation, and jargon, so with the overall presentation of a written document: Lawyers fail to distinguish among their audiences. With thoroughness (correctly) constantly in her mind, Jane Doe covers all bases, but she probably has lost her audience long before the game has ended.

What are the principal goals of this letter? Only the writer knows for sure, of course. But, as I discuss more generally in Part IV, most legal writings reveal their goal—at least after several close readings. The idea, perhaps particularly in writing to nonlawyers whose attention span may be shorter and who are, after all, usually not paid to be attentive readers, is to place the goal or goals *prominently*. In so doing, the lawyer need not sacrifice thoroughness; instead, she gains reader responsiveness and quick receptivity to her aims.

Ms. Doe apparently intended Mr. Jones to do four main things:

1. Receive a copy of the Easement
2. Read it
3. Recognize that Jones's company (Z) is still indemnifying A, a situation unchanged by the Easement
4. Acknowledge receipt of several related documents by signing a copy of the letter and returning it to Doe

While the first goal is articulated in the first paragraph, it is the most obvious and need hardly be mentioned at all. (*See* §7.2.1, the "attachment convention.") Readers usually can see for themselves what has been attached. The second goal is implicit; it might better have been directly conveyed. "Please read the Easement," Ms. Doe might have said in her second sentence, and continued, "After making the changes we discussed in its property description and adding the proper acknowledgement form, I forwarded it to the Valley Public Service District."

Now Ms. Doe is ready to make her third point and to make it relatively quickly and clearly:

■ The B Power Company had not assumed any liability connected with the Easement, and we assume that was Z's choice. Since, under Section 19 of the lease between A and Z of June 3, 1956, Z has fully indemnified A against all losses connected with use of the service station property and against any failure of Z to comply with the lease, Z's obligation remains fully in effect and is unchanged either by the Easement or the service station property.

Paragraphs two and three have thus been merged and the point politely but powerfully made. (Note that, under certain circumstances, a yet stronger tone might be adopted, for example, "Company Z continues to indemnify A against all losses . . . ," only then filling in the background information relating to B, the lease, etc.) Instead of burying her third goal, which is also her most substantive remark in the letter, Jane Doe achieves it unambiguously but professionally.

Goal four should have been easily attained, since it was a mere "return receipt requested." Instead, Ms. Doe encumbered it with the jargon of her final two paragraphs. A direct request would have sufficed:

■ Please acknowledge receipt of the Easement, and related survey and cover letter, by signing and returning the enclosed copy of this letter.

The rest of the letter—background, file-perfection data, and so on—should of course be included. But thoroughness, a basic professional trait, clearly can coexist with effective presentation of the document's goals.

The fault lies not in our (professional) stars but in ourselves. When lawyers write for the laity, extra time must be expended on a strategy that will respond to the audience's expectations without sacrificing thoroughness. In the process, the lawyer will reap a twofold benefit of increased audience responsiveness and increased lucidity in understanding her document's major aims.

§8.3 FINDING THE MORE DIRECT TONE

Legal writers distrust colloquialisms. Indeed, as we have seen once or twice already (pages 96-97), they sometimes seem awkward attempting to sound trendy or simply "laid back." Yet nonlawyers find the usual stilted lawyerisms disconcerting and mystifying. How can the lawyer locate a happy tonal medium when writing directly to the laity? The answers to that question should be reiterated here:

1. Use a personal voice.
2. Use strong nouns. (Strong verbs will follow.)
3. Avoid words that only lawyers use.
4. Paraphrase legal data simply instead of repeating the statutory, regulatory, or judicial language. (If you use the legal language, be honest and place the language in quotation marks.)
5. Locate the central aims of your document *before* you begin to write it.
6. Feature these aims instead of burying them.

A final example may serve to exemplify all six of these points. The writer had mastered many of them, but she still was grappling with the final two:

> ☐ I received a copy of the book contract your publisher sent to you. I know you are under a deadline, and I will review it quickly and get back to you with my comments. The

other day I indicated that in addition to the contract I need to see the sample chapter you submitted to the publisher. This has not crossed my desk.

On balance, in terms of awareness of audience, the paragraph above gets fairly high marks. Writing to an out-of-town client, the lawyer has adopted a direct but cordial tone and has eliminated jargon in all but her last (fairly innocuous) six words. However, the "recapitulation convention" (§7.2.1) manages to prevail over the featuring of central aims. Somewhat buried in the paragraph, the vital reminder of the penultimate sentence may be lost to the reader.

Naturally the writer was faced with one of the strategic conflicts so typical of nontechnical legal writing; here it is less one of thoroughness versus presentation as *tone* versus presentation. The lawyer needs to reiterate an earlier (but unfulfilled) request without antagonizing her client. Perhaps the structure of the paragraph as written represents a conscious compromise between these conflicting contextual realities. If so, then the writer *did* fulfill item 5 in the list above because ameliorating the client's feelings while urging him to forward the sample chapter was, indeed, a central aim of the letter. If, however, as is more likely, the writer did not devote sufficient time to locating her aims before writing the letter, then the resultant tone is haphazard and potentially ineffective. The lay correspondent may not read far enough into the paragraph to see the urgent request or, if he does, he may still feel somewhat offended by the critical tone of its final sentences.

In concluding this chapter, I urge the reader to redraft the paragraph above in order to marry tone and presentation. In so doing, try to follow all six of the listed points. A sample edit follows.

■ Thank you for sending me the proposed book contract from your publisher. Please keep in mind however, that I will also need to see your sample chapter in order to comment fully on the contract. Since you wish to move quickly, I suggest an expedited mailing of the sample chapter. If overnight mail service is not available, please contact me by phone and we will make other arrangements.

9

Universally Inappropriate Legal Writing Habits

In Chapters 7 and 8 I urged the legal writer to be conscious of his varying audiences and to match the goals of his document with the needs of his likely readership. Something of a dichotomy has been established between lay and professional audiences: Particularly as regards jargon and tone, the correctness of a document may depend on that dichotomy.

The next two chapters dissolve the dichotomy. Everything discussed from this point until the end of Part III applies evenhandedly to all legal writing. These elements are central to awareness of audience, for their use—and abuse—can make or break a document's effect on the reader. Examples abound for each element. Indeed, I draw on no fewer than 43 actual writings to exemplify these points, which characterize legal writing across the spectrum of training, competence, and specialty. This chapter emphasizes the negative, but its effect on future writing should be strongly salutary.

§9.1 RAMBLING SENTENCES

Long sentences spell trouble for the legal writer, yet like a moth to the flames he is drawn fatally to them. If he can come to control them, he will enter into "Cardozo territory," the rarified atmosphere of great legal prose. Then he may impress his reader through the interplay of long and short sentences that lends stylistic spice to substantive analysis. But before attaining those heights, the average lawyer must first avoid the many pitfalls of mediocre lengthiness. This section singles out most of these hazards.

§9.1.1 Double and Triple Negatives

As Jane Doe's letter in Chapter 8 exemplified, long sentences overwhelm the writer and lead to unwise syntactical decisions. Jane Doe allowed one of the more prevalent misjudgments to come to fruition:

> ☐ . . . notwithstanding the absence of an assumption of liability by B . . . Z's obligation to indemnify . . . will in no way be limited.

Clearly the thought emerges better when at least some of its elements are cast positively. Hence for example "Z continues to indemnify . . . despite [because of?] B's nonassumption of liability."

Similarly, the next passage demonstrates how quickly negativity comes to pervade lengthiness:

> ☐ Although it is doubtful that the mortgage loans will generate enough revenue to service the interest on the Bonds, retire the Bonds pursuant to the sinking fund, and pay the principal on the Bonds as they mature, it is not a certainty that the Bonds will not be self-sufficient.

Again, the sentence's needless complexity would be sharply reduced by couching the triple negative as positively as possible:

> ■ The Bonds may be self-sufficient even though the mortgage loans may not generate enough revenue to . . .

§9.1.2   Run-On Sentences

A run-on sentence has too much in it to be grammatically correct. The converse of the equally ungrammatical sentence fragment ("Without understanding the reason."), the run-on afflicts lawyers and preys on their proclivity to sentence length.

☐ It must, however, be recognized that the benefits attributable to the allocation of power from these projects to the source's residential customers results in a different fuel adjustment change per Kwhr for this class, it does not produce two separate fuel adjustments for each residential customer.

The final "it" begins a separable, grammatically complete, new thought. (Drill yourself at this point. Can such complete thoughts be attached within one sentence to another complete thought? Of course. But not the way this writer did. *See* Chapter 6.) As drafted in this rambling passage, the second thought exceeds the tolerance of a single sentence. I surmise that the writer erred less from poor training in English than zeal to express (at long last) his central thought. Had he begun the passage with what comes last, he probably would have avoided both lengthiness and error:

■ The allocation benefits from these projects do not produce two separate fuel adjustments per customer but instead a different fuel adjustment charge per Kwhr for the residential class.

Thus, as in many of this chapter's examples, the hazards of lengthiness derive from poor thinking and planning about the sentence's goals. Most lawyers whose prose seems unintelligibly convoluted give that impression because they fail to think before writing. Grammatical errors rarely produce bad thinking; the reverse, in fact, is the case.

§9.1.3   Dangling Participles

Related to the run-on as a risk of long sentences is the dangling participle. (*See* §5.5.):

☐ In analyzing the potential liability of XYZ for plaintiff's attorneys' fees, it is apparent that similar factors should receive serious consideration.

Here, too, many factors contribute to the unclear referent for the participle "analyzing." The sentence is not so much long as needlessly lengthy, and this is caused by its impersonality. But the writer's (typical) unwillingness to name his real subject (see §4.1) leads here to the ambiguous participle: Who is "analyzing"? Surely not the "it" that follows the comma. The participle forces the writer to name the subject performing its verbal action ("In analyzing the potential liability . . . , *I* determined that similar factors . . ."); if the writer continues to insist on impersonality, he should avoid the participle altogether and also shorten the sentence:

■ Similar factors must be considered seriously when analyzing XYZ's potential liability for plaintiff's attorneys' fees.

§9.2   NEEDLESS REPETITION

The first page of Chapter 1 raised the famous subject of redundant noun and verb clusters. In technical documents, phrases such as "Last will and testament"; "give, devise, and bequeath"; and "release, relinquish, and remit" drip off the lawyer's pen. Such contexts have their own traditions, and I treat them later in §17.2. Shockingly, however, redundancy and repetition lengthen sentences penned in the far freer domains of correspondence and memoranda. Here is a central paragraph in a memo from a young associate to the head of his firm's tax department:

☐ Therefore, it can be argued that the origin of the rights and claims that the parties seek to limit and define is not an overriding consideration in determining the deductibility of expenses relating to the negotiation and drafting of an antenuptial agreement.

As might be guessed, nothing in the memo's context draws any analytical distinction between "rights and claims," "limit and define," or "negotiation and drafting." The clusters merely inhibit the reader's comprehension of the sentence. Compare:

☐ The cosigner assumes obligation and responsibility, and any act in violation of the contract renders it null and void.

☐ First and foremost, we must hear a true and correct interpretation of the statute before attempts are made to alter and change it.

☐ He confessed and acknowledged that his penalty was right and proper.

RULE 14.   Redundant noun and verb clusters should be excised from the freer flowing forms of legal writing, such as correspondence and legal memoranda.

More prevalent perhaps are other kinds of unnecessary repetitiveness. Again, the longer the sentence the greater the risk of such repetitions. In the next two examples, the nonheroic word "that" attains center stage at least twice too often.

☐ The court concluded that because the essence of the transaction was not merely the purchase of the tangible ticket, but rather the contractual right to occupy a seat, that the intangible aspects of the admission tickets dominated over the tangible aspects such that the tickets were not "commodities" within the Section.

☐ However, the court in *Blanton I* ignores that the consequence of 21 Henry VIII, Ch. 4, is that a requirement that all executors act jointly must be explicit in the will.

In the next sentence, a lallapalooza of syntactical complexity, it is the tiny preposition that attacks the reader repetitively:

☐ Rule 10b-6 is designed to prevent manipulation in connection with distribution of securities by precluding a person engaging in such a distribution from at the same time purchasing or offering to purchase such securities for a manipulative purpose.

Two points about length and repetition emerge from this sentence. First, a thought is probably overextended when it requires *eight* prepositions to complete (in, with, of, by, in, from, at, for); second, a single phrase may be verbose if it consists of a noun sandwiched between two prepositions. Thus, this sentence's "in connection with" should have been reduced to "in" or "regarding." Lawyers misuse prepositions in both these verbose ways. Compare these original preposition sandwiches with the bracketed improvements:

☐ Plaintiff's brief contains several misstatements *with respect to* [regarding] the facts in question.

☐ *At such a time as* [When] the judgment is entered, you will hear from me.

☐ *On the basis of the above* . . . [Thus . . .]

☐ The debtor is indebted to the Company in the sum of $10,000. [The debtor owes the Company $10,000.]

☐ *In the event of the party's default* [Should the party default], the contract will terminate.

(See also §18.1.1.)

§9.3   VERBOSE PHRASES

Apart from literal repetitiveness or redundancy, lawyers waste their audience's time through sheer verbosity. Technically, wordiness occurs most often through poor verb choice (the reader should refer carefully on this subject to §5.2), but the following sentences may remind lawyers of other verbose patterns in their writing:

□ The notice of default judgment came *at a time when* [when] our legal staff was extremely busy.

□ *There can be no doubt but that* [Undoubtedly,] the statute applies in this case.

□ You will hear from us *in about two weeks' time* [in two weeks].

□ The plaintiff filed suit *despite the fact that* [although] she knew that the case was weak.

The italicized parts of these sentences display the profession's timeless proclivity toward verbosity. Ungrounded in any technical variation such as verb choice, literal repetition, prepositional sandwiching, or redundancy, these phrases simply waste effort and ink. The bracketed simplifications leap out at the self-editor, if he only takes the time to re-read before exposing an audience to such prose.

RULE 15. Edit every sentence you write, to spot redundancy and to eliminate verbosity.

§9.4 SYNTACTICAL AMBIGUITY

Long sentences carry a greater risk than shorter ones of distorting the writer's meaning. This is simply because the syntactical combinations increase as the sentence proceeds. "I love you" seems straightforward enough; "I love you since you love me" starts to get complicated. So, in the following sentence, the writer unwittingly confused his reader by failing to control an increasingly lengthy thought:

☐ The Privacy Act of 1974 (88 Stat. 1896, codified at 5 U.S.C. 558a) regulates the collection, maintenance, use, and dissemination of information by federal agencies to protect individual privacy.

Do the federal agencies wish "to protect individual privacy" by collecting (etc.) various information? Or does the Privacy Act itself seek to do so? On re-reading, we can glean the writer's probable intention. But why did he force us to re-read?

Editing in this context requires less the cutting of verbiage than its rearrangement. As has happened so often in this chapter's examples, what came last should have been placed first. If those final four words had started the sentence as an introductory infinitive phrase, no ambiguity would have ensued.

The longer the sentence the greater the risk of syntactically rooted ambiguity. The writer has the obligation to rearrange his phrases for maximum clarity; the reader should be spared the necessity of mental editing through re-reading:

☐ On behalf of X, a Delaware corporation, we request that the SEC grant to X an exemption from the requirements of Rule 10B-6 under the Securities Exchange Act of 1934, as amended, with respect to the transactions described below.

As with the first example, this passage's last phrase creates the ambiguity. (Note its redundant preposition sandwich, "with respect to," which is a hint of stylistic breakdown.) Where should the final seven words have been placed to avoid the ambiguity?

Still in the field of securities law, our next passage demonstrates that even a relatively simple thought, if expressed in a fairly long sentence, can throw its reader for a loop:

☐ The SEC has sued Y based on the failure to account properly for such payment (among other things).

To what does the parenthetical final phrase refer? Additional reasons for the SEC suit? Additional nonaccountings by Y? The reader is left to make his best guess.

Yet again in SEC territory, the following sample tries to describe a recent release:

> ☐ In Sec. Act Rel. No. 33-6205 and Invest. Co. Act Rel. No. 11114 [Current Transfer Binder] Fed. Sec. L. Rep. (CCH) 82,488 (April 4, 1980), the Commission proposed for comment a new rule under the Securities Act and amendments to Form S-6 under the Securities Act and Form N-1 under the Securities Act and the Investment Company Act which would eliminate routine review of certain post-effective amendments filed by investment company registrants on these forms.

Putting aside for now the dubious use of the word "which" (*see* §10.1), the reader is still left to guess whether the Commission proposed one new rule or one new rule, various amendments, and a brand new form. Even the specialist reader is coerced by this memo writer to re-read for a mental edit of the sentence.

Lest my reader believe that only securities lawyers inflict syntactical ambiguity on their readers, I close with a litigator's sentence that must have stymied its judicial audience:

> ☐ This is the same receptionist who directed another process server approximately three years prior to Mr. Carl Forward, a claims manager for the company.

Here the words "prior to" wreak havoc with the reader's sensitivities. The preposition "to," of course, is meant to link "directed" with "Mr. Carl Forward"; however, the reader legitimately misinterprets the sentence as written and must work his way through it at least a second time.

The writer controls his syntax and is fully responsible for distorting it to create needless ambiguities. *Short sentences limit this particular risk.* Over time, however, and with care, the writer can master syntactical complexity and resume confident use of longer sentences.

§9.5 CONFUSING SHIFTS IN TENSE

More than other expository writers, lawyers rely largely on the present tense. Lawyers are typically in the business of analyzing or ordering presently available data and only rarely dabble in history, for which purpose the basic compound past tense ("courts have exercised equitable power . . .") suffices. When they do speculate as to future events—say judicial resolution of unclear legal questions—they shift to conditional or even subjunctive modes (*see* §5.4), as well as the occasional simple future tense; generally, however, the present tense predominates.

Like any other writer, legal writers can disorient their audience if they fail to control shifts from the present tense:

□ This was part of the discretion that Mr. Scanlon had bestowed upon Ann Jackson. When Mr. Jackson is out of the office, she would handle many matters.

Here, the brief-writer shifts from the present tense with a vengeance; the sample involves four separate tenses:

This was part (simple past)
Mr. Scanlon had bestowed (pluperfect)
When Mr. Scanlon is out (present)
she would handle (conditional)

The problem for the reader is the unsettling mixture, the bouncing around between past and present. The first sentence seems set completely in a past time that now has ended, but the second sentence at first shocks the reader back into the present and then equivocates with a dissatisfying middle ground ("she would handle").

The lesson so far is simple: The writer must figure out when the action occurred (way in the past, in the past but still happening, once in the past, now, etc.) and then convey that unambiguously to the reader. Hence for the passage above, the office procedures described either still exist at the time of the writing

120

("This *is* part of the discretion that Mr. Scanlon *has* bestowed . . .") or have ceased to exist ("When Mr. Scanlon *was* out of the office, she would handle . . ."). The two sentences cannot coexist as written without confusing the audience.

Violent shifts between past and future can be even more disorienting:

☐ In that Opinion, the Commission had ordered the company to develop experiments so that the Commission will be in a better position to evaluate the proposal.

The pluperfect in the first clause requires not the future but the conditional ("*would* be") in the second. Similarly:

☐ It was contended that this provision expressed the intention of the testator that Mills shall not execute the will alone.

Generally, lawyers tend to bring even deeper grief on themselves and their readers when they structure whole analytical sections or paragraphs through the use of exotic tenses:

☐ Even before such time as the proposed amendments were adopted, compelling arguments could be presented to a court in behalf of recognizing reliance on an OCC ruling. . . . The party so arguing would have obtained a written opinion of the Comptroller. . . . It could be argued that the Section 86 defendant had exercised good faith and had reasonably relied on an appropriate official determination and therefore that the official interpretation exception should properly be invoked.

All those "coulds," "woulds," and "shoulds" not only add verbiage but also finally conspire to set the reader adrift: Where and when is the analysis taking place? The temporal confusion comes to a climax in the last sentence's pluperfect "had exercised and had reasonably relied," a tense ordinarily expressing an action sometime in the past but long ago discontinued, with a present resolution ("should properly be invoked").

121

A moderate revision bestows the double benefit of tense simplification and reduction of verbiage, the need for which is often intertwined in legal writing:

■ Even before the proposed amendments were adopted, compelling arguments were available to a party seeking reliance on an OCC ruling. . . . Such a party obtained [might obtain] a written opinion of the Comptroller. . . . It then was argued [then might be argued] that the Section 86 defendant exercised good faith, reasonably relied on an appropriate official determination, and was therefore entitled to the official interpretation exception.

The revision's major benefit to the reader is its tense clarification; the writer's intended restriction of his analysis to a distantly past set of circumstances finally comes through clearly.

Although the present tense frequently suffices, these examples indicate that tense variation is both necessary and easy to convey to the reader. As with every other aspect of awareness of audience, however, the document's competent use of tenses first requires the legal writer's complete understanding of his sentence's temporal framework.

§9.6 THROAT CLEARING

Example after example in this chapter has demonstrated the lawyer's tendency to push his main message to the end of the sentence, paragraph, or document he is writing. Many otherwise unrelated difficulties have been resolved by placing the central thought first, where it often belongs. As though deliberately to avoid assertiveness, however, lawyers find a variety of ways to bury their principal written message.

One of these ways has been called "throat clearing," the written equivalent of that physiological gesture used by nervous speakers to put off the moment of truth. The profession has found dozens of analogous mannerisms.

☐ Furthermore, there is language in the *Rochester* case that suggests that a post-high school may not be entitled to the same benefits as a pre-high school.

The phrase "there is language in" can be omitted without altering the statement's meaning. These four words constitute classical throat-clearing. Similarly:

☐ The proposed statutory amendments would appear to make it likely that reliance on the regulation would be appropriate.

Here throat-clearing interrupts the main assertion at several points. The words "would appear" are redundant and can *always* be replaced by "appear"; "to make it likely" continues the delaying maneuver and even "would be appropriate" signals a continuing obfuscation. How tentative can a lawyer be without completely losing his reader's confidence? Even if he retains his audience's respect, will he lose its attention?

In both examples, of course, fear of naming strong subjects (*see* Chapter 4) contributes to the throat-clearing effect, with weak verbs automatically following (*see* Chapter 5). Sometimes tense misuse (*see* §9.5) can contrive to weaken even the briefest assertion:

☐ It is anticipated that this formula will require extensive negotiation.

☐ It would be preferable to provide instead a clause similar to the above.

The first writer clears his throat by pushing a present tense assertion into the future, as though this were somehow softer than declaring forthrightly, "This formula requires extensive negotiation." The second conditionalizes, aiding the lawyer to avoid both the true subject (*who* should provide the clause?) and, less acceptably, the appearance of present time assertiveness: "A clause similar to the above must be provided."

Professionalism requires the long view but not wishy-washiness. If uncertainty in the analytical framework exceeds the inevitable doubts we all have about the future, the lawyer should say so quickly and forthrightly instead of making his insecurity the very soul of the sentence.

§9.7 CLEARLY, MERELY, AND OTHER ADVERBIAL EXCESSES

One part of speech not yet treated here is the adverb, the *-ly* word[1] that modifies verbs, adjectives, or other adverbs. Lawyers fare poorly with adverbs. Vying for leadership in legal prose, the adverbs "clearly" and "merely" exemplify this weakness; we thus begin with passages from an internal tax memorandum:

☐ May lessor report the rental payments . . . or is the lease transaction merely a financing arrangement?

☐ Thus, the question is whether lessor is a vendor for purposes of Section 453 or whether it will be deemed merely a financing agent.

☐ Furthermore, the purchaser of installment contracts from a dealer cannot use the installment method because it is not the vendor but merely a money lender.

☐ The court stated that such provisions, and the provisions that gave the lessee a substantial portion of the ownership risks, merely indicated XYZ's desire to minimize its business risks.

☐ . . . XYZ merely purchased the contracts from dealers rather than purchasing the equipment. . . . These conditional sales do not affect the "financing transaction" determination but merely make lessor a vendor.

[1] Although many adverbs end in *-ly* not all do. "Never," "always," and "very" are all adverbs. Likewise, some words that end in *-ly* are not adverbs ("a *lovely* day," "a *likely* story").

The sample indicates both the strength and weakness of the adverb "merely." Used occasionally, it can be effectively deprecating. Used repetitively, however, it jars the audience and becomes annoying. The force of the word diminishes and may result in a counter-productive attentiveness to the thing or argument that the writer intended to minimize. The risk is particularly great in advocacy prose:

> ☐ X fails to address, in concrete terms, what is meant by "preserving the status quo." The citation of passages from cases that are factually unrelated is merely surplussage. And the definition of *status quo ante litem* is merely tautological.

Ironically, the adverb works against its author and serves to highlight the deprecated, opposing position. In the same way and even without repetition, the adverb "clearly" can cast doubt on the thing or concept supposedly too obvious to debate:

> ☐ The Company's involvement if any, in the design of other items is clearly not relevant.

If the statement stands as a given, it will do so on its own terms. The word "clearly" serves (merely?) to center the reader's attention on the declaration and to increase his skepticism as to its transparent veracity.

Aside from "clearly" and "merely," lawyers tend to overdo adverbial usage, particularly in adversarial situations. Consider the following selections from an affirmation in opposition:

> ☐ Surely, the "class" as described is patently overbroad. . . . One is compelled to rationally conclude therefore that plaintiffs' claim cannot stand. . . . Incredibly, there has been no showing that any representative plaintiff . . . has the finances to vigorously pursue this action. Yet, in order to adequately and fairly represent the class. . . .

Note that in three instances the adverb also splits an infinitive (*see* §7.3). From another brief writer:

☐ The Court was emphatically reluctant to interpret the Oklahoma legislation as defendant would have hoped.

Adverbs can be powerful tools of legal prose. For the average legal task, however, they should be used most carefully. Otherwise the reader will rebel against the usage and see the sentence in exactly the opposite light from the one intended by the writer.

§9.8 "TYPOS"

Finally, I turn to the most upsetting and avoidable of audience destabilizers, the "typo." It may be a commonplace to reiterate that only the writer—and never his secretary, typewriter, or word processor—is responsible for his finished document; yet typos seem to produce less guilt than other kinds of mistakes. Despite the tendency to gloss over the typo, it disturbs the reader for at least two important reasons. First, it shows disrespect for the audience. The writer apparently did not value the task enough to re-read the document before sending it out. Second, the typo can all too easily be confused for the kind of error otherwise highlighted in this chapter. Thus, for the reader inclined not to see the error as a typo, it is the mark of an untrained or unskillful writer. Both effects decrease the chances of success for a document.

The author of the next example assured me that the first mistake was "merely" a typo, an assertion that the second mistake tended to ratify. But even though he convinced me, what was the combined ultimate effect on his judicial reader?

☐ Since defendants cannot be expected to know what is on file, it is rare that access to confidential files are [N.B.] granted on the basis of exculpatory material contained therein. . . . What would constitute reasonable access in the case at hand? . . . If this was an assaulg case and the records revealed that the complainant had committed several prior assaults, that would surely be relevant and discoverable.

RULE 16. "Typos" are inexcusable. Re-read your document with a dictionary at hand before inflicting the draft on your audience.

10

A Dynamic Duo to Keep Your Audience on Track: Herein of That/Which and Parallelism

§10.1 THAT VS. WHICH

As Strunk and White suggest about the classic dichotomy that/which, "it would be a convenience to all if these two pronouns were used with precision. The careful writer, watchful for small conveniences, goes *which*-hunting, removes the defining *whiches,* and by so doing improves his work."[1] For the lawyer, too, the correct use of these common but tricky words can serve as a key audience aid to comprehension.

Strangely, lawyers often resent the suggestion that these two pronouns should be sharply distinguished. Of course, they would not use "that" in place of a "which" to begin a clause properly set off from a main thought by commas:

■ The litigation, which commenced last year, still drags on.

But lawyers often fail to recognize when such a set-off is necessary and, failing that, either delete the commas:

[1] W. Strunk & E. B. White, The Elements of Style 59 (3d ed. 1979).

☐ The litigation which commenced last year still drags on.

or substitute a "that":

☐ The litigation that commenced last year still drags on.

The confusion leads to an erroneous assumption that meanings do not change because of these variations and to the overall acceptance of "which" as an adequate substitute for "that":

☐ At the other extreme, the position taken by the appellant, is the view that no evidentiary privilege exists which would allow a university to carry on its employment decisions in private.

The last sentence proves the fallacy of the nonpurists' casual pronoun mixing. First, the reader is left to guess whether the "which" refers back to (and defines) the phrase "no evidentiary privilege" or whether it begins a nondefining clause stating an effect of the already completely defined phrase. To those who would still casually mix "that" and "which," claiming that no ambiguity ever occurs, I offer these possible contradictory readings:

☐ At the other extreme, the position taken by the appellant, is the view that no evidentiary privilege exists, which would [therefore] allow a university to carry on its employment decisions in private. [Private decisions permitted.]

☐ At the other extreme, the position taken by the appellant, is the view that no evidentiary privilege exists that would allow a university to carry on its employment decisions in private. [Private decisions prohibited.]

In the first reading, the university may conduct its employment procedures privately; in the second, it may not. And while, upon further reflection, the second reading seems far more likely, the first reading is not impossible and the reader (in any event) is forced to do the writer's work.

Similarly, and further down in the same document:

☐ However, no single rule of law, which is dispositive of the issue on academic privilege, can be extracted from the common law.

The inserted commas only compound the writer's original error in substituting "which" for "that." Unless she means to say that any "single rule of law" would dispose of the issue, she must further define that four-word phrase by using "that." And, of course, the nonrestrictive commas disappear.

Generally speaking, "that" should be used to define a specific antecedent subject; "that" begins a restrictive clause—a clause that is essential to the meaning of the sentence:

■ The film that I saw yesterday was excellent.

The words following "that" define which film, and the sentence would be incomplete without the clause.

"Which," on the other hand, introduces a nonrestrictive clause; it adds extra information—one of several possible attributes of the antecedent—and usually begins a clause that is set off by commas from the sentence's main thought:

■ The film, which I saw yesterday, was excellent.

This clause adds more information about the film, but the sentence would still be a complete thought without it.

Lawyers have at least as much trouble keeping the two pronouns straight as do other expository writers. In the following sentences, a Strunk and White "which-hunt" should have occurred:

☐ Since through the announcement of the agreement in principle to the merger a distribution of X Common Stock was commenced, Rule 10b-6 would appear to preclude X from entering into agreements for the purchase of Y Common Stock *which* is convertible into X Common Stock at the consummation of the merger.

☐ An engineering contractor defaulted under a construction contract *which* contains a liquidated damages clause limiting the liability of the contract to $1,000,000.

In both cases, the language following the wrongly used "which" defines the subject immediately preceding it: *that* should have been used. If, in the first sentence, the last 12 words were just one of several descriptive qualities of "Y common stock," the writer might have retained the "which"; then, however, a comma setting off the descriptive language would have been required. Similarly, but quite less conceivably, if the last 13 words of the second sentence offered only one of many descriptions of "a construction contract"—instead of the single precise quality defining that particular contract—"which," preceded by a comma, would have been accurate.

The next sentence uses both pronouns correctly. The sole fault is in the punctuation. Can you spot the error?

☐ Mr. Peters asked me to send you a copy of the *State Teachers* case *which* decides four interesting securities laws questions *that* concern the announcement of corporate information.

The "which" correctly demarcates the beginning of a phrase that merely describes—and does not define—the *State Teachers* case. (Note: if there were several *State Teachers* decisions, denominated *State Teachers I, State Teachers II,* etc., the word "that" might sometimes be used definitionally.) On the other hand, "that" introduces language specifically defining the "four interesting securities laws questions" that precede. It, too, is correct. The error? The writer should have set off her "which" clause with a comma after the word "case." (Note: "That" clauses are *never* set off, since they define.)

In terms of awareness of audience, the use of "that" and "which" in the last passage guides a reader analytically through the thought. Misuse can engender costly ambiguity, as the following sentence shows:

☐ In SEC Act Rel. No. 33-6201 the Commission proposed for comment amendments to Regulation S-K *which* would require that certain companies include information on the effects of changing prices.

The word "which" leads the reader to assume that the rest of the sentence describes Regulation S-K when in fact it *defines* the antecedent "amendments." The writer should have used "that" instead of "which."

■ In SEC Act Rel. No. 33-6201 the Commission proposed for comment amendments to Regulation S-K that would require certain companies to include information on the effects of changing prices.

Note that this revision eliminates the second, repetitive "that." The next sentence is structurally similar:

☐ This memorandum purports only to explain generally the export controls of the Departments of State and Commerce *which* may be triggered by the transfer of these contracts.

Again, had the writer thought of the specific way in which the final phrase connects with "export controls," she would have replaced *that* for *which*. Once more:

☐ Furthermore, there is language in the Rochester case *which* suggests that a post-high school may not be entitled to the same benefits as a pre-high school.

In this sentence, as with all four of these ambiguous examples, the only factor saving the reader from complete confusion is the absence of a comma before the word "which." If the comma were there, the subsequent phrase would clearly modify "The Rochester case," descriptively, as though summarizing its holding. Of course, the writer intended that phrase to define "language," for which purpose only "that" (without a comma) suffices.

Sometimes the audience's confusion derives not only from misuse of "that" and "which" but also from the poor placement of those pronouns within the sentence (compare §9.4):

☐ I have attached an excerpt of the report *that* presents the nine recommendations of the task force and a discussion of each by staff.

Which possible meanings does this sentence hold? Too many. "That" may be correct, but it is unclear whether it defines "report" or "excerpt." If the latter, perhaps the writer should have tried, "I attach from the report an excerpt presenting the nine recommendations . . ." and avoided "that" or "which" altogether.

Even more disorienting to the reader is the following:

☐ A crucial factor in each of these rulings was the absence of a tax treaty between the U.S. and the foreign nation *which* would require a court in either jurisdiction to aid in the collection of taxes owing to the other.

Here the word "which," even if correctly used, is asked to bear too much of the burden of meaning for the sentence. Placed closest to "the foreign nation," "which" at first appears wrong, and it remains possible that the writer intended the final 18 words to define "foreign nation." The logic of the full sentence, however, militates against that meaning. After some work the reader figures out that the pronoun relates either to "absence" or "tax treaty." She then must dig out from the remaining that/which ambiguity. As written—and with the needed comma introduced after "nation"—the final 18 words describe "absence." But if, as is also possible, those words define "tax treaty," then "which" must be replaced by "that." Note that the sentence may well mean something different than was intended. Meaning 1 (the sentence as written, with a comma before "which"):

■ A crucial factor in these rulings was the absence, which would require a court in either jurisdiction to aid in the collection of taxes owing to the other, of a tax treaty between the U.S. and the foreign nation.

Meaning 2 (the sentence with "that" replacing "which"):

■ The absence between the U.S. and the foreign nation of a tax treaty that would require a court in either jurisdiction to aid in the collection of taxes owing to the other was a crucial factor in these rulings.

RULE 17. A restrictive clause, one that precisely defines a preceding term, should begin with "that"; a nonrestrictive clause, which only describes a preceding term, should begin with "which" and be set off by commas.

§10.2 PARALLELISM

Just as mastery of "that" versus "which" guides a reader through the law's complex sentences, effective use of *parallelism* can aid the audience to persevere and comprehend. Parallelism, briefly defined, is the coordination of two or more elements in a sentence by stating them in the same grammatical form. Noun is matched with noun, verb (and form of verb) with verb, phrase with phrase, clause with clause. Matching is signaled by coordinating conjunctions, by correlative conjunctions (either . . . or, neither . . . nor, not only . . . but also), or by a repeated pattern of word order.

Parallelism does not necessarily create equal emphasis, but it does show that items share a single extended thought.

■ either Jones or Smith

■ not Jones but Smith

■ not only Jones but also Smith

Parallel structure advises the reader that a group of ideas is to be considered in a common light or in a common relationship to some other, previously defined, sentence element. The key is to define the common element, which is italicized in all the following sentences.

■ The plaintiffs are *known to* Smith, Jones, Brown, and Hobbs.

■ We will shepherd the *legislation* out of committee, through the Congress, and, if necessary, to the White House.

■ X *wishes* to rely on constitutional claims and to discuss other theories more fully.

■ Y *understands fully* neither the tactical situation nor the cast of characters.

■ *Y* neither understands fully the tactical situation nor comprehends the cast of characters.

Parallelism is a valuable device, but only if the sentence's grammar and punctuation clearly signal the items to be linked to subsequent language. An excellent example of a breakdown in identifying and signaling the key parallel word comes from an authoritative daily paper's sports pages:

☐ The season has been a disappointment and the enforced time on the disabled list has given him both time to rest his arm and to take stock of himself as a pitcher.

What word should have been placed before the word "both" to guarantee its applicability to both parts of the rest of the sentence? "Time," of course (And, were it not for my aversion to split infinitives, *see* §5.3, "time *to*" might be placed before "both" and also made doubly applicable.) As it stands, "time" does not apply to the language after the subsequent "and." If the sentence is broken down, its meaning is:

☐ . . . given him both   1. time to rest his arm
                                   2. to take stock of himself

Once "time" is moved, however, the parallel structure is obvious:

■ . . . given him time both   1. to rest his arm
                                        2. to take stock of himself

The writer should be especially aware of *faulty parallelism*—an attempt at parallel structure that does not work because of poor word choice or placement.

☐ The court's decision is both intelligent and a necessity.

This sentence, with its awkward pairing of an adjective and a noun, is not parallel. "The court's decision is both intelligent and necessary," however, is. In the following sentence the writer tries to match an abstract noun, a gerund, and a noun modified by a phrase:

☐ The allegations included fraud, embezzling, and a charge of malfeasance.

A better, parallel structure would use three abstract nouns:

■ The allegations included fraud, embezzlement, and malfeasance.

Note that the redundant "charge of" is also eliminated by the parallel structure.

In the next example, the writer again makes a poor word choice:

☐ In that case, Surrogate Bennett construed Article VI, section 12(d) of the state constitution to include within the court's jurisdiction such aspects of an inter vivos trust *as* relate to the affairs of a decedent and *which* need resolution in order to complete estate administration.

The switch from "as" to "which" disrupts the parallel flow. The writer should have repeated "as."

In using parallelism you must be careful not only about word choice but about word placement (as demonstrated in the "both" example above).

☐ Such a generalization provides X neither with an idea of the causes of action nor of their material elements.

137

"Neither" must come after "idea," otherwise "with an idea of" does not apply to the second half of the sentence—the words following "nor"—and the sentence does not really make sense.

Finally, if you begin repeating any word within a series, you should do so consistently until the series ends.

☐ It is his investment, his choice, vote, and risk.

Once the second "his" appears, the writer is committed to supplying the last two: "It is his investment, his choice, his vote, and his risk," or "It is his investment, choice, vote, and risk."

Similarly, in the following sentence the preposition "by" should have been repeated:

☐ Under section 7 of the guaranty agreement, X and Y may terminate the respective guaranty agreements by giving notice to the purchaser and all note-holders and, on the "effective date," each executing and delivering the stockholders' agreements in a form specified in the exchange agreement.

In order successfully to complete the parallelism that would have linked "each executing and . . ." back to "X and Y may terminate . . ." the word "by" should have been repeated before "each."

The writer must also be careful to avoid *false parallelism,* the situation where parallelism appears to exist, but the writer did not intend it:

☐ We are authorized and required and intend to pursue and collect this debt through litigation if necessary.

What the writer really meant was:

■ We are authorized and required to collect this debt, and we intend to pursue the matter into litigation if necessary.

The next long sentence finally loses the reader because the writer chose the wrong defining principle of parallel structure.

☐ These laws and regulations may require that additional steps be taken by the parties to these contracts [1] *to amend* export licenses *and* any documents submitted in support of an application for an export license *and* [2] *to submit* to the Department of State any amendments of the manufacturing licenses *and* technical assistance agreements, if amendments are necessary, to reflect the transfer of the contracts of X to Z.

All the operative words have been emphasized. The problem arises because the word "and" serves too many roles. The first and third italicized "and" each link two closely connected parts of a series; the middle "and," however, seems to draw back in the words "that additional steps be taken." This creates what turns out to be a false parallelism (demarcated by "[1]" and "[2]"). In fact, the writer wanted to set forth a separate requirement of the "laws and regulations" having nothing to do with "additional steps." The key parallel word is not "and" but "that."

■ These laws and regulations may require that additional steps be taken by the parties to these contracts to amend export licenses and any documents submitted in support of an application for an export license and *that they* submit to the Department of State . . .

Note that this revision also eliminates the otherwise confusing infinitive "to submit."

Review Exercises for Part III[*]

■ **Revise the following sentences *twice*. First, assume that your immediate audience is a fellow attorney; then, assume that the audience includes at least one nonlawyer.**

1. In the aforementioned matter, the basis of the motion is that defendant, as owner of the premises and plaintiff's customer thereat, is liable for payment of said bills.

2. Attached hereto are exhibits A and B, hereinafter referred to as "A" and "B."

3. The John Doe Company, heretofore known as The Doe Store, is obligated under said contract to perform such services as listed in Schedule I, annexed hereto.

4. The latter lays down the rule of just compensation and one could argue thereunder that insofar as courts treat excessive or large amounts of liquidated damages as penalty they ought to treat inadequate amounts of liquidated damages as inverse penalty and thus void.

■ **Reduce the verbiage in the following sentences by *at least 25 percent*.**

1. Automobile manufacturers are aware of the potential danger associated with the use of alcohol or drugs by those employed

*See page 291 for suggestions about these exercises.

at automobile plants and have developed and implemented policies that include stringent disciplinary measures should drug or alcohol use by those at automobile plants be found to occur.

2. The appropriate standard by which the existence of a *prima facie* case may be measured in a discharge case is modeled on the test articulated in *McDonnell Douglas Corp. v. Green.*

3. The zoning cases, holding in the main that a purchaser of land is not estopped to contest the validity of a preexisting ordinance, seemingly lend support to the argument that Mr. A does have standing to contest the treaty.

4. Thus, it is clear that a filing party who does not produce a privileged document pursuant to the government's specific request therefor will be deemed by the enforcement agencies to be in noncompliance with HSR—and thereby precluded from consummating the proposed acquisition.

5. The court is required by the governing Delaware law to apply a fairness standard in determination of whether to enforce a contract that was secured through the efforts of an officer or director of a corporation who has a financial interest in the agreement.

■ **Revise the following sentences by effective use of parallel construction.**

1. I submit this statement in support of the cross-motion for an order (1) dismissing the petition for an order compelling X to remove certain of its facilities or, in the alternative, (2) to grant inverse condemnation of the property where those electrical facilities are located.

2. We need one Grade 11 to assist in the investigation required for subpoena compliance and light typing.

3. We are pleased to have you represent us at the forthcoming hearing and to actively lobby on our behalf.

4. We shall not be responsible for the accuracy of any particular document or any other information that we furnish to you in connection with the permits or this agreement.

■ **Rearrange the syntax of the following sentences to make their meaning more clear to the reader.**

1. In the United States-Iran hostage case, the ICJ distinguished the request for provisional measures that was denied in the *Factory at Chorzow* case, from the request presented by the U.S. on the basis of the facts.

2. Specifically, under the "sales" method, the average cost of widgets is computed by multiplying the quantity of widgets purchased during the previous twelve-month period by the supplier rates and charges divided by the quantities of widgets sold to specified customers.

3. Equipment, defined as any article not including technical data, on the U.S. Munitions List cannot generally be exported from the United States until an export license has been obtained from the Department of State.

4. Resort must, therefore, be had to cases interpreting the 1924 Code's refund provision to arrive at a conclusion on the issue presented here.

5. Proper supervision of these personnel by federal certified applicators and monitoring of the work by XYZ Corp. employees has proven to be sufficient to insure that the work of these seasonal and temporary employees is conducted in a proper manner, consistent with federal regulations.

■ **Correct that/which usage.**

1. The fact that the defendants appealed the court's preliminary injunction on April 1 which deprives the court of jurisdiction "over all matters involved in the appeal" during the appeal perhaps explains why Judge Jones painstakingly avoided using the language "invalid" or "unconstitutional."

2. A preliminary list of work items which contain electrical, mechanical, civil, and insulation work is attached.

3. There are few state court decisions and even fewer federal court decisions which are on point.

■ In each of the following sentences, identify the specific writing habit that is at fault: redundancy, preposition sandwich, throat clearing, or typo.

1. The bill establishes a liason between the Commission and the SBA.

2. The definition of *status quo ante litem* as "the last uncontested status which preceded the pending controversy" is merely tautological.

3. Paragraphs (a) and (b) have been modified so as to provide for computing collections on the basis of sales.

4. The facts presented here are very diverse, ranging from global warfare to the American game of baseball.

5. It would be preferable to provide instead a clause similar to the following.

6. In the event of the party's default, the contract will terminate.

7. The Sixth Circuit rejected the plaintiffs second argument.

IV

Organization

11

Overall Organization of the Document

§11.1 INTRODUCTION: PUTTING IT ALL TOGETHER

When the research is over and the facts have been amassed, all the meaningful work lies ahead. Surprised? Probably, because my experience with legal writers indicates their almost culpable neglect of the sole procedure that will guarantee the quality of their document. If the lawyer ignores that procedure, everything that comes before—the exhaustive compilation of data—disappears into everlasting chaos. Part IV elaborates on the task of bringing it all together—in sentences and paragraphs as well as documents—and recommends to the reader several procedures to bridge the gap between chaotic research and organized writing.

A phase between research and writing marks the custom of the effective writer and sets him apart from the rest. More than technical writing competency or stylistic eloquence, the behind-the-scenes technique of "bringing it all together" maximizes the document's potential for success. Some technique of organization must be applied to each writing, however small. The simplest letter, as we have seen already, can stand and fall on its structure. And the loftiest judicial opinion may achieve authoritative status equally for its "architectonics" (Cardozo's word)[1] as for its legal acumen and thoroughness.

Lawyers encounter at least two pitfalls not met by others seeking good organization. First, their quest for thoroughness too often seems to them to supercede the need for effective structure. Second, their tendency to parse any thought to its logical extreme shows up on paper in sentences and paragraphs that literally bury what is vital. A third trap, which confronts all busy writers, lies in wait for the lawyer who apportions 95 percent of his time to research and only 5 percent to writing.

These three pitfalls, or any one of them, inhibit the lawyer from bringing it all together. The first—thoroughness—*lulls* the writer into thinking his goal is realized simply by putting everything on paper. The second—logical complexity—*lures* him into forgetting what is central to his audience and how best to present it. And the third—lack of balanced time planning—*loses* him the chance to interpose an organizational procedure between research and writing.

All three blocks tripped up the writer of the following letter. Although he has great facility with words and is a fine lawyer, he frequently (as here) forgets to bring it all together.

Sue Steady, Esq.
Anywhere, USA

Dear Sue:

Enclosed please find two complete original copies of the subject lease and the side letter agreement executed on behalf of XYZ. Kindly have them executed on behalf of your client by signing the lease and side letter agreement and initialing both pages of the preliminary plans (Exhibit D) and the first page of the preliminary specifications (Exhibit E). One fully executed copy should be returned to me.

Also enclosed is the Certificate of Insurance required by Paragraph 41 of the lease.

Please be advised that pursuant to Paragraph 64(A) of the lease,

[1] Benjamin N. Cardozo, Law and Literature, Selected Writings 352.

XYZ thereby elects to pay for Landlord's Work during the progress of such work, pursuant to the method described in subparagraph (x).

The execution copies of the lease documents which I am enclosing herewith have been modified as follows from the copies you submitted to me with your letter of June 28, 1980:

1. References to Exhibits "D" and "E" were typed in the appropriate spaces in the lease.

2. Exhibits "A-1," "A-2," "D," and "E" were attached to the lease.

3. The lease documents were dated and the name of XYZ's signatory added.

4. The side letter agreement was dated, the word "course" in line 7 was changed to "cause," and the word "lease" in line 14 was changed to "Lease."

At your convenience, please send me the landlord's partnership information and affidavit which we discussed on the telephone yesterday.

It has been a pleasure working with you on this matter.

Best regards.

Sincerely,

Steven Zilch, Esq.

The letter is certainly not bad. It includes everything Steady needs to know. Eventually, she will be able to detect what she needs to do to be responsive. And she will also piece together what is enclosed and how those enclosures have been revised since she last dealt with Zilch about the matter.

But we cannot say that Zilch took any time to organize his letter. His organizational scheme, probably arrived at haphazardly, tracks the following path:

I. First paragraph
   A. attachment convention (*see* §7.2.1)
   B. request for execution
   C. (ambiguous) request for (one?) fully executed copy

149

II. Second paragraph
    A. additional attachment convention

III. Third paragraph
    A. assertion of client's election

IV. Fourth paragraph
    A. assertion of modifications 1-4

V. Fifth paragraph
    A. request for data already discussed

Had Mr. Zilch taken the minute or two necessary to make an outline—a commendable step—he would surely have restructured the letter in one way or another *before* "leaping into prose." He might have rearranged it as follows:

I. Attachment convention
    A. lease and side letter
    B. Certificate of Insurance

II. Modifications made in Lease Documents

III. Assertion of client's election

IV. Request for Zilch's responses
    A. execution of lease by client
    B. execution of side letter agreement by client
    C. (clarified) "fully executed copy"
    D. forwarding of previously requested data

This new structure puts everything in its place, maximizes the reader's comprehension, and lessens the risk that one or two of the four things Zilch wants Steady to do will remain unperformed. Instead of jumping from one subject to another (both within and among paragraphs) as in the actual letter, this act of outlining disciplines Zilch's thoroughness into an effective form. There is a logical development, available to the reader, yet no information is sacrificed.

§11.2 CREATING THE ARCHITECTONICS OF YOUR DOCUMENT

In his wonderful essay, "Law and Literature," Cardozo establishes the primacy of the organization of a judicial opinion, the correct placement of particular words and arguments "so as to produce a cumulative and mass effect" on the reader. The document's "architectonics" surpasses in importance the "mere felicities of turn of phrase."[2]

The word "architectonics" is carefully chosen. Cardozo creates in our minds the image of a scrupulous draftsman working out on paper *before construction begins* his complete plan for the finished project. Legal writers, no matter how constrained by time, owe it to their readers and to their professional traditions to preplan their written projects.

Wonderfully enough, most jobs allow the lawyer to choose his own structure. Letters, most memoranda, even contracts, as well as many other everyday forms of writing, may be structured as the lawyer sees fit. Other writings, partially prefabricated with boilerplate, still permit what Cardozo calls "emancipation in our very bonds."[3] No legal document worth writing denies the lawyer the challenge and the opportunity of creating most or all of its structure.

Since only the writer knows the full range of his document's goals and readership, no simple "rule of organization" can be provided for, or plugged into, each situation. The sole architectonic rule, and it is a fundamental one, reads:

RULE 18. Before writing a single word, consciously grasp, and physically set out, the architectonic system of each document.

Corollaries to the rule: (1) amass all the information collected for the document; (2) subdivide such data into categories and sub-

---

[2] Benjamin N. Cardozo, Law and Literature, Selected Writings 352.
[3] Benjamin N. Cardozo, The Growth of the Law, Selected Writings 225.

categories; (3) decide which subcategories are relevant and then which are vital; and (4) decide how to order each piece of relevant information.

Only after Rule 18 and its four corollaries have been followed should the act of writing begin. For only then will the lawyer have created the document's architectonics. The remainder of Part IV will consistently refer to this rule. We begin with beginnings, appropriately enough, exemplifying with the two most widely used forms of legal writing, correspondence and memoranda.

§11.3 WHAT GOES UP FRONT

§11.3.1 Correspondence

As a very general rule, what you decided was "vital" (corollary 3 above) goes first. Legal writing has its prerogatives, and we have seen cases of lawyer-to-lawyer correspondence in which this generalization may be skirted. Even the lay reader may need some tonal "softening up" before the most "vital" message of a letter is conveyed. Another way of looking at this, however, is to assert the conventional or "softening up language" overtly as a vital part of the letter's architectonics. Under this analysis, the writer knowingly places a priority on file perfection or tone and can then decide the relative placement of introductory material and vital substantive message as he sees fit. Thus the generalization would hold.

In most letters, unreflectively, lawyers begin with one of three conventional mannerisms that have little to do with tone or vital data communication. These are the "attachment," "recapitulation," and "social" mannerisms, all exemplified earlier for their tonal effect (*see* §7.2.1). They may sometimes fit the architectonics of what follows, but they usually do not. Instead of factoring in these conventions at a stage of organization under Rule 18, the writer mindlessly begins with them. Where a weighing process should occur (i.e., how vital to this audience is the attachment, recapitulation, or social mannerism compared with other aspects of the letter), the lawyer instead short-circuits his planning by "plugging in" a banal, conventional opening.

Most readers, for example, would rather have their uniquely attuned minds bombarded right away by hard information than by any of the following conventions:

☐ Please find attached copies of the Notice and the Amendment to the Landlord's Waiver you will be utilizing in protecting our interest in X's inventory that will be stored on two other recreational vehicle dealers' lots. (Attachment.)

☐ This is in response to your letter of December 31, 1986, in which you asked about the notice you received from the Bank announcing their succession as Trustee under the Trust Indenture. (Recapitulation.)

☐ I am sorry you had so much trouble getting hold of me last week; unfortunately, I spent a good part of the week in court. (Social.)

RULE 19.   Unless the letter-writer consciously sees the file perfecting or tonally softening effect of conventional openings as vital, they should be avoided in favor of stronger, information-conveying beginnings.

Even when, as was most likely the case in the second example above, the writer simply sets down for the record what has already been discussed orally, substance should be placed up front. More often than not, the convention can be merged with the primary message of the letter in its first sentence. Hence:

▪ In answer to yours of December 31, 1986, the Bank's announcement of their succession as Trustee is [is not] proper under the Trust Indenture.

The files can always be perfected further down in the letter. Even fellow lawyers will appreciate getting the basics first. A nonlawyer may simply fail to get the message altogether if a letter pushes convention over hard data or requests for responsive action.

153

§11.3.2   Memoranda

While experienced lawyers see the memo as a way of communicating information directly (and therefore expect to see vital data first), novices (correctly) seek a form that sometimes seems to demand *suppressing* the basics. The typical internal memorandum "form" may go like this:

Question(s) Presented
   1.
   2.
   3.
Conclusion(s)
   1.
   2.
   3.
Discussion
   I.
      A.
         1.
         2.
      B. . . .
   II.
   III. . . .

Often the writer will also have a "Facts" or "Background" section (*see* page 156). Analysis reveals that this time-honored form favors Rule 18 and its corollaries. The most essential data, having been discovered only through the lawyer's post-research quest for the memo's architectonics, gets placed first. The "questions" reflect, of course, the lawyer's determination of which issues need to be discussed; they should be placed in descending order of importance. The "conclusions" parallel the questions and give the reader an immediate sense of the memo's import.

Too often, younger lawyers blame organizational lapses in their memoranda on the traditional form. (*See also* §15.3.) This doesn't make sense, however, since the form seems to coerce a *better,* and not a worse, written structure. The fault, perhaps, is an *over reliance* on the form to do the organizational thinking that only the lawyer can do. In the following sample, the lawyer failed to identify as many Questions (which he calls "issues") as his Conclusion section patently reveals:

☐ *ISSUES:*

   1. What duty of care does Company X, as landowner, owe to Mr. and Mrs. A, as adjoining landowners, for acts of trespassers?
   2. What alternative means does Company X have to satisfy that duty?

CONCLUSION:

   Company X has a duty to adjoining landowners, or any person on adjoining property, to exercise reasonable care to abate a known dangerous condition on its land. Reasonable care is determined by a balancing test based on factors such as degree of danger and opportunity to exercise control. It is my opinion that Company X has exercised reasonable care by posting the property and alerting the police. I suggest that Company X notify the police and the Department of Environmental Conservation that trespassing on posted property is continuing. Mr. and Mrs. A should continue to report any known violations to these authorities but should not attempt to patrol the land themselves.

The dense Conclusion section breaks out of the issues and leaves the reader immediately puzzled as to the writer's goals in the memo and therefore as to what the reader will find emphasized in the Discussion section. Analytically, sentences three and five of the Conclusions impermissibly raise issues not articulated earlier. Sentence three answers a question not asked: "Has the landowner fulfilled its duty of care?" And sentence five launches the memo into uncharted territory, opining suddenly as to "Mr. and Mrs. A," toward whose standard of behavior the memo had not previously turned. The ensuing memo nowhere elucidates the relationship of

Company X to Mr. and Mrs. A, thus leaving the reader in the dark about the legal import of sentence five. But even if the Discussion had been thorough, the opening of the memo would still be fatally disorganized. Again, as in letters so in memos, the reader should know early *and fully* what the document intends to cover.

The same policy of stating all structurally vital data up front should inform those memo writers who include a "Facts" (or "Background") section to their opening format. This choice is fine but only really helps the reader if the Facts are selected carefully to match the Questions and Conclusions chosen architectonically by the writer. If, instead, the Facts section becomes a catch-all to guarantee "thoroughness," or if, conversely, any vital fact is carelessly omitted from the opening, the writer again risks confusing rather than guiding his reader.

One lawyer, for example, meticulously explains the long history of client X's receiving a $500,000 credit line when (on page four of his memo) it becomes clear that the sole issue treated has to do with the legality of X's issuing a guarantee in blank. The reader gradually sees that that issue marginally touches on the credit line because *part* of the funding for the guarantee could come from the credit line. But the four pages of "facts" as to the latter seem grotesquely disproportionate within the memo's structure.

The urge to "throw in the kitchen sink" derives, of course, from the lawyer's salutary compulsion to be thorough. Combined with this, perhaps, is the natural frustration when he is forced to eliminate a large chunk of research as irrelevant to the final memorandum. Both factors will cede to effective architectonics only through experience and discipline. (*See* §15.3.)

Less understandable is the converse tendency to *omit* vital facts and to insert them later. Here the writer simply has not taken the time to think through his structure and is grasping at straws as though under extreme time pressure. No error more clearly indicates to the reader the failure to follow Rule 18 and its corollaries. In the next example, the writer acts out all too publicly what should have been a calm, private process of architectonic planning.

☐ *Facts:* Z Corporation ("Z") proposes to implement a Stock Purchase Plan (the "Plan") through which Z employees may purchase equity securities issued by Z. It is contemplated that some or all of Z's officers and directors will participate in the Plan. These officers and directors are subject to the reporting requirements of section 16(a) of the Securities Exchange Act of 1934, and will therefore be required to file on Form 4 a statement of changes in beneficial ownership within 10 days after the close of each calendar month in which a change of beneficial ownership occurs.

Issue: When, under the terms of the Plan, are Z officers and directors deemed to acquire beneficial ownership of securities purchased through the Plan so that the running of the period within which they must report commences?

Conclusion: The Securities and Exchange Commission (the "Commission") applies the "firm commitment" rule to determine when a change in beneficial ownership of stock occurs. Under this rule an officer or director participating in the Plan would become the beneficial owner of Z stock at the time when he no longer had the right to receive cash, but could only receive Z stock. The date when stock is actually purchased is irrelevant to this determination.

The Plan as currently envisioned contemplates twice monthly payroll deductions as authorized by each Plan participant. On the last business day of each month the accumulated deductions will be forwarded to the Plan's agent. The agent will purchase Z stock in the open market that day. Stock purchased for Plan participants will be held by the agent for the account of the participant until such time as the participant requests that certificates be issued in his name for the shares in his account. The Plan also contemplates the automatic reinvestment of any dividends paid on stock held for the account of the participant. Finally the Plan allows participants to contribute additional cash to the Plan for the purchase of additional Z stock on an annual basis.

Discussion: . . .

Here, the last paragraph preceding the demarcated Discussion section, but coming after the Conclusion, seems thrown at the reader as a kind of challenge. "Stick me where you will!," it cries, "Help me to find my place in the memo! Am I a fact, an issue, or a conclusion? Or should I be the first paragraph in the Discussion section?"

Now in fairness to the writer, he at least placed the needy paragraph on his first page; vital though its information is, many writers are disorganized enough to bury such paragraphs pages and pages further on. (*See* §11.4.) Also, he seemed understandably torn by the choice of either including that fourth paragraph under Facts or delaying it until the SEC's rule had been articulated in the Conclusion section. But the interplay of facts and law is always a subtle one in legal analysis. The writer, not the reader, must figure out how and when to convey vital information.

A Facts or Background section usually aids the reader, but we have just seen that it is a double-edged sword. The chaotic, if thorough, mass of data compiled in researching the memo cannot be regurgitated in such a section. Nor can any single piece of truly relevant data (relevant, that is, to the Questions and the Conclusions) be omitted. The writer, using Rule 18 and its corollaries, must think and organize, not blindly rely on the memorandum's formal headings. (Note that this applies equally to all other genres of legal writing not covered in this section, from opinion letters to last wills, from contracts to judicial opinions. No Blumberg form, no in-house boilerplate, no formula can replace architectonic thinking.)

§11.4 AVOIDING UNPLANNED SHOCK TO THE READER

Legal documents often look like caricatures for a variety of reasons, but near the top of the explanatory list is their occasional inversion of the vital and trivial. We have just seen how a failure to organize can confuse the reader of an internal memorandum by placing key facts outside of the opening structure or by throwing useless facts into it. (*See* §15.3.) But our primary example here comes from a different legal universe, that of the judicial writer. The opinion chosen lacks an organizational sense generally; its particular fault is the "unplanned shock":

HOLLARIS v. JANKOWSKI
Appellate Court of Illinois, 1942
315 Ill. App. 154, 42 N.E.2d 530

SCANLAN, Presiding Justice. A suit for damages for personal injuries sustained by the minor. A jury returned a verdict finding defendants guilty and assessing plaintiff's damages at $20,000. Defendants appeal from a judgment entered upon the verdict. . . .

The complaint charges that defendants were driving a truck in an alley and (1) carelessly and negligently drove it so as to injure the plaintiff, a boy four years of age. . . . Defendants filed a general denial to the allegations of the complaint. . . .

Defendants strenuously contend that the manifest weight of the evidence is in favor of defendants. After carefully reading the entire evidence that bears upon the instant contention we are satisfied that the contention must be sustained. As this case may be tried again we refrain from commenting upon the evidence.

Defendants contend that the trial court erred in permitting Clyde Hollaris, the minor, to testify; that a child of eight years of age should not be permitted to testify to an accident that happened to him when he was between four and five years of age. Defendants argue that the child would not have been competent to testify as to the accident if he had been called as a witness directly after it occurred, and that the mere fact that he has now reached the age of eight years does not now make him competent to tell what happened when he was between four and five years of age, and counsel argues that "many children do not walk until they are two years of age and do not talk until they are three. At four a child is very apt to be in the prattling age in which impressions are nebulous and conversations vague." Counsel for plaintiff argues that "it is the intelligence and understanding of the witness, and not his age, that determines his competency." Upon the first trial of the case the court refused to allow the minor to testify. Neither the Legislature of this State nor our Supreme court has laid down a hard and fast rule with respect to the minimum age at which a minor is permitted to testify. . . .

In the instant case the testimony of the minor does not show that he is a very intelligent boy. Moreover, his testimony shows that he had little, if any, memory of what actually occurred at the time of the accident. He testified that "the lawyers have talked about it to me, I don't know how many lawyers"; that he remembered the facts better at the time of the first trial; that "My memory is not very good about what happened at that time, so long a time has gone by. After I heard my brother and other people talk about it, I didn't remember so much more about it.

Q. In other words the more they talked about it, the less you knew about it, is that what you mean?

A. Yes, sir.

Q. Do you really remember about it, Clyde?

A. No, not so well.

Q. You said something about the truck turning over to you? Did you see the truck turn over to you at that time?

A. Well, my brother told me.

Q. Your brother told you, and that is the reason you thought the truck kept turning over to you?

A. Yes, sir.

Q. Did you see the truck come out of the garage?

A. No, that is the only time when my brother yelled.

We are not obliged to hold, however, that the minor was an incompetent witness solely because of his age. Undoubtedly there are some very smart, precocious children, who, at eight years of age, can remember the details of an accident that happened to them when they were between four and five years of age, but the record shows that the minor in this case was not a very smart, precocious child. Moreover, it affirmatively appears that he had been talked to so much about the accident by members of his family and lawyers that the child had little, if any, independent recollection as to the facts and circumstances surrounding the accident. In any future trial he should not be allowed to testify. Defendants argue, and with some force, that the minor was placed upon the stand not because it was expected that his testimony would have any material probative force, but solely for the emotional effect that the one-legged boy would have upon the jury.

The judgment of the Circuit court of Cook county is reversed, and the cause is remanded for a new trial.

Architectonically, the opinion lacks force and a coherent vision. Beginning with the dry procedural posture (two paragraphs), the opinion then conveys defendant's point of view (third and fourth paragraphs), managing at the same time to bury its judgment in the middle of paragraph three.

Paragraphs four and eleven, the longest and most "substantive" of the opinion, purport to deal with different reasons for the holding; in fact, the opening sentence of paragraph eleven mischaracterizes the earlier discussion, which is not about "age" at all. It turns out that *intelligence* is the principal factor in both paragraphs. The court's structure is thus both repetitive and misleading.

But the heart of this opinion's organizational scheme (and perhaps of its reasoning) comes only in the last 12 words of that long, penultimate paragraph. Here for the first time we learn that the plaintiff is a "one-legged boy," and that defendant's main concern was that putting him on the stand would prejudice the jury. The reader, his own senses dulled by the preceding prose, suddenly jerks himself awake, realizing that the essence of the situation has been relegated to the lowest and last structural place in the opinion. Such shocks to readers often occur in legal documents. Lawyers frequently leave the "best till last" (*see* page 55) for reasons rarely clear after the fact. Perhaps the judge felt more comfortable reciting procedure instead of the grim facts of the auto accident, so he began with it. Or perhaps he could not perceive the link between the boy's "intelligence" and the traumatic effect of the injury. His structure seeks to bury what indeed is vital, not only on a human but also on a legal level.

Analogously, a memorandum of law should not bury essential information so as either to surprise a reader or to leave him uninformed if his attention has by then flagged. In many cases, almost all explainable by an absence of organization, key information seems literally stuck into a middle or late page, unforeshadowed by anything in the Questions, Conclusions, or Background sections. In a typical example, a writer replicates the error of Justice Scanlon's opinion by burying on his ninth page the principal suggestion of the memo, nowhere else articulated:

☐ [P.1] *Question Presented.* What is the appropriate procedural vehicle to present expeditiously the constitutional issue to the Court for an immediate appealable determination of the Act's constitutionality?

Conclusion. Defendants' answer should be amended to state a counterclaim for declaratory judgment that the Act is unconstitutional. . . .

[P.9] A finding by the Court, however, of "no just reason for delay" would make the ability to appeal whatever order issued an absolute certainty. It is therefore suggested that the Court be asked to make such finding and that plaintiffs be asked to consent thereto.

A 50-50 risk arises that the reader will miss this suggestion, which bears precisely on the question asked but is *not* one of the formal conclusions. As sometimes happens, the lawyer discovered this point late in his research and—rather than carefully integrating the data into a well-conceived architectonics—literally inserted it at a convenient point.

Surprises may have a place in a Hitchcock film or an O. Henry story; they do not belong in legal documents and can be prevented by some attention to organization.

§11.5 TRANSITIONAL FLOW

Within most documents, and all fairly complex or lengthy ones, the writer must move deftly from topic to topic. Major headings often help the lawyer to alert the reader to a discussion shift, but these aids are not always available. Thus, while the memorandum's discrete "Discussion" headings and the brief's subtitles afford demarcations, none may exist for a long letter, a judicial opinion, or a consumer-related document. These must be provided by the writer through either explicit numerical headings or transitional language (*see* Chart 3), or both.

CHART 3
Transitional Words

1. Words and phrases that signal a shift of topic from paragraph to paragraph within a document
   moving now to a related point
   on the other hand
   associated but not precisely the same as
   another topic worthy of treatment here is
   analogously

2. Words and phrases linking one paragraph (or sentence) to another within a section (subdivided according to context)

   A. Words that signal the addition of ideas

similarly	too
in the same way	furthermore
in addition	nor
moreover	next
and	likewise
besides	last

   B. Words that signal the contrast of ideas or the concession of a point

but	although
still	in contrast
however	conversely
on the contrary	yet
nevertheless	granted
even though	in spite of
notwithstanding	

   C. Words that signal the introduction of an example

for example	for instance
to illustrate	as proof
specifically	

   D. Words that signal a cause and effect relationship

as a result	since
thus	accordingly
so	then
therefore	consequently
because	

   E. Words that signal emphasis

certainly	truly
surely	in fact
indeed	undoubtedly

   F. Words that signal a summary or a conclusion

thus	to sum up
therefore	accordingly
finally	in short
in conclusion	in summation
consequently	

Even when a form of numerical subheading is used, transitional language may be needed to provide *flow* between paragraphs of each section. Lawyers seem strangely reluctant to use such language, but readers deeply appreciate it. *See* Chart 3, on the previous page, for some representative words used for transitional flow between major sections or paragraphs (*see also* §12.3).

§11.6 HOW TO CONCLUDE

The safest and most accepted way to conclude almost any document is to reiterate in the last paragraph the essential concepts conveyed in what has preceded. Since the document's first paragraph (or at most its first few paragraphs) should have left the reader sure of just that essence, the ending may be a paraphrase, perhaps with an eye to the precise audience anticipated, of the beginning.

In a letter, for example, the writer should leave his correspondent no doubt at the end as to what the latter is expected to do to further the situation. Instead of the formulaic "Best regards," the writer might try, "I look forward to working with you again and anticipate receipt of your mark-up of the enclosed draft," all of which (except for the first eight words) should also be found in the opening paragraph.

Legal writing, however, otherwise generally shuns elaborate conclusions. (An exception, besides letters, is the law review article.) Given the stress in this chapter on the opening into the document, I would not insist also on full-circle endings. If the writer has done his work early (and this is a big IF!), he need not reiterate at the close. Instead, closings can be used for additional emphasis, rhetorical flourish (where appropriate), or advice to the reader about follow-up potential or related source information.

If your front door is sound and reveals a strong and coherent internal structure, your reader will be quite content to exit quietly.

12

Paragraph and Sentence Organization

§12.1 TOPIC SENTENCE

The equivalent in each paragraph of the full document's vital opening section is what grammar school teachers still call the *topic sentence*. Just as the document's architectonics stands or falls with its beginnings, so the paragraph's success lies in its first impression on the reader. And, just as the opening section should prepare the reader so that there are no surprises later in the document, no paragraph should be permitted to exceed the bounds established by the topic sentence.

This does not mean that paragraphs must be monoliths, treating only one subject. (Such an approach, on the other hand, has much to recommend it, particularly for less secure writers.) It does mean that each principal thought should be fully evoked in the first sentence. Thus, in each of the following examples, the first sentence of a paragraph is matched with two possible second sentences. Which of the two goes best with the topic sentence?

- ■ 1. Days seem to differ always one from another.
  - a. Sunsets make me sad.
  - b. Yesterday's sunset was special.

■ 2. Three years ago I went to summer camp, and part of the itinerary was a wilderness expedition.
   a. I played no tennis for two months.
   b. There was, however, no sports program.

■ 3. The President of the United States must be at least 35 years old.
   a. Young people find it hard to get ahead.
   b. We seem to think of maturity as a virtue.

Even though we do not know the remaining sentences of these paragraphs, we can tell that, given each topic sentence, only alternative "b" seems structurally correct in all three cases. The opening sentence raises expectations of inclusiveness that are violated in each alternative "a."

Of course, the lead sentences above could each have developed in many directions. The essential mark of the better organized writer—the writer of alternative "b"—was that she launched into a *covered* area, while the other choice leapt away from the topic sentence's protection. Such structurally attuned writers plan their paragraphs in advance, either by a process of trained intuition or (if they are less gifted) of an actual pre-prose stage.

Lawyers, with their allegiance to thoroughness (sometimes needless, to the detriment of effective presentation), often make a choice like "a" instead of "b," surprising their readers and making them deduce the relationship to the topic sentence of the rest of the paragraph. Here are some representative samplings:

☐ Plaintiff sued the defendant in the County Court, Kent County, for $300,000 for personal injuries. On May 11, 1978 plaintiff's vehicle was struck in the rear by a truck.

Here there is no clear relationship between the topic sentence and the second sentence. Among other jarring features, the writer failed to decide which organizing principal to use: the procedural posture of the case or a factual chronology of events. (*See also* Review Exercises for Part IV.)

☐ Several weeks ago A, B, C, and I met with the people from Tuskaloosa to discuss the takeover of XYZ Corp. The issue that generated the most discussion and the greatest resistance from the marketing staff was the provision in the dealer contract requiring them at our option to obtain public liability insurance.

The topic sentence does not pin down the relationship, if any, of "the people from Tuskaloosa" and the second sentence's "marketing staff," and the result is that the two sentences seem to be discussing two completely separate situations.

The examples indicate that, at best, lawyers frequently rely on third, fourth, or fifth sentences in paragraphs to unite what seem until then to be disparate facts. The yearning for thoroughness compels the professional to disgorge information; but the presence of an *audience* should equally urge her to place the clarifying and unifying elements at the *beginning* of the paragraph. As the next section discusses, the topic sentence can and should serve as a road map for the full paragraph.

§12.2   A COHERENT PATH

The topic sentence is a map prepared *in advance* that demarcates all the major paths to be taken through the paragraph. Nobody wants to be surprised by unexpected detours encountered en route. The expectations raised by the map must be respected. If the paragraph deals with a single theme only, one emphasis suffices. Hence:

■ In October, 1980, Mr. X and Ms. Y executed an antenuptial agreement (the "Agreement"). Under the Agreement, all property other than home furnishings that either party owned at the time of marriage would remain the sole property of that spouse and would not be subject to any rights of the other spouse that might otherwise arise as a result of their marriage. The Agreement also limited the amount of any maintenance payments that Mr. X would be required to pay to Ms. Y in the event of a divorce or legal separation.

Everything in this paragraph faithfully pursues the route established in the topic sentence, and that route is marked "antenuptial agreement."

Some of the best journeys, of course—like some of the best paragraphs—involve more than one roadway. Again, however, *all* major paths must be indicated to the reader as the trip begins, that is, in the topic sentence. Thus:

■ The Treasury Regulations also support the conclusion that separate but interdependent units of equipment will not be placed in service until installed in conjunction with related equipment. Although the regulations that define "place in service" indicate that component parts may be considered to have been placed in service before they become part of a machine that is capable of producing a product, the rule applies only if they serve the function of replacement parts, which permit the owner of the equipment to "avoid operational time loss." Treas. Reg. 1.46-3(d)(2)(i). Thus, the parts are placed in service before being utilized to produce a product because their possession facilitates smooth operation of a piece of machinery. Therefore, this treatment of replacement of parts does not seem to apply to units of equipment that do not serve a function as appendages to machines that are ready to function, and such components should not be treated as having been placed in service before they are assembled.

Here there are two principal topics: "separate but interdependent" and "placed in service." Both having been demarcated in the lead sentence, they consistently structure the paragraph. Sentence two explicitly introduces the exceptional case of component parts being considered "placed in service" for tax purposes before a full machine is productive, but the topic sentence guides the reader in recognizing that "separate but interdependent" explains the exception. Sentence three retains the unity by explaining the policy behind the exception. And, with the help of the transition word "Therefore" (*see* §§12.3, 11.5), the reader completes her perfectly directed journey by recognizing that nonreplacement component parts—being "separate but interdependent"—will *not* be considered as "placed in service," for tax purposes, until installed.

Dense, analytical paragraphs can be the best ones produced by lawyers. Especially when written to fellow specialists, these mini-treatises increase the body of knowledge and elucidate technical points efficiently. However, they require caring attention to paragraph organization in order to guide the reader along. No surprises, no potholes, no detours. Simply law.

§12.3 FLOW

Instead of a "bullet point" itemization of independent facts, we have seen that, at its best, the paragraph is a unified pathway to the communication of data. And if the topic sentence is a kind of roadmap, small transition words act as service roads, smoothly facilitating voyage from mainroad to mainroad, from sentence to sentence. A full list of transition words has been set forth in Chart 3 on page 163. The function these words serve within the paragraph has further been exemplified in this chapter. Recall the way in the last example that the word "Therefore" created a smooth flow between sentences of a complex tax memorandum. Or how, in the second example of §12.1, the word "however" effortlessly linked a topic sentence to the paragraph's succeeding, related point.

Unfortunately, lawyers tend to skip these by-roads, leaping without transition from fact to fact and forcing the fellow traveler—the reader—to provide the missing flow. The assistance provided to the reader by flow may become clearer by comparing two versions of the same paragraph. The first adequately and thoroughly sets forth the facts; the second adds the transitional language.

☐　A corporation can be liable for fraud. Plaintiff has to prove defendant corporation possessed an actual intent to deceive him in order to prove fraud. Unless a defendant admits possessing the intent, specific intent can only be inferred from the facts and circumstances surrounding the alleged fraud. The Court has held "It is enough to say as to this prospectus that a fraudulent intent on the part of the author and publisher may be inferred from the falsity of the statements therein contained and that alone." [Cite omitted.] To hold a defendant liable for fraud, an intent to deceive must be inferred from the surrounding facts and circumstance. At issue here is the method of establishing the intent of a corporation.

■　A corporation can be liable for fraud. *Specifically,* plaintiff will have to prove defendant possessed the actual intent to deceive him. *But* unless a defendant admits possessing the intent, specific intent can only be inferred from the facts and circumstances surrounding the alleged fraud. *So* the Court has held in stating "It is enough to say as to this prospectus that a fraudulent intent on the part of the author and publisher may be inferred from the falsity of the statements therein contained and that alone." [Cite omitted.] *Usually, then,* to hold a defendant liable for fraud, an intent to deceive must be inferred from the surrounding facts and circumstances. At issue here, *however,* is the method of establishing the intent of a corporation.

Each of the underlined words or phrases provides transition of a precise sort. (*See* Chart 3.) The first ("specifically") alerts the reader that an example of the topic sentence's generalization is about to be provided. The second ("But") signals that a complexity in the previous sentence will now be revealed. The third ("So") links that complexity with a source of authority. The fourth ("Usually, then") applies the authority to the topic sentence's continuing concern (corporate liability for fraud). Finally, the fifth transition word ("however") makes clear that, as to corporate defendants, there is yet another complexity in proving fraud, one the writer is about to treat fully in her next paragraph.

Thus the writer guides the reader through several related by-paths, never deviating from the topic sentence's map but still negotiating complex twists and turns with the help of transitional flow. While the five transitions obviously add no substantive information, they are as important to the audience's comprehension as the raw data.

Objections to striving for smooth flow usually are grounded in "time constraints." When Rule 18 and its corollaries are not kept in mind, lawyers do sometimes run out of time and economize destructively at the writing stage by leaving out everything but the "bare facts." Just as often, however, transition words are left out because the paragraph actually lacks any organizational sense to begin with. Facts are strung together haphazardly; it would be difficult to provide the right transitions even if the writer wished to. The following paragraph could *not* be improved by transitions alone; rather it would have to be rethought and recast in the context of all the data the writer wanted to communicate in the document.

> ☐ Y is suing X because of an allegedly defamatory headline on the news page. The news page had just been added to the Newsletter in that issue, and Y is claiming it therefore attracted considerable attention among X's readership. X's readership consists of some 5,000 readers. They live all over the State of Z. The State of Z has a population of 12 million, mostly living in three main cities.

As important as flow is for the reader's path through a paragraph, it cannot alone guarantee a smooth trip. When paragraphs, like this one, run out from under a topic sentence and (literally) jump all over the map, no amount of transitional assistance will suffice. (*See* §13.2.) Flow must factor into all the other principles of organization discussed in Part IV. But once a paragraph reflects thinking that legitimately sets it apart as a discrete system of information, flow greatly enhances reader responsiveness.

§12.4 ENDINGS

A paragraph usually should, at its conclusion, provide ample evidence of what the next paragraph is likely to discuss. This must be done substantively—through content—although transition words can also help.

Generally, if the topic sentence of, say, paragraph two, has nothing whatsoever to do substantively with the closing sentence of paragraph one, the reader will be jarred into at least temporary confusion. The writer may attempt to cure this later, but some damage nonetheless will have been needlessly inflicted on the audience. The following two paragraphs form the substantive heart of a memorandum testing the fourth amendment constitutionality of a state's "Tender Offer Disclosure Act."

☐ XYZ is a foreign corporation and the transaction that Middleplace seeks to regulate took place outside the state. XYZ's presence, Middleplace would argue, gives the state a valid interest to protect. By requiring purchasers of large blocks of shares to disclose their intentions with regard to control of the company, the state can protect its interest. This argument would have greater validity if XYZ were a Middleplace company. If that were the case, then Middleplace, exercising its power to regulate the affairs of the corporation, might be able to validly regulate purchases of the shares of the corporation.

Under the Supreme Court's due process, "minimum contacts" analysis, it is often instructive to determine the foreseeability by the defendants of regulation by the forum state. [Cite omitted.] In this case, if Middleplace were the state of incorporation, it might have been reasonable for the defendants here to have expected regulation of their stock purchases by that state. But it is unfair to expect every investor to determine whether his purchase of securities is subject to regulation by every state in which the corporation has substantial assets.

No relationship between the ending of this example's first paragraph and the beginning of its second exists (beyond their mere physical proximity). The writer moves, with insufficient substantive verbal indication, from a "foreign corporation" to a "foreseeability of regulation" argument. The final sentence of paragraph one bears the burden of indicating its link to the next paragraph. If, as here, the burden is not carried, the ending cannot be deemed successful. Did the writer ask herself what the link was? It only becomes clear to the reader in the second sentence of paragraph two, and this is unnecessarily late.

Of course at least one kind of paragraph need not bear the "linkage" burden, and this is the last paragraph of a section of the document as a whole. (*See* §11.6.) But as an ending, the final paragraph of a section or a document should provide "reverse linkage" to everything that has come before. The writer gains, in such ending paragraphs, the potential to summarize the section just completed. Lawyers rarely capitalize on that summation potential; ironically, in a profession that uses summation so effectively in oral advocacy, little time goes into written summation. But as the next example indicates, final paragraphs can assist readers (legal and lay alike) to emerge from a section or document fully aware of its main points:

■ In summary, it is possible that a strict construction of the statutory language regarding an "express agreement to the contrary" would find that the language of the Oak Street lease did not go far enough to exclude the statute's application and that XYZ Corp. has the right, under Section 456 of the Real Property Law, to surrender the demised premises and terminate the lease.

While correct *memorandum* form (§§11.3.2;15.3) places major summations first, most other documents benefit from this kind of section ending. Indeed, even in memos, discussions of minor points may be helpfully summarized. And no reader objects to seeing the writer's basic arguments repeated at the end, as long as summation is not used as a remedy for disorganized earlier argument.

13

Planning Tips on Outlines and Alternative Approaches Prior to Prose

§13.1 RULE 18 REVISITED OR "DON'T LEAP INTO PROSE"

Earlier I set out one of this book's most important rules, one that covers almost everything in Part IV. Rule 18 and its corollaries (page 151), if religiously followed, will lead to well-organized, and hence to professionally competent, writing. For no matter how technically and stylistically *strong* a document, if it is poorly organized it will be marked weak by its reader; and no matter how technically and stylistically *weak* a document (within a normal range, of course), effective organization will permit its reader to derive some benefit from it.

The basic lesson of Rule 18, negatively expressed, is the same as Rule 2: "Don't leap into prose." Except for very gifted lawyer-writers, in whom the architectonic sense almost magically parallels the absorption *and* regurgitation of raw data, a separate, pre-first draft organizational state *must* take place. Overwhelmingly, however, the lawyers with whom I have worked jump haphazardly into a prose form from a state of chaotic data compilation. By prose form ("p.f.") I mean of course a draft that reads very much like the final document, indeed often is the final document; by chaotic data compilation ("c.d.c."), I mean the pre-writing phase of researching or otherwise amassing the information needed to write the document.

Whether authoring a two-paragraph letter or a mini-treatise of a legal brief, lawyers typically spend at least 90 percent of their time doing c.d.c. and at most 10 percent "writing it up." Although I challenge the wisdom of these proportions a bit later (§14.1), my point here is to separate clearly—to create a chasm between— the 90 percent and the 10 percent. This should be done even if the time commitment needed to create the chasm robs a percent or two from the writing phase, although of course the real "fat" is usually on the 90 percent c.d.c.

Thus, whatever the proportions, the graphic of effectively organized writing looks like this:

c.d.c. p.f.

He who leaps the gap, he who leaps into prose is doomed. He who rationalizes the leap of doom by pleading time constraints is a fool. And he who, having taken the leap, thereby inflicts on his reader the task of organizing the document is not only a sadist but also a lawyer with an ever-diminishing base of clients. But how does the scrupulous writer, eager to avoid the fatal leap, safely bridge the gap between c.d.c. and p.f.? This is the subject of the next two sections.

§13.2 THE ROMAN OUTLINE

A minute or two of reflection will remind many of us of the most popular form of gap-bridging, the Roman outline. We mastered that ancient form in junior high school, but can it be revitalized to further a legal career? Of course. Let us see how.

First, what exactly is a Roman outline? The titular key is in the use of Roman numerals to set out each major subject of the eventual document. In a memorandum of law, for example, the writer will establish his Questions, Conclusions, and Discussion sections acccording to the precise contours of the Roman numerals. If he has found four such major categories in his research, then there should be four divisions in the Questions, Conclusions, and Discussion sections. Irrelevant or minor data will have been rigorously excluded from Roman numeral status *before* writing begins. (All other kinds of legal writing—including the shortest letter or the most technical kinds of contract, securities, or testamentary work—can use the Roman outline as well.)

Data falling under each Roman numeral are then organized into subcategories. Each principal subcategory takes a capital letter, from "A" to "Z" if necessary. These letters may become separate paragraphs at the prose stage. But should the writer, in increasing his compilation under any letter, discover a separate and relevant *major* category, he has time (again, *before* entering the prose phase) to recast his Roman numbers and to add to or modify the main topics.

If time permits, and time must be allotted to this essential pre-prose phase, further subdivisions may be added to the outline. These begin with Arabic numbers under each capital and extend to lowercase letters under the Arabic numbers where necessary.

Give and take literally defines the construction of the Roman outline. Flexibility prevails, as the writer has the luxury of not yet being locked into prose. (*See* §13.4.) Checking his notes constantly, perhaps even adding moderately to his research as he organizes, the lawyer is in a position to change the form of his outline before etching his architectonic scheme in stone. A good Roman outline takes raw data and eventually finds the proper structure in which to convey it to the reader. The prose document simply incorporates that structure.

As an example, let us recall the defamation problem raised in a paragraph earlier (page 171). The "raw data" compiled by the researcher-lawyer typically consisted of a mix of facts and law. Gathering together the legal pads, index cards, small slips of paper, marked-off sections of photocopies, or whatever else he used during the research phase, the lawyer might have found himself with these fragments:

> Y is suing X. X challenges Z's defamation laws, constitutional defect? Z statute says: [marked off section of statute book].
>
> Discussed 3/28 with a reporter. Sports, X is a newspaper publisher. Small paper (Check circulation figures with editor.) Two years old. News page, sports page, ed. Sports coverage has grown a lot. Covers sports all over state and even elsewhere. Editorial page has also grown. Some syndicated columnists.
>
> Discussion of 3/29 with editor. "Y didn't like our headline on news page. He thinks people especially would remember it cause we just added a news page. Used to be mainly ads and then got into sports." (Asked him about circulation.) "About 5,000. But we have them all over the state."
>
> Z's population is about 12 million, 3 large cities.
>
> *Legal analysis.* Y is not a public official or figure. [Cites] Z stat. thus only requires that headline, "Y found Drunk in Street" (64-point type, lead item) satisfy common law defamation. (Look up Prosser and Z cases.)
>
> Discussion 3/30 with actual news reporter. Says that on 3/3 a man looking like Y *was* found drunk on street.
>
> Newsletter itself published 3/4. Only on 3/5 did police announce it wasn't Y, who was actually out of the state.
>
> Senior attorney here continues to think X is right in thinking Z stat too easy on plaintiffs. Says Supreme Court requires more, even of private plaintiffs.
>
> On 4/2 asked X editor if retraction has been printed. "No."
>
> 4/3 Call from senior attorney. Wants me to summarize situation in a short preliminary memo.

Now, suppose the lawyer "leaps into prose" with this haphazard data. The memo to his senior attorney will read like this:

☐ Memorandum of Law: *Y v. X*

X, as part of a suit against him by Y, is challenging the constitutionality of Z jurisdiction's defamation laws. A new Z statute says "Unless a plaintiff is a public official or figure [cites omitted], his action in defamation is established when he shows that the alleged utterance was made by the defendant, about the plaintiff, published to a third person, and defamatory."

X is the publisher of a small newsletter in the State of X. The newsletter opened for publication two years ago; it has a news page, a sports page and an editorial page. Over the two years, it has expanded its sports coverage considerably. It now covers sporting events not only in Z, but in neighboring states as well. The editorial page has also expanded, now including some syndicated columnists.

Y is suing X because of an allegedly defamatory headline on the news page. The news page had just been added to the Newsletter in that issue, and Y is claiming it therefore attracted considerable attention among X's readership. X's readership consists of some 5000 readers. They live all over the State of Z. The State of Z has a population of 12 million, mostly living in three main cities.

The constitutional issue relates to the fact that Y is neither a public official nor a public figure [cites omitted]. Hence, under the Z statute, Y claims that he need only show that the utterance, "Y Found Drunk in Street" (contained in a 64-point headline as the lead item on the news page) was made about him by X, was defamatory, and was published.

On March 3, 1980, a man looking like Y *was* found drunk on the street. The Newsletter was published on March 4, 1980. On March 5, the police announced that the man was *not* Y; Y was out of the state at the time.

X claims that the Supreme Court has established for the states a greater burden on nonpublic defamation plaintiffs than Z's statute requires.

X never printed a retraction.

If this is a mess, it deviates not far enough from what lawyers produce for their readers every day. A mere 15 minutes between c.d.c. and p.f. would have produced the following Roman outline.

Outline

I. Background as to facts
   A. The newsletter itself
      1. general description
      2. the alleged libel of Y on news page
   B. Events of 3/3-3/5
      1. man looking like Y found drunk on street
      2. X's headline
         a. exact language
         b. typeset
      3. police announcement
   C. X's lack of retraction

II. The litigation
   A. Y's suit and its statutory base
      1. defamation
      2. the new Z statute (cite)
      3. Y's private status
   B. X's defense
      1. Supreme Court precedents
      2. effect on even nonpublic plaintiffs
      3. constitutional challenge

In the ensuing short memo, there is no need for formal headings. But the Roman outline does provide a way for the lawyer to restructure his original, chaotic data into a coherent whole. The two principal categories allow him to sort out facts from law (a reasonable architectonics in this situation); each capital letter becomes a paragraph of unified information, subdivided sentence by sentence.

Much needless information in the first version can be eliminated given this structure. Certainly I(A)(2) need not tolerate the added baggage about the sports page, gathered at the research phase but irrelevant to the real issues clarified by the outline. On the other hand, when the lawyer learns on April 4 (just as he finishes the outline) that Y never formally *asked* X's editor for a retraction, he is able to add that information to I(C) and thus to incorporate it effortlessly and felicitously in the prose version:

■ Memorandum of Law: *X v. Y*

X has been publishing a small newsletter in the state of Z for two years. It runs many ads, has a sports page, an editorial page, and the recently added news page. On the news page's first day, it allegedly defamed Y.

On March 3, 1980, a man resembling Y was found intoxicated on a street. On March 4, X's newsletter printed the headline "Y Found Drunk in Street," in 64-point type (or 8/9 inch high); it was the lead item on the news page, the third section newly added that day. On March 5, the police announced that the man resembling Y was *not* Y, who had been out of state on March 3.

X has never printed a retraction, but Y never formally requested X to do so. Y has sued X for defaming him in the headline of the news page. He established a claim to defamation under Z's new defamation statute, which states:

Unless a plaintiff is a public official or figure under [cites omitted], his action in defamation is established when he shows that the alleged utterance was made by the defendant, about the plaintiff, published to a third person, and defamatory.

Y is neither a public official nor a public figure. He believes he has enough on these facts to bring a cause of action.

X, however, claims that the Supreme Court has established for the states a greater burden on nonpublic defamation plaintiffs than Z's statute requires. He is therefore challenging the constitutionality of Z's statute.

§13.3 OTHER WAYS TO FILL THE GAP

The advantages of stopping to organize before leaping into prose should be clear by now. Some time *must* be allotted to creating and then filling a gap between research and writing. The Roman outline serves this need best, but it is not the sole showstopper available to the writer.

Some lawyers may feel more comfortable using their personal computers to dash off the main lines of their factual data and legal analysis. A one-page print-out summarizing, say, a month of re-search, helps to focus the mind and to sort out otherwise chaotic thoughts. Data can also be easily rearranged on the computer simply by moving a cursor and pushing a key. (*See* §17.4.) A writer discovering new facts or arguments need not place them at the bottom of a page or squeeze them in between the lines of a legal pad. Instead, all ideas of the same general sort are put together, as available, exactly where they belong on the screen.

Again, the lawyer learns to *avoid prose* as much as possible at this structuring phase. Brief descriptions and phrases, sometimes one- or two-word codes meaningful only to the writer suffice ("private figure plaintiff," "*Gertz* test," or "negligence standard" might have been code words for the memo writer above). Where prose is avoided, flexibility reigns, and flexibility is the path to supple architectonics.

For those disliking the Roman outline but lacking a personal computer, the "index cards" approach remains. Code words or common factual headings ("newsletter's format," "police report," "retraction") are placed on index cards, and then every relevant piece of information may be encoded on the appropriate card as it is discovered or recovered from the lawyer's notes.

Or, more space consuming but even less analytically pigeon-holed, "small surfaces" may be used to organize. These may range from 3″ by 5″ index cards to tiny slips of paper. Each has a single fact, legal source, or analytical approach on it. As the research phase ends, the lawyer gathers together on his desk all these papers. He then sorts them out into common themes. He clips together each grouping. He then ranks them by importance to his topic and sorts out what is left, usually items of lesser importance. Some of these latter may be discarded as ultimately irrelevant (e.g., the sports page data in the first version of the defamation memo); others may be subcategorized and clipped together with a grouping from the first stage. The result should be a series of clipped papers, virtually organized into section, paragraph, and even sentence form. Now only the easy part remains: to translate these phrases and codes into prose.

The gap assures, paradoxically, the best possible relationship of research to writing. For, whichever method of filling it the lawyer may choose, the very act of organizing forces him to clarify his own intentions and to realize exactly what he has to say. The time-honored—but needless—dichotomies of research time vs. writing time and thoroughness vs. effectiveness disappear. A sterling and long-lasting written memorial to the ephemeral fact and law gathering phase now will emerge. The gap has been filled.

§13.4   A FIRST DRAFT IS NOT *STARE DECISIS*

While the organization phase is a necessity, the first, second, and ensuing drafts often seem like luxuries. To the lawyer foolish enough to accept one part of writing time for every twenty parts of research time, more than one draft may seem like a hopeless dream. But unless and until his architectonic sensibilities are razor-sharp, he may find himself doing several drafts to perfect his structure.

Given this reality, no treatise on organization would be complete without a word or two on the pitfalls of early drafts. They are wonderful for correcting grammar and typos and improving syntax and style. But be careful! *Lawyers, once into prose, tend to regard their own writing as binding precedent.* Their ingrained respect for what is written and set down distracts them from recalling that, in this situation, they have total freedom to revise, repeal, and even remand for further research.

If the lawyer feels that the analysis in his first draft must be altered, or if he discovers new information blasting open the structure of that draft, he must sit down and redo (quickly) his outline, print-out, index cards or small-surface compilation. He should not try to get away with crossing out a few words or sticking in a new argument where it simply cannot fit. Unavailing to his reader are subsequent arguments of time pressure. In most such cases, the reader will not even notice the new analysis or new fact, buried as it will be in a structure that was never meant to support it. Everything else can be improved from one draft to another. Not organization. Where new realities require new architectonic methods, a new gap must be created. The draft does not bind the lawyer. The lawyer all too often binds himself. The stronger the original structure, of course, the less likely that any such changes will be required from one draft to another. If Rule 18 and its corollaries are followed, the lawyer will almost always produce a first draft that, though it may have technical or stylistic faults, is a model of effective organization. That alone will bring him almost all the way to a competent finished document.

§13.5 PUTTING TOGETHER "PUTTING IT ALL TOGETHER"

1. In any document you write, insist on a structure that presents your thoughts in the most efficient form for your probable audience. This means creating a stage between the conclusion of your research or analysis and the actual writing. Be sure to give yourself time for that stage because it is vital to effective communication.

2. In the phase of your project between the research and the writing, prepare some kind of intermediary structure. One way to do this is to organize your thoughts into an *outline*. There are other ways of organization: The main idea is to stop yourself before you "leap into prose." Choose the approach you are most comfortable with in terms of the length and complexity of the project you are about to commit to writing.

3. Make sure that the outline (or other intermediary structure) leaves you prepared to observe the following crucial elements of organization as you enter the writing stage of the project:

   A. *Totality*. The document should be logically organized around one or more *central* idea. It should be *unified*, in the sense that nothing belongs in it that does not relate to the central idea or ideas. Each *paragraph* should support that unity. Furthermore, each *sentence* should relate to the main idea (set forth in the topic sentence) of each paragraph.

B. *Structure.* Each important topic deserves its own paragraph. Within each paragraph, further development should be provided by arguments and examples. Concrete illustrations (such as cases or statutory language) should thus be placed in their maximally effective position. Lengthy examples should support major, not minor, ideas.

C. *Audience.* Never forget that you are writing for someone else (or for more than one reader, not all of whose identities you can know). If you simply duplicate the chronology of your research or thinking in your written product, your reader will never be able to follow your analysis. If you assume that your reader knows vital facts, which you therefore do not state, you risk losing the reader. If you bury vital data on page six when it belongs on page one, you have lost sight of your reader. Your writing loses the efficiency it would otherwise have.

D. *Flow.* Move from idea to idea in a manner that facilitates reader understanding. Use *transitions*. Make sure that each transition is verbally and syntactically proper.

The mnemonic for A-D above is "TSAF," or "fast" backwards. Since the writer at the organization stage must, in fact, reverse gears and refuse to rush into prose, TSAF offers an appropriate reminder of this chapter's lessons.

Review Exercises for Part IV*

■ **In each of the next two cases, restructure the raw data provided to produce a better organized document.**

1. Prepare a Roman outline based on the following information. Wishing to draft a cross-motion requesting items for trial preparation, the lawyer has noted:

> $1m. lawsuit. Injured 3/12/82. P suing XYZ. We represent XYZ.
>
> Files reveal: suit started 10/27/85. P was riding motorcycle. Summons and complaint. We answered 11/13/85. Two notices sent P for discovery and inspection, returnable 11/30/85. Can't prepare for trial without those items. EBT on 8/27/86. P admitted he has photos of accident cite as of 3/12/82. His counsel refused to give over such photos. Notices demanded photos, physicians reports, copy of Notice of Claim, witness's statements, copy of Comptroller's hearing.
>
> P hasn't complied with notices. He admitted at EBT that he used the photos to refresh his recollection prior to testifying. And didn't show up for physical exam on 6/21/86. Physical exam (conversation with B of this office): 2d

---

*See page 294 for suggestions about these exercises.

notice returnable 11/30/85 called for exam by MD on or before 6/21/86. Gave office of our MD and address.

2. Prepare an outline and then completely rewrite the following document (without deleting any necessary data), making as many architectonic improvements as you can.

MEMORANDUM TO SUPERVISING ATTORNEY FROM DEFENSE COUNSEL

Plaintiff sued the defendant in the County Court, Kent County, for $300,000 for personal injuries. On May 11, 1986 plaintiff's vehicle was struck in the rear by a truck. The rear brakes on the truck had failed.

Plaintiff suffered a severe back injury and was hospitalized for two weeks. He has not worked as a taxi driver for close to four years. Defendant's doctor examined the plaintiff and found that plaintiff could no longer work as a taxi driver. Plaintiff has had a wage loss in excess of $25,000 and had medical expenses of over $4,000. He now wears a back brace.

Plaintiff demanded $100,000 at opening of the trial, and the trial judge recommended $65,000. After further negotiations, the plaintiff agreed to accept $50,000. A $50,000 settlement would be advantageous to the defendant. We have no defense to the happening of the accident and our doctor found that plaintiff has suffered a severe back injury. A jury could reasonably award plaintiff a verdict in excess of $150,000.

V

Writing in the Special Context of Law Practice

We now have completed the basic approach to establishing and maintaining legal writing skills. Every feature of writing, from the technicalities of grammar to the creative potential of organization and style, has been presented with a special sensitivity to the ingrained habits and increased risks of lawyerlike expression. In Part V, I add something new to this sensitivity, for here I emphasize the practical aspects of everyday professional life that are likely to affect writing.

From my own experience in varied forms of practice and from my consultancies with lawyers and judges through the years, I cull here the essential situational sense that informs legal writing as it actually takes place. For no matter how fully a lawyer has mastered the lessons of Parts I-IV, he or she will only be able to display that mastery *contextually*. And context makes its own demands when lawyers write.

14

Time Pressure, the Universal Concern

§14.1 THE "25 PERCENT RULE": ON DEVELOPING A WRITTEN WORK PRODUCT

Everyone involved in the law, from academics to corporate lawyers, from Supreme Court justices to first-year law students, complains of insufficient time to prepare and complete assignments. Overwhelmingly, these perceived time pressures take their toll in one area of professional practice: writing. Few lawyers will admit to short-changing their research or their client nurturing; perhaps because it seems so passive, the document alone takes the brunt of the alleged absence of time.

Without any doubt, I believe that professional improvement will follow hard upon a willful reversal of this time restraint fallacy. Writing *must* take a preplanned, logically appropriate, and professionally mandated ascension over other elements of a project.

RULE 20. At the beginning of each project, estimate the number of hours needed to complete it. Then mark on your calendar (even if it is for the same day) a date (and time) 75 percent into the estimated time period. Enter the inscription: "Begin writing phase" at that spot. This leaves you at least 25 percent of the time allocated for your project in which to write it up.

As an example, Rule 20 dictates 10 hours for the writing phase of every 40-hour job requiring a document. The brief-writer under a judicial deadline to file her document by, say, June 15, and beginning her work on June 8, should (assuming regular work days and two days off) mark her calendar to start the writing phase at 3 P.M. June 13. Folding in here the dictates of Rule 18 and its corollaries (page 151), the brief writer should utilize the last two hours or so of June 13 to organize her research and prepare a Roman outline or similar nonprose architectonic system. June 14 can serve as the day for first draft, revision, and final draft and, by the deadline on June 15, the written document can be delivered to the court.

Rule 20 cannot be counted on to create new time or to relieve the inevitable sense of time pressure. What it does, however, is to reverse the fallacy that poor writing, squeezed into a panic-ridden last few minutes of a project, may escape notice or be excused by the reader. Instead, the pressure of time exerts itself where it should—*at the research or data amassing stage*—and not at its most obvious but least fruitful expansion point, the writing stage. It is especially inappropriate for time pressure to influence the written document, since it alone survives for immediate, as well as ultimate audiences to peruse at their leisure.

§14.2   KEEPING COOL BY ASKING KEY QUESTIONS AS YOU EMBARK

Time pressure has its psychological component, but it is also a function of pragmatic strategies (or the lack of same) adopted by the legal writer. At every stage of seniority and experience, whenever a project is destined to become a document, the following rule must be followed.

RULE 21.   Always ask questions.

Each matter has a beginning, although it is not always easy
to identify when an amorphous situation crystallizes into a project.
For the law firm associate, it may be the 20-minute conversation
with a senior colleague (*see* Chapter 15) outlining a specific set of
issues to be researched. For the senior colleague, it may be a quick
give-and-take with a key client who throws out a chaotic spurt of
facts and questions. For the law clerk or legal secretary, it may be
when litigation commences or when a motion is made. For the
attorney writing a will, it may be a long interview with the prospective testator, for the writer of a contract, an attempt to determine her client's aims and those of the other party. The securities
lawyer may find out the terms of a proposed public offering; the
appellate litigator may have thrust upon her a thousand-page trial
record.

Whatever mysterious process transforms a vague mass of potential into a concrete matter requiring some kind of writing, the
lawyer must recognize the transformation and immediately begin
to prepare for the writing. At the earliest stage, a crucial mistake
is often made, one that colors the rest of the project and finally
produces the time pressure syndrome we all know and rue. This
mistake is the failure to ask key questions. Let us exemplify by
rehearsing the previous paragraph's litany of beginnings, with
snapshot anecdotes that everyone in the field will understand.

A junior associate embarks upon a three-week research project. She never once returns to the senior attorney to ask for elaboration upon any aspect of the original conversation. It turns out
that she pursues at length a theory that has little relevance to what
her senior colleague needs. Or, a law clerk or legal secretary may
be most of the way through a draft when a brief encounter with
the judge reveals that a new issue has become central and others
have been relegated by events to a trivial role. A will writer relies
on her only long interview with the prospective testator, even
though lingering questions arose at that stage. When the 32-page
will has been completed, the client suddenly calls. Sure enough,
there is an illegitimate child lurking in the situation. The whole

will must now be changed, although one timely follow-up question might have revealed the truth earlier on. A contract writer relies too heavily on her client's representation of a business's viability; one phone call to that company's treasurer might have saved last-minute changes in the contract that detract from the whole. A securities lawyer, caught up in the technical details of a public offering, fails to pursue questioning of the offeror's treasurer and much later learns of a key fiscal detail that must change the structure of the prospectus and the opinion letter. An appellate litigator chooses not to phone an in-house trial lawyer to ascertain firsthand impressions of an issue in the case.

In each of these hypothetical situations, something short of professional disaster has occurred. Mistakes or omissions were discovered during, not after, the document's submission. But early or even periodic questioning of knowledgeable sources would have spared each writer needless "time pressure" that always diminishes the quality of the ultimate written product.

§14.3 BOILERPLATE AS A HAZARD

When time seems to run out, lawyers run to boilerplate. The pros and cons of in-house forms are discussed fully in §17.2, but the urge to substitute preexisting models for time-pressured original thinking needs analysis here. Particularly when the "25 percent rule" is abused, lawyers find themselves pinched for writing time and hence eager to plagiarize. Now some lawyers do rely on boilerplate or in-house forms for reasons other than time pressure. The novice may feel insecure about her assignment on a substantive level. Boilerplate comforts her. This too, is hazardous. (*See* §15.2.) But no small number of legal writers, experienced or inexperienced in the subject of their project, simply crib from forms appropriate to some other project, and they do so in order to save time.

For example, the following passage flowed from the pen of an experienced litigator filing a notice of motion for leave to appeal to her state's highest court. Or, more accurately, it did not flow from *her* pen; rather she cribbed most of it from a long-departed colleague who had established the in-house form for such documents. The notice was written last, under considerable time pressure, and tacked on at the beginning of an otherwise plainly written affidavit and brief of some 25 pages in support of the motion:

□ NOTICE OF MOTION FOR LEAVE TO APPEAL

Please take notice, that upon the annexed Affidavit of Joan J. Jones, sworn to the 17th day of February, 1984, the annexed order of the District Court, Anywhere County, dated October 16, 1982; the resettled order of the District Court, Anywhere County dated May 5, 1983; the order of the Court of Appeals, District 8, affirming the order dated October 16, 1982, said order being entered in the office of the Clerk of the Court of Appeals, Ninth Department on the 18th day of January, 1984; the record on appeal to the Court of Appeals; and briefs served in conjunction therewith, and upon all of the papers, pleadings and proceedings herein, including the brief submitted herewith, the defendant-appellant will move at a Term of the Supreme Court of the State of Kent, on the 28th day of February 1984, at 9:30 o'clock in the forenoon of that day, or as soon thereafter as counsel can be heard, for an order granting leave for the defendant-appellant to appeal to the Supreme Court from the said order of affirmance of the Court of Appeals pursuant to Kent Stats. Ann. 2042-08(e) upon grounds that the present determination has left unclear and uncertain the applicability of the State's Probate Code to transactions involving after-acquired property; has left unclear and undefined the basis upon which an executor may reasonably effect a rescission in such situation upon misrepresentations of fact; and denied defendant-appellant opportunity to have very serious factual issues involved in this case determined by jury; in addition to all of the foregoing, the order of the Court of Appeals has adversely affected plaintiff's right to contest damages in this action contrary to the provisions of the resettled order of the District Court, Anywhere County dated May 5, 1983; and for such other and further relief as is just and proper the premises considered. Dated: Anywhere, February 17, 1984.

Yours, etc.,

Joan J. Jones

Joan J. Jones apportioned less than 25 percent of this project to writing. She did manage to draft a reasonably effective affidavit and brief, but she ran out of time at the "Notice of Motion" stage. Perhaps assuming that the court expects stilted and archaic speech in such a Notice, she took exactly five minutes and adapted paragraphs, some of them threescore or more years old, to the present facts. The effect on the court, since the Notice *precedes* the affidavit and brief and therefore hits the court's eyes first, will not be salutary. The most Jones might wish is that the court will not read the Notice at all. But courts do, more often than not, read consecutively, and they always expect each page submitted to them to represent the best work of the litigator and to convey information relatively clearly.

Sometimes, of course, litigation-related language is dictated by statutory provisions. But this occurs quite rarely, and hardly ever is the kind of jargon and archaic tone found here demanded by law. Joan J. Jones simply "ran out of time," and she is fully responsible for every word in the motion. Upon reflection, she found it strange to be declared the author of so many "herewiths" and "therewiths," of phrases such as "9:30 o'clock in the forenoon of that day" or "the premises considered." Finally, she shuddered to notice that the series of reasons offered after the phrase, "upon grounds that the present determination," retained its parallelism for only three parts of the series and then broke down completely.

Jones again fell back upon "time pressure," although she also noted that the form was still used, even by presumably less pressured lawyers, in her office. But Jones, as a more senior litigator, had the power to *alter* the form (*see* §17.2) and by using it only encouraged her juniors to propagate such poor writing. As a further irony, Jones found herself authorizing a document that resulted in at least one-third more verbiage than if she had drafted it with relative freedom from forms. Thus, even the excuse of time pressure faded, given the added time needed to draft, type, proofread, and correct all those extra words.

Boilerplate looms as a hazard to the experienced as well as the novice lawyer, particularly when insufficient time is apportioned to *all* the writing required by the matter at hand. Had Jones followed Rule 20, she would have demanded of herself *in advance* the few extra minutes required to write her own, jargon-free Notice. Her chances of success with the court could only have improved with such planning.

§14.4 THE CALENDAR, THE UNEXPECTED, AND THE SKILL OF JUGGLING

What I have said so far about predicting the time frame of a project and apportioning 25 percent to its written components assumes, of course, no major *extrinsic* surprises in the lawyer's calendar during that period. But unpleasant shocks to the system do occur: A dormant matter suddenly heats up, an ill colleague needs covering, a professional or charitable association makes a demand that cannot, in good conscience, be refused.

Before suggesting an approach to the unexpected, I offer three caveats. First, this section does *not* relate to unexpected aspects of the immediate project. The "25 percent rule" must subsume some latitude for *intrinsic* surprises. This means simply that new cases coming down on point, or new parties entering the matter with new information or demands, or collegial support on the project somehow breaking down—these and other exigencies must be factored in when the lawyer makes her original determination of the time needed for the project.

Second, lawyers conjuring the extrinsic surprises noted earlier should be honest with themselves. Surprises, by their nature, work two ways. Just as frequently, a "hot" matter dies down, a trip is canceled, an issue is mooted, and so on. (I freely admit, however, that lawyers should never expect a sudden influx of collegial work hours. Once a lawyer assumes responsibility for a matter, it remains hers. This hard fact merits elaboration a bit further on.) Thus on balance, if a lawyer begins a matter accurately predicting the amount of time it will take, the 25 percent rule will usually allow her ample time for producing the documents irrespective of extrinsic influences during that period.

Finally, even if the extrinsic does adversely impinge upon the lawyer's calendar, she may still abide by the 25 percent rule on any given project by extending the deadline for that project. Unless the document is due on someone else's desk by a date certain, and even then unless no extension may fairly be obtained, the time frame for a project's completion (not the absolute number of hours devoted to it) may be extended to accommodate the extrinsic surprises.

If we put these caveats aside, we can proceed on the assumption of an inflexible deadline and a reasonable estimate of hours needed for the project. With the goal still to maximize the chances of unpressured writing, what can the lawyer do to reckon with extrinsic shocks to her calendar? Here are three basic suggestions, applicable to lawyers at all stages of their careers.

§14.4.1   Learn How to Say "No"

The only acceptable time to decline participation on a project is when it is first proposed. Almost all colleagues respect a negative response at that moment, and it is often cost free to seek another lawyer for the task. Particularly attuned to the occasional negative will be a colleague who learns that the lawyer is already involved with one or more matters that will occupy her—through the writing stage — for a specific number of hours or days. This ability to be precise when saying "no" represents another advantage of abiding by Rule 20.

Each new proposed project must be weighed against existing responsibilities. At this point, the lawyer must assume the possibility of dormant matters heating up, new professional duties suddenly arising, and so on. If the 25 percent rule cannot be followed for the proposed project, given known and unknown contingencies, the project should be politely declined.

§14.4.2 Juggle Efficiently

Few professional lives escape occasional comparison with the circus juggler, she who keeps a dozen plates spinning in the air at the same time. The key to mastery lies in the performer's athletic efficiency: no single second of wasted energy. When matters arise in tandem, as they inevitably will, the lawyer must become an athlete (or at least a circus performer), forgoing all wasteful activities.

Lawyers and executives like to talk about efficiency, but anyone who has attended a single business meeting knows that the first item on the agenda is lunch and the last is football or the World Series (in my experience, by the way, women attending these meetings are far less inclined to waste time in these ways). The individual lawyer seeking good writing must cut such fat from her schedule when extrinsic shocks attack the professional system. Lunch can be foreshortened or even omitted, collegial socializing temporarily abandoned, the daily newspaper (blissfully) discarded, many evening activities precluded. There are even some little luxuries that legitimately accrue to the overburdened lawyer: Take an occasional taxi to and from the office, keep an assistant around overtime, bring in an associate if budget allows (see §14.4.3). Unless the professional juggles well, she will write poorly. For, as frank reflection reveals, writing always becomes the whipping boy when time pressure mounts.

§14.4.3 Delegate

Almost every lawyer, except perhaps the newest (and best paid!) Wall Street associate, has a chance to delegate at least some of her tasks. The judge has her clerk or secretary, the professor her research assistant, the senior attorney everybody else in the firm, and so on. Even the single practitioner may seek a paraprofessional or a per diem lawyer to help her through the crazy days.

As with other decisions discussed here, the lawyer needs to plan in advance which tasks she will delegate and which she must retain. The lawyer may generally feel comfortable delegating research and bibliographical aspects of a project to others or even fact finding involving little or no client contact. Unfortunately, lawyers tend too often to delegate the writing itself. My suggestion, of course, is that writing should be the equivalent in its sacrosanct quality to client nurturing. In the final analysis, a legal document, the only lasting element of the work product, provides the mark of the responsible professional presence whose name is found upon it.

Thus writing—good writing—can survive the inevitable time pressures (real or imagined) that plague lawyers when they must take up the pen or the processor.

15

The Apprenticeship and Its Particular Confusions

§15.1 RULE 21 REITERATED

Everything about the practical context of writing that has just been reviewed in Chapter 14 applies equally to senior and junior attorneys, and the younger lawyer opening to this chapter should re-read those pages. Of great importance to people just out of law school is Rule 21 (page 193): "Always ask questions." Whether the lawyer takes his novitiate in a firm or in government, with a judge or single practitioner, he often neglects this seemingly obvious principle.

I recall my own first assignment as an associate in a large international law firm. I was third and last in the pecking order as we represented the underwriter for a public offering. The senior associate tossed around phrases such as "cold comfort," "regular way," and "corporate check," and words such as "opine," "indenture," and "bluesky"; all sounded vaguely familiar but totally incomprehensible in the new context. *Yet I did not ask her a single question about their meaning.* Eventually, I came to understand these words and phrases, but in time I saw how much richer the experience would have been had I asked as soon as I felt—quite legitimately as this was my first "deal"—the slightest bit ignorant.

Discussing this with friends, I perceived that my hesitancy to ask obvious questions was both common and understandable. No one teaches you in law school to ask questions. The best teachers hear your questions and try to answer them, but the atmosphere at most law schools discourages voluntary participation. The student, especially in the first "Socratic" year, does not always glean the rewards of speaking out in class. The ingrained lesson is that people new to situations—even bright people—do better learning on their own and not by asking questions.

Now the fact is that most teachers welcome questions. And lawyers with greater experience certainly expect and value the inquiring mind; most even enjoy displaying through answers their own knowledge. Indeed, all lawyers delight in the give-and-take about the profession that only intelligent questioning initiates. But when is a question "intelligent" and when will it make you look like a fool? Again, the novice finds himself in a privileged position, for almost any field of information is obviously fair play for the newcomer seeking enlightenment. Yet I believe I could win a wager supporting the proposition that young lawyers at least once go all the way to writing a document without discovering the meaning of every key word involved in the document's preparation. Certainly it was only *after* finishing her first opinion letter that a friend of mine told me she really understood the concept "cold comfort" and only *after* telexing a foreign bank about a client's loan that another learned what "draw-down" meant.

Whether dealing directly with a client or indirectly through the mediation of an in-house senior colleague, the shortest distance to valuable knowledge is the route from questioner to knowledgeable informant. The first conversation rarely reveals everything about a matter that its source may know. Research and writing based solely on that preliminary talk often pursue false leads that assume too much or too little. Even administrative agencies, or others issuing guidelines, such as courts, can be approached with direct questions about a project. Before leaping into prose, with all its traps (*see* Chapter 13), young lawyers should take the minimal risks involved in questioning others who possess superior knowledge or wisdom. The ultimate document will be more fully informed and more directly to the point.

§15.2 FINDING YOUR OWN VOICE

Turning now to the act of writing itself, I would like to elaborate for the apprentice on some general suggestions about style made earlier. (Again, the reader may wish to turn back, this time to Chapter 1.) Almost everything the law school graduate brings with him to his new job seems to resist the development of a personal writing style. From the blandness of most legal writing courses to the enforced impersonal style of most student law journals, and from the fear of stating a bald assertion to the fear of offending an imperious seeming senior colleague, the young lawyer finds all kinds of reasons to repress rather than kindle his creative, personal style.

Having seen hundreds of legal writers in action and in context, I am absolutely convinced that style enhances career and that a spark of individuality in writing, if controlled and appropriate, brings rewards to the lawyer. As with style in all parts of life, however, style in writing cannot be artificially imported and must faithfully reflect the person who projects it. If a lawyer already possesses a characteristic and energetic style, his practice will provide appreciative audiences for strong prose often lacking in law school or among one's peers.

An example illustrates excellence in novitiate legal writing. I cite two paragraphs from opposite ends of a lengthy memorandum on an antitrust matter. At the outset the young associate makes clear immediately that he has found his own voice and intends to project his legal conclusions with lucidity and force:

■ This memorandum covers the state of the law regarding horizontal mergers. I have been asked to examine all horizontal mergers challenged by either the Federal Trade Commission ("FTC") or the Department of Justice ("DOJ") in which decisions were rendered (i.e., those that were not ultimately settled pursuant to a consent decree or stipulation). In order to insure comprehensive treatment of the state of the law regarding horizontal mergers,

I have read all private merger cases that have relied on both actual and potential competition analyses to challenge horizontal mergers. With respect to actual competition analysis (traditional horizontal merger theory), I have been looking for cases that involve relatively low market shares. In doing so, I have attempted to determine what, if any, evidence has persuaded the reviewing agency and/or court to find the challenged merger legal or illegal. As regards potential competition analysis, I have been looking for cases in which potential competition theories have been used to challenge horizontal mergers.

Some 90 pages later, the writer maintains his vigorous presence. His prose indicates that professional writing and strong writing need not be at odds:

■ Another salient point of Justice Stewart's analysis of the acquisition data was his conclusion that the Court sustained its view that acquisitions had continued by "indiscriminately lump[ing] together horizontal and market-extension mergers." *Id.* at 294. He found that only 29 stores, representing 13 acquisitions, were acquired in horizontal mergers, and that 9 of the 29 were acquisitions in the course of dispositions in bankruptcy. Therefore, the horizontal merger data reflected only a *de minimis* level of 10 acquisitions involving 20 stores. In light of the substantial economic distinctions between market-extension and horizontal mergers, Justice Stewart felt it was improper to rely on this evidence to prove a tendency toward decreased competition. *Id.* at 295.

It could be argued that the Court, in *Von's Grocery,* did examine the structure of the market; however, the accuracy of that examination is questionable in light of Justice Stewart's evaluation of the evidence relied on by the Court.

Admirable in the passage from early in this lawyer's memorandum is the straightforward exposition of his task and of the methods and limits of his memo. He embraces the first person pronoun, seizes responsibility immediately for his conclusions and achieves both a competent and an intimate relationship with his audience. The repetitive usage of the compound past ("I have read," "I have attempted," etc.), instead of replicating the annoying passivities more typical of legal writing, establishes a convincing cadence of information. Other effective stylistic nuances worth noting include the introductory subordinate clauses used in sentences three through six and the implication of ongoing research conveyed through the past perfect progressive ("I have been looking for").

In the judicial analysis taken from the last few pages of the same memo, other stylistic strengths appear. The adjective "salient" strikes at the heart of the writer's admiration for Justice Stewart's approach to antitrust law, sustained throughout the passage with strong verbs such as "found" and "felt." If the last sentence seems to retreat into more traditional passive drabness ("It could be argued . . . is questionable"), the writer has earned that stylistic choice. After all, even impersonality and passivity have their place as variations on an otherwise forceful style—but not if employed endlessly to mask the writer's presence and force the reader to squeeze the essential information out of a mass of verbiage.

Another excellent passage authored by a first-year lawyer typifies sharp adverbial word choice and strong use of verbs:

> ■ Although the Supreme Court of Germany has not squarely held that the Convention supersedes national law, two decisions indicate that courts of that country have applied the Convention exclusively to questions involving the validity of the arbitration agreement. In an untitled decision reported in the Yearbook of Commercial Arbitration, the court in Germany was asked to enforce an award rendered in France. Apparently rejecting the French seller's argument that the agreement was invalid under French law, the German court stated that "the validity of the award had to be judged under the New York Convention since both France and Germany had ratified the Convention." In another case, the court was asked to analyze the validity of an arbitration agreement contained in a sales con-

firmation which was in writing but not signed by the parties. Rejecting the German buyers' contention that the agreement was invalid (apparently because the sales confirmation was not signed by both parties), the court held that the Convention was applicable.

The words "squarely," "exclusively," and "apparently" demonstrate the power of adverbs if lawyers will only deviate from their obsessive use of "clearly" and "merely" (see §9.7). Although the passage, again, contains some passive constructions ("the court was asked"), verbs tend primarily to strength without in any way being exotic. Surely the words "held," "indicate," and "stated" are accessible to any graduate of a law school; these and similar verbs invigorate a passage and keep the reader attuned to the substantive analysis.

This writer can only perhaps be criticized for the overuse of what should be a device of syntactical variation. Like the earlier writer, he correctly spices his sentence structure with introductory clauses; the problem here is that the device itself becomes a habit and threatens to inflict what it is meant to cure, audience inattentiveness ("Although the Supreme Court," "In an untitled decision," "Apparently rejecting," "In another case," "Rejecting the German buyers' contention"). The trick, of course, is to *vary* longer sentences with shorter, to keep the reader's attentive juices flowing through the use of syntactical alternation.

Despite these young writers' stylistic faults—and who besides the writer of a book like this would throw stones?—they stand as models for the young lawyer. Unwilling to mask their personal presence (or in other words, eager to take responsibility for their substantive arguments), both lawyers assert their positions strongly. Each avoids ornateness or inappropriate brashness, but each manages to find his own voice and to make it vibrate in the required language of the assignment. The sometimes seemingly endless writing required of many new lawyers thus becomes at once more pleasurable, more personalized, and more effective. (*See* §1 of the Bibliography for selected titles on style.)

§15.3 YOUR MAJOR MODE—THE INTERNAL MEMORANDUM

Unless the new graduate courageously hangs out his shingle as a sole practitioner, he will probably spend a good part of his apprenticeship researching and writing memoranda for senior colleagues. Young litigators and some government lawyers may do a bit less memo writing than their classmates at small or large firms, but they will also frequently write memoranda in which factual and legal data must be amassed and communicated to an immediately interested audience. Most of what follows, then, applies to all.

Again, I point the reader first to earlier sections of this book dealing with the memorandum of law. (*See, e.g.*, §§3.4.2; 11.3.2; 11.4; 12.4.) There I identified the formal and tonal elements appropriate to the internal memo and discussed the particular challenge of organization that faces the memo writer. Here I will stress the special features of memo writing that affect younger lawyers. I begin with a generalization so widely ignored and yet so vital that it deserves status as a rule:

RULE 22. Assume, in writing a memorandum, that your audience is virtually ignorant of the factual and legal elements under discussion.

There is nothing simple about this rule. The apprentice, properly deferential to his senior colleagues, often extends polite respect to an assumption of omniscience.

This works two ways. On the one hand throwing in the factual kitchen sink, the young lawyer may well omit important legal data, the thought being that "Ms. X knows everything about the field anyway." On the other hand setting forth (as other lawyers will) every crossed "t" and comma of a lengthy statute only partially apposite to the matter, the novice may omit a vital factual element without which the memo is incomprehensible. When questioned about this kind of omission, lawyers usually explain that "Ms. X knew that fact because she mentioned it to me in giving me the assignment."

Both approaches are fallacious. Most obvious perhaps to my readers should be the mistaken assumption that "Ms. X" will be the only audience for the memo. (*See* §3.4.2.) A writing lasts forever, and numerous readers may wish to learn from it. Without the relevant law and facts, their task is impossible. Less obviously, but just as verifiably, Ms. X herself has probably long forgotten (or never read) the statute or case studiously omitted by her junior colleague. And, although the omitted factual element Ms. X mentioned while giving the latter the assignment may well be part of an important conversation recalled in every detail by the novice, Ms. X herself has long since moved on to other matters. The naive assumption that key facts will be remembered is even less secure than the view that Ms. X has mastered the relevant law.

To be safe and to be thorough, the young lawyer simply should include the basics as though writing for a lawyer who, however intelligent, is ignorant of the memo's subject matter. To illustrate: An apprentice finishes a six-page memo about his state's law of contractual rescission with a citation to Rule 8(a) of the Federal Rules of Civil Procedure. That rule, which deals with pleading in the alternative in federal court, seems to have nothing to do with the memo. It turns out that Ms. X apparently asked the young lawyer to include the short section on the small chance that federal court relief might be sought. But, without any transition or prior explanation, the section seems grotesquely extraneous to the first six pages of discussion.

Or, as another example, the fourth page of a lawyer's memo makes reference to "John Doe of the Department, who indicated that their agency's operating procedure" allowed the activity centrally discussed in the memo. This is the first and last mention of John Doe, and no reference is made to the form in which Doe communicated the vital data. Again, of course, Ms. X had given the writer Doe's name, so Ms. X must surely know who he is and how the data was obtained. But will the busy Ms. X recall Doe? And, in any event, will Ms. X be the memo's only reader? What will the third, fourth, or fifth reader, not privy to the conversation between the writer and Doe or between the writer and Ms. X, be able to make of this important information?

The frequent omission of key law and fact stands in ironic contrast with the novitiate habit best handled by the following rule.

> **RULE 23. No matter how dearly bought, in time and analytical effort, information that is irrelevant to the issue section of a memorandum should be excluded.**

An extreme breach of Rule 23 occurred when an eager apprentice, writing up a memo of corporate law, threw in the history of the subject corporation back to its original charter and by-laws in 1794. He had been asked to ascertain whether, under the existing corporate law, a quorum could be attained by a director phoning in his proxy. Other examples, less extreme perhaps but similar in kind, are found on pages 156 and 179.

Yet the rule speaks to a serious aspect of professional pride, particularly evident in new lawyers. The urge to thoroughness, discussed often in these pages (*see, e.g.,* §3.1), is nowhere stronger than in apprentices, for it is inscribed in their law school examination experience ("spot every issue; being right or wrong in your conclusion is less important than being thorough") and reinforced in their work on journals. Added to that acquired instinct is the natural reluctance to discard any piece of information extracted from midnight divagations through the library or Lexis.

How much of any research project should survive to the final document? For the 75 percent of an assignment spent in the library, the lawyer pleases himself, deliberately barking up trees that may yield little prey, testing analytical theories to illogical conclusions, checking every conceivable source. This is fine. But the 25 percent of the project devoted to writing is for the benefit of at least one other person. (Our old friend awareness of audience ultimately unifies us behind yet another rule of legal writing.) That "other" has a completely legitimate disinterest in the compendious but largely irrelevant research phase. Like a gold surveyor, he wants the rarified nuggets, not the sludgework.

Earlier, I suggested that the organization of an internal memorandum, despite its time-honored structure, remains in the hands of the lawyer-writer. (*See* page 158.) Control also attaches to the writer in the decisions discussed here. How to manage that self-generated mass of data, knowing that it must be readied for someone else, and whether the mass will devour its creator—Frankenstein-like—these are the questions that the novice will face and overcome through pragmatic control of his context.

§15.4 FORGOING UNIMAGINATIVE MODELS: READ ONE NOVEL PER MONTH

Bombarded by boilerplate, intimidated by a seeming atmosphere of conformity, reluctant to call attention to himself, the new lawyer needs constant assurance of his own unique style. For, as I hope this chapter has indicated, he will excel professionally because, and not in spite of, what is special within himself. His writing, without ostentatiousness, can resist blandness and help him to express a firm and colorful professional presence.

How to avoid the real or imagined pressure to fall back upon shades of gray? I have found that a mix of stylistic models permits the observer to recognize what is best in his own written work. Since every day the lawyer reads forms, cases, statutes, and regulations, every weekend he should read novels. To be precise, "great" novels, and to be more precise, great novels *about law*. Since such works exist in abundance, I have included a representative list in §§7 and 8 of the Bibliography.

I recommend novels because they replicate the prose medium to which we as lawyers are bound, great novels because they show us how powerful that medium can be, great novels about law because they will interest *all* lawyers on many different levels. A good number of such works, indeed, discuss precisely the way lawyers speak and write. Dickens's *Bleak House* and *Great Expectations* or Faulkner's *Intruder in the Dust* not only afford varying examples of brilliant style but also point out thematically the pitfalls and the potential of lawyerlike speech. Melville's *Billy Budd* or Katherine Anne Porter's short story "Noon Wine" similarly meld form and theme as they depict the effects of law on the individual; Twain's *Pudd'nhead Wilson* or John Barth's *The Floating Opera* humorously portray lawyers in their attempts to overcome what Barth's lawyer Todd Andrews calls "imperfect communication."

Imagination and style play vital roles in law. Anyone doubting this needs only to return to Cardozo's classic essay, "Law and Literature," which rightly heads the list of the bibliographical section on style. (*See also* pages 41 and 255.) Novels replenish and sustain the lawyer's creative urge. Younger lawyers, often seemingly pulled toward the more humdrum (if equally important) aspects of the practice, can refine through novels their sense of professional style.

16

Moving On Up: Learning to Edit Another's Writing

§16.1 DISSOCIATING YOUR CRITIQUE OF WRITING FROM OTHER PROFESSIONAL JUDGMENTS

As the lawyer strides upward in her career, she usually becomes at least a part-time editor. Fully 80 percent of lawyers with three or more years experience do some editing of others' writing, yet the skill of editing is not taught to the profession. As with so many other anachronistic aspects of the field, this absence of formal training in editing reflects the genteel old-world apprenticeship practice of nineteenth century American practice. There the master craftsman would take the novice under her wing, teaching the "whole lawyer" everything necessary to enter the guild, including, of course, good writing. Editing complemented the conveying of corrective advice in courtroom technique, indenture drafting, or any other slice of professional life. And the assumption was made, of course, that a senior lawyer would be as good a writer as she was a litigator or draftsman.

Today, like the faded rose in many a romantic poem, the parent/fledgling metaphor has dissipated. When, in our more impersonal environment, a lawyer acts as the editor of another lawyer's writing, she must summon a variety of skills probably unavailable to her. The first of these is her own excellence and authority *as a writer*. Although one need not be a fine writer to be a competent editor, it "wouldn't hurt," and it surely enhances the confidence brought to the task by an editor.

But even if, with the help of this book perhaps, today's editor has attained distinction in her own writing, the disappearance of the apprenticeship model makes many other abilities necessary. First and foremost, the contemporary editor must reverse the method of her nineteenth century forebears: Editing for stylistic and technical writing faults must be *dissociated* from all other professional judgments. Too much rides on the correction of the smallest grammatical error, and too little remains of the paternalistic atmosphere of terror-but-trust, to permit any confusion of skills. When a younger lawyer hears "You dangled a participle," she understands "You're not much of a lawyer." The editor must make clear, by saying so explicitly, that one has nothing to do with the other. Where an editor fails to clarify this segmentation of skills, no improvement of the junior lawyer's writing will occur. Convinced that her entire existential being as a lawyer risks insult and injury, the junior misses the point. Grammar and syntax remain just as confused as she does.

What can a busy lawyer-editor do, short of taking a series of courses on social psychology, in order to forestall trepidation and produce writing improvement in her colleagues? If my principal suggestion (to state simply and directly that a critique of writing is not a critique of lawyering) seems insufficient, there are two other possibilities. First, hire an outside writing consultant. Such an outsider carries none of the potentially injurious baggage of a senior colleague and can criticize writing with impunity. Or second, make clear at orientation sessions for all new lawyers that their work will be edited for technical mastery of the language, but that continuing improvement in writing is all that is asked and that substantive legal abilities are judged completely separately. Repeat this announcement at any periodic evaluation session with junior colleagues.

§16.2 EDITING WITHOUT REWRITING

If clear differentiation among skills should be the major theme of in-house legal editors, saving time is the second. Countless hours disappear into that special inferno preserved for nonbillable and nonproductive time as editors mark up other lawyers' writings. Furthermore, extensive rewriting often takes place not only of the work of juniors but even that of fellow seniors engaged collegially on a written project. Thus any technique designed to save time at the editing stage will yield significant dividends at all levels of the professional enterprise.

There is such an editorial technique, and it is fairly obvious: Take the basic structure of the writing given to you and work with it. The writing may be deficient in ways clear to you, and these can be signalled later to the writer; but acting as an editor rather than a rewriter saves time as well as the original writer's feelings. If the technical aspects of the document's language pass muster, the fact that it might not satisfy every stricture imposed by this book can be overlooked temporarily. There is much to be said for getting a literate, if not a brilliant, piece of writing dispatched with minimal editing.

Of course, ideally each law office or department would have its own in-house, full-time editor. Some have taken this step, but few can afford it. Short of delegation to a permanent editor, the busy senior lawyer must trust her editorial intuition on the key questions: "Is this a passably literate document as drafted? Can I work within its structure to make it as effective as possible in roughly its present form?" If the answers to both are affirmative, the editor should save specific comments about grammar, syntax, word choice, and organization for a calmer time. A conference called with the writer *uniquely for the purpose of writing comments* is more effective (*see* §16.1) and more efficient.

How to distinguish the document requiring a complete face-lift from the passable if not perfect one needing only some fine-tuning? Two litigation examples illustrate the difference. First, suppose an editor meets these sentences in the opening page of a brief to her state's supreme court:

☐ Plaintiff is a Delaware corporation, which, in 1983 was engaged and presently is in the business of, among other things, manufacturing and selling widgets. Defendant in early 1983 was interested in acquiring widgets. This mutual business interest eventually led to contacts between the parties, subsequent negotiation, and decisions by defendant to execute initial and subsequent letters evincing an intent to acquire widgets manufactured by plaintiff and being marketed under the trade name "Widgeteriffic." . . . It is urged on the appeal that error exists which justify reversal of the order entered below and the court to issue an order in favor of defendant dismissing the complaint.

Next, assume that the same editor receives from another associate a brief containing the following sentences in its opening pages:

☐ The Supreme Court, focusing on the inter-vivos nature of the arrangement, held that the Orphans' Court was without jurisdiction to hear the petition. Unlike the inter vivos trusts in the more recent cases discussed above, however, the subject trust in *Zilch* was not an element of an organized estate plan. There was no provision for the trust corpus to "pour over" into the testamentary estate of decedent or for the assets of the estate to "pour over" into the trust. Therefore, there was no basis for the court to find that the trust "related to the affairs of a decedent." Furthermore, none of the considerations of judicial economy which today's courts have found so compelling were present in *Zilch*. An additional ground stated by the *Zilch* court for its holding was that the Orphan's Court could not exercise jurisdiction over the trust, since upon the death of the trustee, legal title to the trust corpus vested in the Supreme Court pursuant to the predecessor to Kent Stats. Ann. 802.36.

Both documents are flawed. Both need editing. The trick is to exercise editorial judgment as to which, if either, can remain more or less intact and which must be essentially rewritten. If the reader now has the judgment to make that choice, she already edits efficiently. If not, I ask the reader to peruse the samples again and then to close the book while reflecting on their relative merits.

The samples, on reflection, are distinguishable. The first might really embarrass the firm if submitted without rewriting. The second will suffice with certain corrections. The first example's first sentence does not make sense, its third is terribly verbose, and its fourth is plagued by a glaring error in agreement, a flaw in parallelism and a reversal of that and which. Taken alone, any of the sentences might be corrected by simple editing; taken together, they alert the editor to a document that probably needs substantial rewriting.

The second example reads better throughout. Basically, the author's control shines through. True, sentence five has its own agreement error "none . . . were present" (*see* §4.4), and some of the sentences are poorly punctuated. On balance, however, once these aberrations are handled, the editor can retain the rest and submit it to the court without further anxiety.

Lawyer-editors need to protect themselves against overediting, which is simply another way of saying underperforming as a substantive attorney. Allowing various levels of writing, from superb to merely competent, to pass muster, the editor frees herself for her own work and for the arduous task of literally rewriting the occasional disasters that inevitably cross her desk. Correcting mistakes, but relegating discussion of them until the task at hand is completed, the editor acts efficiently and benefits from the writer's prior work.

§16.3 SUPERVISING TEAM WRITING PROJECTS

Considerably different from editing alone, leadership of a team writing project demands its own skills. Here the desired result is a single document authored, so to speak, by a committee. The situation arises most frequently when an outside agency or court needs to be addressed on an issue vital to an entire section of a law department or firm. Such documents sometimes run to hundreds of pages, and they can take weeks to prepare. The supervisor of the team document may be a senior attorney in the section involved, but she is more often a lawyer with five or six years' experience. She should be a good writer and editor who is flexible in her collegial dealings but also capable of some firmness. Hers will be the task of keeping people to deadlines, of correcting errant writing, and, finally, of harmonizing disparate styles into a coherent, single-voiced document.

Since the latter element has not been discussed earlier, we might dwell on it a bit here. Throughout this book, I have been arguing for the lawyer's discovery and retention of a personal voice, of a genuine writing *style*. But the leader of a team project, if faced with colleagues who have accepted my argument, necessarily meets a paradox. She must now reconcile those individual, dearly won approaches to professional writing. Even if—and sometimes *especially* if—the members of the team produce universally excellent drafts, the final document will appear disjointed to its audience if some harmonization does not occur prior to its completion.

At this difficult juncture, the leader must somehow resist the mediocrity that frequently emerges from team writing. Reducing the multiple effort to its lowest common denominator, some lawyers at this point surrender to a base commonality, typified by the passive, impersonal, and verbose style all too often correctly associated with legal writing. Instead, the team's leader should seize both the opportunity granted her by her role and the *best* aspects of her team members' individual styles. If one member excels at strong verbs, she should extend that strength to the entire document. If another mixes syntax effectively, she should make that a staple of the whole effort. Throughout, the leader should seek the colorful adverb, the precise locution, the most accurate use of pronoun and tense, and all the other points discussed in Parts II and III of this book.

If the team leader lets herself be guided by a variety of her colleagues' writing strengths, she will save time and achieve a fine document all at once. The sole task remaining to her will be the document's final organization. She will have already developed a preliminary architectonics, of course, before apportioning responsibilities to the team members. But, inevitably, as the results come in to her, new questions of structure arise. Two members' research may have taken them into overlapping areas, so there is some repetition, or an especially strong argument may have emerged in an area of the document the leader first thought to be quite secondary.

Such architectonic quandaries are really no different in kind for the multiauthored document than for any other legal writing. (*See* Part IV.) The team leader should treat each of her member's submissions as a piece of "raw data" needing to be integrated with the rest. She should "create a gap" (*see* Chapter 13) between the time she receives that data and the editing phase. This gap should be filled by at least a half-day of reflection on the document's optimal final form. A Roman outline then can assist the leader best to utilize the raw data, shifting some sections around, eliminating others, and so on. In other words, the team leader stands as a master-writer. The document produced by her team will impress its audience as somehow remarkably unified and uncharacteristically forceful.

In variety there can be strength.

17

At the Top: Professional Responsibility and Taking Steps to Improve the Breed of Writing Lawyers

§17.1 THE REFORM OF IN-HOUSE WRITING

One of the strange outgrowths of the nineteenth century apprenticeship model was the twentieth century aversion to central administration in the law firm or department. Even though the numbers of lawyers grew beyond the apprenticeship model's tolerance, senior attorneys resisted thinking of their places of work as corporate or bureaucratic structures. By some magic or other, each lawyer would learn his craft, and each section would make its decisions in line with the "spirit" of the whole. The ship would sail on, somehow. Yet, despite lawyers' historic reluctance to administer, a degree of internal organization haphazardly occurred. Documents, for example, did find their way not only to files distinctly related to the given matter but also to a central place where lawyers assigned to similar cases in the future could find them. No matter how weak the writing, it passed unreformed to the central location, there to guide generations unknown along the path of tortured legal prose.

Lawyers in the late 1980s have become more conscious of the need to devote firm or section resources to administration. And, although the trend began with law office management committees, budget committees, and the like, it has trickled down to exercising control over questions of in-house writing. For the first time in the history of the profession, senior attorneys are making and implementing systematic decisions about the general quality of writing in their professional environment.

As in almost all reform situations, this new approach to writing skills can be ascribed to the enlightened dedication of a mere handful of leaders in law firms and legal departments. In the main, they have capitalized on a vague uneasiness, shared by many of their senior colleagues, regarding the standards of in-house writing. They have acted on this concern, moving effectively to improve the situation. Extrinsic goads to such action, discussed in Chapter 2, often dovetailed fortuitously with the internal receptivity to both centralized decision making and writing reform. But only these people at the top could take the tangible steps necessary to improve their own and their colleagues' writing.

No two programs organized by these leaders are exactly the same. Each must reckon with in-house traditions. Each must answer the special concerns of occasionally skeptical colleagues. Some of the latter feel that "it ain't broken, so why fix it?," although fewer and fewer lawyers still cling to the view that legal writing is unassaultable. Others see the problem but wonder why the old apprenticeship approach no longer does the job; they often can be made to see that points such as those raised in §§16.1 and 16.2 against the internal instruction model are difficult to answer.

The better known and more successful centrally administered in-house writing programs nonetheless do have certain elements in common. First, they all go beyond remediation to universal reform. That is, they avoid stigmatizing the few in favor of requiring improvement for the many. Good writers as well as deficient ones must participate in writing programs and become self-conscious about this vital skill. Second, at least for the first several years, such programs enlist the support of outside consultants. Third, they make clear, symbolically and programmatically, that better writing has become a *priority* within the firm or department. Senior lawyers accomplish this by enrolling and appearing and by having their own writing criticized along with everyone else's. They also contribute by constant support, through in-house memoranda and posted announcements, for stylistic reform. Strong writers are rewarded for their writing skills as those skills become a formal element in annual evaluations. Poor writers begin to sense the professional costs of failing to focus on the problem.

There are other ways, more variable, to enhance in-house style. Some firms hire full-time editors. Others invite consultants at fixed times every month to edit specific documents and to answer any questions on writing. Writing guidelines are prepared (or revised) to reflect the educated expectations of the leading in-house lawyers. These guidelines are then distributed to each lawyer, made a part of orientation programs, and established as a basic reference tool available to all. They stress the basics; they do not dictate style. Checklists itemizing particular areas of concern (verb use, jargon, passive construction, architectonics) are printed and utilized both for self-editing and eventual objective evaluation.

Style, of course, cannot be imposed. But leaders can take the invaluable step of instilling an *awareness* of writing throughout their bailiwicks. Here form is just as important as substance. The firm, department, agency, or judicial chamber headed by people who are constantly emphasizing good writing *will produce* better writing. Ideally each lawyer, in such an environment, will be encouraged to nurture his own professional style within the liberal constraints of the organization's expectations.

The costs of such a focus? Putting aside the funds allotted for consultants (which can be balanced against the savings in editing and teaching time of in-house lawyers), there are some preliminary psychological hurdles. People grumble when they are asked to return to the very source of their liberal education, literacy. But, almost universally, they quickly see the advantages of such programs. Many come to perceive writing training as a "fringe benefit" of their jobs. Finally, no superb lawyer has been lost because of in-house attention to writing style, but one or two diamonds in the rough have been discovered. If an inability to write well has kept some talent unexpressed, in-house writing reform will surely bring it to light. It thus pays for itself many times over.

§17.2   THE REFORM OF BOILERPLATE

Typically, when confidence in the idea of stylistic reform has spread
to a majority of an institution's department heads, boilerplate can
be refashioned. Few tasks, in such a benign atmosphere, give lawyers as much pleasure as eliminating two thirds of a standard form's
verbiage. Archaic usage disappears forever. Lawyers leap suddenly
but safely forward into the world of everyday speech habits. Before
exemplifying with a representative sampling, I should reiterate that
boilerplate reform occurs only when leaders are willing to pursue
it. For, as I have stated in varying context earlier (*see* Chapter 13;
§14.3), lawyers by training respect the written word. All forms of
prose take on the mystical qualities of *stare decisis*. In-house boilerplate, with its implied leadership imprimatur, seems impregnable
even where it is at its most unreadable. Department heads alone
can tamper with such time-honored formalism; certainly only they
may extirpate precedential language with impunity.

Under the aegis of committed and enlightened leaders, the
work of boilerplate reform proceeds apace. In one situation with
which I am familiar, a team of lawyers and consultants edited some
300 litigation forms in the course of just four half-day sessions.
Many of these documents had survived, unaltered, threescore or
more years, and their prose evoked a quainter world in which lawyers seemingly had more time to spin out their counterclaims and
"wherefore" clauses as verbosely as possible.

Seven of those documents fairly accurately suggest the full
group and thus can offer the reader an idea of the scope of boilerplate reform within a department. Originally consisting of a total
of 1551 words, they emerged from revision at a crisp 985 words.
That reduction of 37 percent lies toward the lower edge of the
average cut, which is about 42 percent. Substance unaffected, the
pithy new boilerplate serves at least three highly salutary ends:

1. Encouraging through example in-house pithiness and
   strength in nonboilerplate areas of litigation drafting;
2. Influencing boilerplate reform by proving that verbosity
   is needless;

3. Reducing the amount of paper and ink expended on frequently used forms.

All seven documents, first in their original and then in their revised versions, follow.

DOCUMENT 1

Original

As a Complete or Partial Affirmative Defense:

First: That the plaintiff(s) caused or aggravated any injuries suffered in the accident by failing to use the available automotive safety restraints.

Revision

As a Complete or Partial Affirmative Defense:

First: That the plaintiff caused or aggravated any injury by failing to use seat belts.

DOCUMENT 2

Original

WHEREFORE, the defendants, XYZ Company of Anywhere, Inc., demands judgment dismissing the complaint herein as to it, with costs, and further demands that it have judgment over and against the defendant, pursuant to Section 007 of the Anywhere Code Annotated, and/or against the defendant for all or part of any verdict or judgment which shall or may be recovered herein by the plaintiff against the defendant XYZ Company, of Anywhere, Inc., together with the costs and disbursements of this action and any expenses incurred in the defense thereof.

Revision

WHEREFORE, XYZ Company of Anywhere, Inc., demands both judgment dismissing the complaints as to it, with costs, and judgment against the defendant pursuant to Section 007 of the Anywhere Code Annotated, or against the defendant for all or part of any verdict or judgment that may be recovered by the plaintiff against XYZ Company of Anywhere, Inc., together with costs, disbursements, and expenses.

DOCUMENT 3

Original

As a First Cause of Action

First: That at all times hereinafter mentioned the third party plaintiff, XYZ Company of Anywhere, Inc., ("the Company"), was and still is a domestic corporation existing by virtue of the Laws of Anywhere.

Second: That at all times hereinafter mentioned third party defendant, DEF ("the Contractor") was and still is a domestic corporation existing by virtue of the Laws of the State of Anywhere.

Third: That prior to the date of the accident alleged in the plaintiff(s) complaint, the Company and the Contractor entered into a contract, wherein the latter agreed to perform certain work indicated on the portion of the contract attached, the contents of which contract the Company requests permission to refer to at the trial of this action, as if the same were set forth herein.

Fourth: That the plaintiff(s) commenced this action, alleging that injuries and damages were sustained due to the negligence of the Company. The Company will refer to plaintiff(s) complaint at the trial of this action.

Fifth: That on or before the date of the accident, the Contractor had performed or was performing work provided for in the Contract, and was in charge of the work, performed by its agents and/or employees.

Sixth: That the General Conditions of the Contract between the Company and the Contractor state in part: . . .

"26.   Indemnification . . . "

Seventh: That if the plaintiff(s) sustained the injuries and damages alleged, they were sustained either through the negligence of the plaintiff(s) or through the negligence of the Contractor, or by reason of the Contractor's breach of the provisions of its contract with the Company, and not through any negligence on the part of the Company.

Eighth: That because of this action, the Company has sustained costs and expenses none of which have been paid by the Contractor.

Ninth: That because of the Contract, entered into between the Company and the Contractor and of the matters set forth herein, if any verdict or judgment is entered against the Company, the Contractor is obliged to indemnify and save harmless the Company and reimburse it for all costs and expenses incurred in the defense of this action.

As a Second Cause of Action

Tenth: The third party plaintiff, XYZ Company of Anywhere, Inc., reiterates every allegation made above in paragraphs One through Nine, as if the same were fully set forth herein.

Eleventh: That if the plaintiff(s) sustained the injuries and damages alleged, they were sustained either through the negligence of the plaintiff(s) or through the negligence of the Contractor, and not through any negligence on the part of the Company.

Twelfth: That because of the common law of indemnification and of the matters set forth herein, if the third-party plaintiff, XYZ Company of Anywhere, Inc., is held liable to the plaintiff(s), such liability arose out of the negligent conduct of the third-party defendant, its agents, and/or employees, in causing and creating the alleged unsafe condition, and the third-party plaintiff, Company, is entitled to be indemnified in whole or in part by the third-party defendant for the amount of any verdict or judgment which may be recovered against the Company.

WHEREFORE, the Company demands judgment dismissing the complaint herein, as to it, together with the costs and disbursements of this action, or in the event that the plaintiff(s) recover judgment against it herein then the Company demands judgment over and against the Contractor for all or part of the amount of said judgment together with the costs and disbursements of this action.

Revision

As a First Cause of Action

First: That XYZ Company of Anywhere, Inc., ("the Company"), is a corporation under the Laws of the State of Anywhere.

Second: That DEF ("the Contractor") is a corporation under the Laws of the State of Anywhere.

Third: That before the date of the accident alleged in the complaint, the Contractor agreed with the Company to perform certain services indicated on the portion of the Contract attached.

Fourth: That the plaintiff(s) commenced this action, alleging that injuries and damages were sustained due to the negligence of the Company.

Fifth: That the Contractor had performed or was performing services provided for in the Contract.

Sixth: That the General Conditions of the Contract between the Company and the Contractor state in part: . . .

Seventh: That if the plaintiff(s) sustained the injuries and damages alleged, they were sustained through the plaintiff's negligence, the Contractor's negligence, or through the Contractor's breach of the provisions of the Contract, and not through the Company's negligence.

Eighth: That because of this action, the Company has sustained costs and expenses that the Contractor has not paid.

Ninth: That because of the Contract, and because of the matters set forth here, if any verdict or judgment is entered against the Company, the Contractor is obliged to indemnify the Company and reimburse it for all costs and expenses.

As a Second Cause of Action

Tenth: That the Company reiterates every allegation made above in paragraphs one through nine.

Eleventh: That if the plaintiff(s) sustained the injuries and damages alleged, they were sustained either through the negligence of the plaintiff(s) or through the Contractor's negligence and not through the Company's negligence.

Twelfth: That because of the matters set forth here, if the Company is held liable to the plaintiff(s), such liability arose out of the Contractor's negligence in causing the alleged condition, and the Company is entitled to indemnification by, or contribution from, the Contractor for the amount of any verdict or judgment against the Company.

WHEREFORE, the Company demands judgment dismissing the complaint, together with costs and disbursements of the action, or in the event that the plaintiff(s) recover judgment against it, the Company demands judgment against the Contractor for all or part of the amount of the judgment with costs and disbursements.

DOCUMENT 4

Original

As and for a Separate, Distinct and Complete Defense to the Alleged Cause(s) of Action, the Defendant, XYZ Company of Anywhere, Inc., Alleges, upon Information and Belief:

First: That at all the times mentioned in the complaint herein the defendant, XYZ Company of Anywhere, Inc., was and still is a domestic corporation duly organized and existing under and by virtue of the Laws of the State of Anywhere, and was and still is a widgets corporation within the purview of the Business Regulations Law and the Manufacturing Corporations Law of the State of Anywhere, and was and still is engaged in the sale and distribution of widgets in the Township of (Ourtown) and elsewhere, under franchise or franchises duly granted to or acquired by it, and that (any and all work that may have been carried on or conducted by it—OR—any equipment which may have been installed and/or maintained by it) in the vicinity of (location) in the Township of (Ourtown), City of Kent at or about the times mentioned in the complaint, was (carried on or conducted by—OR—installed and/or maintained by) the said defendant under and pursuant to the rights granted by law to widget corporations, and under and pursuant to permission or license of the proper municipal authorities having jurisdiction thereof.

Revision

As a Separate and Complete Defense to the Alleged Cause(s) of Action, the Defendant, XYZ Company of Anywhere Alleges, upon Information and Belief:

First: That the defendant, XYZ Company of Anywhere, Inc. is a corporation under the laws of the State of Anywhere and is engaged in the sale and distribution of widgets under franchises. All work conducted, or equipment installed, at the times mentioned in the complaint was pursuant to the rights granted by law and the permission or license of the proper municipal authorities.

DOCUMENT 5

Original

As and for a Fifth Affirmative Defense:

First: That the furnishing of widgets by the defendant, XYZ Company of Anywhere, Inc., to its customers is subject in all respects to the provisions of the Company's Widget Component-Part Schedule and any amendments thereto as approved by the Manufacturers Control Commission of the County of Midville, the contents of which the defendant begs leave to refer to on the trial of this action as if the same were set forth herein more particularly at length.

Revision

As a Fifth Affirmative Defense:

First: That the defendant, XYZ Company of Anywhere, Inc., furnishes widgets to its customers subject to the provisions and amendments of the Company's Widget Component-Part Control Schedule as approved by the Manufacturers Control Commission of the County of Midville, to which schedule, as amended, the defendant may refer at trial.

DOCUMENT 6

Original

SIR:

You are required to serve upon the undersigned, the attorney for the defendant, XYZ Company of Anywhere, Inc., within ten days after service of this demand, a verified bill of particulars, setting forth the following:

1. The post office address and residence of the plaintiff.
2. The age of the plaintiff at the time of the accident.
3. The exact day, month, and year and the approximate hour of the day or night when the alleged occurrence took place.
4. The location of the accident indicating the street or avenue, and, with compass directions, the exact distance in feet from the nearest intersecting street or avenue, and the exact distance in feet from the nearest curbline.
5. A detailed description of the manufacturing defect or condition which caused the alleged occurrence and the specific nature of the defendant's negligence.
6. The date, time, and form (whether written or oral) of any actual notice claimed. Provide a copy of written notice or indicate the substance and recipient of oral notice.
7. The facts supporting any claim of constructive notice.
8. When and by whom allegedly improper or defective parts were installed, if such are claimed to have caused the occurrence.
9. The specific laws, statutes, or ordinances allegedly violated by the defendant.

10. The nature, extent, location, and duration of each injury allegedly sustained by the plaintiff.
11. The injuries claimed to be permanent or to have permanent effects, including a detailed statement of the allegedly permanent effects.
12. The length of time plaintiff, as a result of the injuries complained of, was confined to (a) bed, (b) home, (c) hospital.
13. The expenses or obligations incurred by plaintiff for: (a) hospitalization, (b) medical care, (c) X-rays, (d) nursing, (e) medicines, (f) medical supplies, and (g) any other medical expenses, specifying the nature and the amount of each.
14. The occupation and average weekly, monthly, or annual earnings of the plaintiff.
15. The length of time plaintiff was unable to work as a result of the alleged injuries and the amount of earnings of the plaintiff.
16. The name and address of plaintiff's employer at the time of the occurrence and at the present time.
17. An itemized statement of all other special damages allegedly sustained by the plaintiff, specifying the nature and amount of each.

Revision

TO PLAINTIFF'S ATTORNEY:

You are required to serve the attorney for the defendant, XYZ Company of Anywhere, Inc., within ten days after service of this demand, a verified bill of particulars setting forth the following:

1. Plaintiff's residence.
2. Plaintiff's age.
3. The date and time of the occurrence.
4. The exact location of the occurrence.

5. A detailed description of the manufacturing defect that caused the occurrence.
6. Whether actual or constructive notice is claimed.
7. The facts supporting any claim of actual or constructive notice of a defect.
8. When and by whose agency defendant's negligence occurred.
9. Any statute, ordinance, or regulation violated by the defendant.
10. The nature and duration of each injury.
11. The length of time plaintiff was confined to (a) bed, (b) home, and (c) hospital.
12. The cost of: (a) hospital, (b) medical, (c) X-rays, (d) nurses, (e) medicines, (f) medical supplies, and (g) any other medical expenses.
13. The dollar value of other damages, item by item.
14. Plaintiff's occupation, name and address of employer, dates absent from employment, and amount of lost earnings.

DOCUMENT 7

Original

Allege(s) upon Information and Belief:

That if the defendant(s) XYZ Company of Anywhere, Inc., (and _____) (is) (are) held liable to the plaintiff, such liability arose out of the negligent and careless acts and conduct of the plaintiff, _____ , and the defendant(s) XYZ Company of Anywhere, Inc., (and _____) (is) (are) entitled to be indemnified in whole or in part by the plaintiff, _____ , for the amount of any verdict or judgment which may be recovered against the defendant(s), XYZ Company of Anywhere, Inc. (and _____).

WHEREFORE, the defendant(s) XYZ Company of

Anywhere, Inc. (and _____), demand(s) judgment, dismissing the complaint as to (it) (them), with costs, and further demand(s) that (it) (they) have judgment over and against the plaintiff, _____ , for all or part of any verdict or judgment which may be recovered herein by the plaintiff, _____ , against the defendant(s) XYZ Company of Anywhere, Inc. (and _____), together with the costs and disbursements of this action and any expenses incurred in the defense thereof.

Revision

Allege(s) upon Information and Belief:

That if the defendant(s), XYZ Company of Anywhere, Inc., (and _____) (is) (are) held liable to the plaintiff, such liability arose from the negligence of the plaintiff, _____ , and XYZ Company of Anywhere, Inc., (and _____), (is) (are) entitled to be indemnified in whole or in part by the plaintiff, _____ , for the amount of any verdict or judgment recovered against (this) (these) defendant(s).

WHEREFORE, XYZ Company of Anywhere, Inc. (and _____), demand(s) judgment dismissing the complaint and further demand(s) judgment against the plaintiff, _____ , for all or part of any verdict or judgment that may be recovered by the plaintiff, _____ , against XYZ Company of Anywhere, Inc. (and _____), with costs, disbursements, and expenses.

§17.3 CONTROL OVER THE WORD PROCESSOR

The advent of computer technology can work a benevolent revolution in law offices. But it can also produce a dictatorship of the machine. The choice rests with the lawyers who lead appropriate in-house committees or who otherwise exercise control over the situation. As regards writing, the main importance of technology lies in word processing. Most decisions involve what gets fed into the computer, or, in an increasing number of offices, who gets his own personal computer (PC).

The risk in using central word processors that I want to address relates to their seeming indifference as to what is spewed out to staff members pressing various buttons. "Why reform boilerplate," some who have just read §17.2 might ask, "if all these forms can be placed on the computer anyway? We no longer need to maintain cumbersome in-house binders containing hundreds of forms that then have to be located, photocopied, and replaced. Instead," they might proceed, "we have all the forms on a few floppy disks, one thin index binder, and a printer that would just as soon print a three-page interrogatory as your slimmed-down one-page version."

In response, I might start with a suggestion. An excellent time to reform boilerplate comes when the machines are rolling into the office. At that stage, few would make the observation above. If the operator of the word processor can be given well-written, revised forms to enter into the computer *ab initio,* a true revolution will have occurred. Later, it seems harder, although of course the very technology that has been installed makes broad-scale revision absurdly simple.

Beyond this, however, the firm or department has reasons (extrinsic to time saving) for improving boilerplate and all other expressions of in-house legal style. The reputation of the office, the improved response from the document's intended audience and all of the facets emphasized in this book, dictate a continuing attention to writing skills. Furthermore, the ink, paper, and support service expenditures—multiplied over years—are probably as high when a computer spews out verbiage as when the forms are assembled manually.

Indeed, the office's centralized word processor creates a marvelous opportunity for constant improvement of in-house writing. Every reasonable suggestion for enhancement of form letters, leases, testamentary documents, indentures, or anything else lawyers draft should be considered. If approved, the supervisory lawyer need only instruct the operator to plug the correction into the processor. Reform succeeds revolution and becomes the order of the day.

As to placing a personal computer in each lawyer's office, what a luxury! Few offices can contemplate such largesse, but more and more may offer PCs to a percentage of their staff. When choices must be made as to distribution of PCs, writing skills should predominate in the calculations. A good writer can only benefit from a ready-to-hand PC. Drafting fairly glibly onto the screen, such a writer now for the first time has real flexibility in editing his own work. The *stare decisis* fallacy vis-à-vis first drafts (*see* §13.4) may be overcome. The finished product thus should be significantly improved over traditional techniques. But the weaker writer faces certain hazards when the new technology is made immediately available to him. A reduction will occur in his willingness to create the needed gap between the research and writing phase (*see* §§13.1-13.3) and to generate an outline before leaping to the PC. Itchy fingers will seize the keyboard before the mind has been readied to produce mature drafts. Then, too, weaker writers rarely edit their own work well, so the unparalleled editing potential of the PC means less in their case.

In every writing-related category, the decision maker must dominate the machine and not permit vanquishment by the new technologies. As the law office's economy grants him the opportunity to invest in computers, the person at the top must concomitantly gather his advisors and committees to guarantee that word processing means better writing.

§17.4 WRITING SAMPLES AT THE HIRING STAGE

Since the chapter title speaks of a *breed* of writing lawyers, the reader may forgive a slight extension of the image. Just as the breeder of thoroughbreds must work with the known quality of horses he has on hand, so the individual or group charged with monitoring writing skills can only build on the talents already to be found in house. What senior lawyers find available—the breed—derives from decisions made by those charged with bringing new lawyers into the barn. For this reason alone, writing should be sampled at the hiring stage. Happily, every year more and more law offices require applicants to submit samples of their written work. Less clear, perhaps, is the mechanism then used to evaluate the sample; also ripe for improvement may be follow-up procedures for borderline cases.

What should the law firm or legal department do with the applicant's writing sample? Three things. First, apportion to the office's best writers—senior or junior—the task of evaluating *comparatively* the applicant's sample. This means grouping samples, anonymously and without reference to any other evaluation criteria (law school record, journal membership, etc). Second, have the evaluator grade the sample from one to ten, by comparison with the group. For this purpose, provide the evaluator with a checklist of writing skills based, if context permits, on the approach of this book, particularly Parts II-IV. Third, use the evaluator's grade as an objective component of the applicant's complete dossier. (Keep in mind that different evaluators will grade differently, so factor in the variations in median average if more than one evaluator is used.)

What weight to grant the applicant's writing grade depends on the values of the employer. I would of course advise making it one of the salient features of any final personnel decision, perhaps even more so at the hiring stage (where little is known of the lawyer's overall practical ability) than later on. But if two or more otherwise equal candidates are vying for a position, their relative writing talents should be decisive.

In the many offices for which September signals the influx of a horde (herd?) of newcomers, some investigation of the applicants' writing abilities may be required beyond the submission of writing samples. There—and in smaller contexts as well—two or more applicants may be quite difficult to distinguish as they compete for a remaining "slot." If the preliminary sample yields little decisive data, I recommend that such candidates be asked to complete some of the writing exercises compiled in this book. Exercises should be graded by a competent writer from among the legal staff. The exercises should be chosen for a mix of skills (syntax, punctuation, organization, etc.), including, if the candidate is a middle- or senior-level lawyer, *editing*. Exercises should also vary in testing contextual strengths (writing under pressure or at greater leisure, writing letters, form documents, etc).

One of the most pleasurable aspects of achieving institutional leadership is the nurturing among juniors of qualities dear to the leader's heart. A lawyer at the top who is sensitive to the vital role of writing can, in our late-century environment, work in-house wonders.

18

Special Tips for Various Kinds of Practice

§18.1 THE DRAFTSMAN

About a month before President James Monroe laid the cornerstone of the first building of Central College, ex-President Jefferson sent Joseph C. Cabell the draft of a bill for the establishment of elementary schools throughout Virginia. He had promised it to this colleague and state senator, perhaps at the midsummer meeting of the visitors, and he prepared it at Poplar Forest, where he had more leisure than in Albemarle. He said that he had sought to avoid the "verbose and intricate style" of modern statutes but was willing for his bill to be corrected to the taste of his fellow lawyers. Accordingly, he authorized Cabell to make every other word a "said" or an "aforesaid," and to repeat everything so many times that only lawyers could untwist the diction.

Dumas Malone, 6 Jefferson and His Time 267 (1981)

§18.1.1 Government Lawyers

Beset with its own traditions, subject to its own peculiar style, writing among government lawyers seemed during the '60s and '70s to receive a disproportionate share of critical barbs. For a

241

while, only governmental writing was attacked. Until the reforms of the past decade, lawyers and the laity alike vented their spleen almost uniquely on some readily available document in the public domain: the tax codes, the regs, the standard form government contracts, and so on. (Another widely accessible and frequently analyzed type of governmental legal writing—the judicial opinion—is treated in Chapter 19.) Recent developments across the spectrum of the profession have taken the pressure somewhat off government lawyers. Reformers see little difference any longer between legal writing within government and legal writing without. They focus as much or more on private, in-house style as on statutory and regulatory language.

On the other hand, and much to their credit, governmental agencies at the federal, state, and municipal levels have kept the question of public legal writing alive. Their enlightened search for improvement encompasses not only those kinds of writing that all lawyers do (memos, letters, etc.) but also writing peculiar to their agency or department. A 1983 edition of the NLRB Style Manual exemplifies this concern for more effective writing within an important government agency. Although the manual is scheduled for revision, it already hits almost all the right chords. Not content merely to replicate the correct citation form for lawyers appearing before the Labor Board, the manual has specific sections on punctuation, spelling, and good usage. From this manual, a concise but competent excursion into the traditional themes of writing reform, come the following passages:

GOOD USAGE

Strunk & White, The Elements of Style (3d ed. 1979) ("the little book") contains such crisp rules (with examples) as "Use the active voice" (rule 14), "Put statements in positive form" (rule 15), and "Omit needless words" (rule 17, stating "Vigorous writing is concise. A sentence should contain no unnecessary words, a paragraph no unnecessary sentences. . . . This requires not that the writer make his sentences short . . . but that every word tell"). Its brief rules of usage and principles of composition are recommended reading.

The Manual then exemplifies Strunk and White's "Omit needless words" as follows:

Along the line of *(like)*

As far as I am concerned *(as for me)*

At all times *(always)*

At about, at approximately *(about)*

At such time as *(when)*

At the present time *(now)*

By means of *(by, with)*

By the name of *(named)*

Despite the fact that *(although)*

Due to the fact that *(because)*

During such time *(while)*

During the course of *(during)*

During the time that *(during)*

Each and every one *(each)*

For the purpose of *(for, to)*

In advance of *(before)*

In connection with *(in, concerning)*

In regard to *(regarding, concerning)*

In a negligent manner *(negligently)*

In a position to *(can)*

Inasmuch as *(because, as, for)*

In excess of *(over)*

In lieu thereof *(instead)*

In order to *(to)*

In respect to *(about, concerning)*

In some cases *(sometimes)*

In spite of the fact *(despite)*

In the amount of *(for)*

In the case of *(if)*

In the course of *(during)*

In the event of *(if)*

In the immediate vicinity of *(near)*

In the last analysis (delete)

In the matter of *(in, concerning)*

In the near future *(soon)*

In the neighborhood of *(near, about)*

In the not too distant future *(soon)*

In this day and age *(today)*

In view of *(because)*

In view of the fact that
(because, considering that)

Notwithstanding the fact
(although)

Of an indefinite nature
(indefinite)

Of an unusual kind *(unusual)*

Of great importance
(important)

On or about *(about)*

On the ground that *(because)*

On the order of *(about)*

On the part of *(by)*

Owing to the fact that
(because)

Prior to *(before)*

The fact that (delete)

The present time *(now)*

There can be no question that
(unquestionably)

Surrounding circumstances
(circumstances)

Subsequent to *(after)*

Until such time as *(until)*

With the exception of *(except
for)*

Whether or not (omit *or not*
when possible)

With reference to *(about,
concerning)*

With regard to *(regarding,
concerning)*

[NLRB Style Manual (1983).]

Other federal agencies, such as IRS and Justice, have also moved along the lines of consciousness raising among lawyers writing in their domains. Most of these branches of government have in common a greater-than-average emphasis on *drafting* and its special requirements. Few writers, including fellow lawyers, who have never tried to codify collective judgment into linguistic form can fathom the difficulties inherent in such drafting. And while a book of this kind can only hint at an approach to drafting generally, the lawyer in public practice can look confidently to a variety of sources for writing improvement. (*See* Bibliography, §3.)

§18.1.2 Private Practice Drafting

When we speak of the *craft* of law, we envision the draftsman. In the unheralded activity of translating inchoate wishes into ordered language, the lawyer achieves perhaps her most literary and certainly her most paradigmatic stature. The finished product may seem to lack some of the flair of the appellate brief or the judicial opinion, but in the very binds that constrain the draftsman and keep her from free-flowing prose lie the potential for superb craftsmanship. Reed Dickerson's fine book on drafting expresses well the elements that distinguish this form from other kinds of legal writing.

> The most important single principle in legal drafting is consistency. Each time an idea is expressed in a legal instrument, it should be expressed the same way. Each time a different idea is expressed, it should be expressed differently. Where comparable ideas are similar in some respects and different in others, their expression should be correspondingly similar and different. Because this highlights the existence and extent of the substantive differences, it facilitates useful comparisons. . . .
>
> The consistency principle also calls for maintaining parallel sentence or paragraph structure for substantively comparable provisions. . . . [I]t facilitates extrapolation, which, too, helps to perfect substantive policy.

Dickerson insists, convincingly, that the draftsman lacks the stylistic freedom of other legal writers. Indeed, synonyms and sometimes even strong nouns and verbs can work a disservice to the goal of the document.

I think it is true that the reformer must move with particular humility among the ranks of the draftsman. Yet some improvement in the writing of private, as well as public, documents is surely possible. Dickerson strikes home, for example, in advising the lawyer against the "drafting sin" of redundant noun and verb clusters. (*See also* §9.2.) My own work with individuals who draft contracts, deeds, and wills further indicates that other principles relating to legal writing generally apply also to these lawyers. Thus,

I would add to Dickerson's consistency principle the following drafting guidelines:

1. *Organize* the document well so that similar subjects are grouped as close together as possible. (Example: if you are drafting a lease prohibiting animals in a building, group all the provisions relating to animals consecutively.)
2. Do not hesitate to use "said" as an adjective. It is irreplaceable in the drafting context.
3. Perfect the use of that and which. (§10.1.) The distinction is vital to the draftsman.
4. Eliminate needless boilerplate. Each document stands on its own as a reflection of the situation's unique demands. Boilerplate adds nothing but verbiage.
5. Avoid ambiguous referents at all costs. (§§6.4; 13.4.) No matter how dense the paragraph or how multifaceted the document, the reader should never be in doubt as to which precise subject is being discussed.

§18.2 THE CORPORATE LAWYER

The practice of corporate law entails almost all the writing genres discussed in this book. Large corporate firms typically contain litigation, tax, and trusts and estates, as well as securities-related departments. A good deal of writing in such an environment touches on and can benefit from this book as a whole. In-house corporate lawyers or those practicing in small or intermediate firms also find themselves writing across the spectrum already covered. In this section, therefore, I will suggest just two additional guidelines.

First, corporate lawyers might consider how their writing style affects the classic tension between themselves and their business clients. Even in-house corporation lawyers meet frequently with a kind of impatience on the part of their "clients," the decisionmakers within their company. For outside counsel this impatience is almost a staple of the relationship.

Generally, the conflicting perspective of business lawyer and client resolves into a truce, subject to frequent small arms fire and an occasional major battle. Businesspeople want to move ahead aggressively; lawyers are paid to discover barriers. Theoretically it is right that the twain should never meet. More typically, both sides finally see it the businesspeople's way. And there is the rare— and highly valued—corporate lawyer who marshalls the business energies of her clients, originating assaults on hitherto well-defended targets.

Writing style, in my opinion, plays a small but nonetheless noteworthy role in the relationship of client and corporate lawyer. General correspondence abounds between these players. Both would benefit if the lawyer agreed to use plain English in her letters to the client, along the lines suggested in Chapters 7 and 10. Corporate clients, many with a faster-paced style, appreciate a more direct tone in documents addressed to them. (*See also* §§2.4; 3.4.1; Charts 1 and 2.) A pattern of simple and straightforward writing can only assist the lawyer to buttress substantive positions that inevitably strike business people as picayune and deleterious.

My second suggestion involves proofreading skills. For the nation's biggest corporate law firms as much as for its smallest, in-house proofreading commands an allocation of time that would shock those who equate law only with complex reasoning or sophisticated wheeling and dealing. Yet few lawyers are taught proofreading skills. Nor is the increasing coterie of paraprofessionals who may handle such tasks (*see* §18.4) always given appropriate training.

Those lawyers or paralegals who spend sleepless nights "at the printer's," waiting for securities-related documents to emerge, realize that this kind of proofreading is of a special sort. The conventions of "team-proofing" of a document differ from techniques associated with proofing one's own work. Both are important enough (*see* §13.8) to merit attention. But the corporate lawyer, especially given the extremely high stakes when registration and prospectus documents are involved, should have her attention explicitly directed to this writing-related skill.

§18.3 THE SOLE PRACTITIONER

The lawyer who works on her own has surely wondered—at least from time to time—if she practices the same profession as everyone else addressed in this part of the book. For the sole practitioner, talk of collegial editing, managerially implemented writing programs or even word processors may seem extraterrestrial. Nor is her alienation from some of what I have said limited to collegial or technological concerns. The sole practitioner may find herself with no in-house boilerplate to reform, with no legal staff to hire, and with no audience for internal memoranda.

Yet sole practitioners, among the noblest and most successful of the breed, do every bit as much writing as their more collegially directed fellow lawyers. Not one word of Parts I-IV of this book is irrelevant to their enterprise. But how, in addition to the present volume, may the sole practitioner gain counsel when faced with those pressing problems of professional writing? My answer is a straightforward nod in the direction of the sole practitioner's bookshelf. (If there is no bookshelf, one should be acquired long before the purchase of a computer!) Where colleagues may be lacking, the friendly influence of books need not be. And here I refer not to Blumberg's. I refer to each and every work on style referenced in this book's bibliographical section. Beyond this, practitioners alone or in groups of two to five might consider remaining alert to the increasing number of bar association, PLI, or Continuing Legal Education programs geared to legal writing skills. These sponsoring organizations allow, at minimal cost, exposure to excellent workshops that can improve writing for the duration of a career.

Writing is, when all is said and done, a solitary venture. Small wonder that some of the profession's finest writers work pretty much on their own.

§18.4 PARALEGALS

A percentage of writing responsibility formerly shouldered by lawyers has now passed to an excellent cadre of paraprofessionals.

Because the paralegal's duties are expanding into many areas of form writing, sections of this book such as Chapters 9, 10, and 14 should be read particularly carefully by the "para" (as the paralegal is sometimes called).

Beyond that, I would note that enlightened supervisors often enroll their paras in writing skills programs along with the firm's (or department's) lawyers. Much can be elicited by the para from such programs even though they may contain technical aspects germane only to those with law degrees.

Finally, the para can and should be exposed to high-level, writing-related instruction in her specific field of duty. Thus, if a para works in a real estate or a trusts and estates department, she should be exposed to PLI or CLE courses touching on draftsmanship in those fields.

§18.5 ACADEMIC LAW

A separate treatise could (but probably should not) be written on legal academic style. Academic lawyers, with rare and notable exceptions, have not garnered trophies in this professional domain. Those who write about legal language, like Zechariah Chafee or Reed Dickerson, often write well. (*See* Bibliography §3.) The self-consciousness that comes with that substantive topic may well provide an incentive that otherwise seems to be lacking in the field of academic writing.

Although much could be said, I would like to dwell here on only one point: the law professor's relationship with her student editor. Few outside teaching understand, and some within it (like Professor Roger Cramton) are beginning to criticize, the enormous influence that law students have on legal academic publishing. Almost all law journals are completely managed by student editors, who select the content and largely control the style of their journal. Style, which alone interests us here, is further controlled by the "Blue Book," a manual of legal style known from their student days to almost all lawyers.[1] A manuscript's final published

---

[1] *But see* Posner, Goodbye to the Bluebook, 53 U. Chi. L.R. 1343 (1986).

form typically reflects transformations derived from a somewhat mechanized and often impersonal editing process.

I have dealt with a fair share of student editors and always found them courteous. On occasion, the editor assigned to a manuscript has training either in English or in editing. More often, the editor sincerely attempts to enter into my style, making suggestions in its spirit. (My colleagues seem to experience this receptivity a bit less often. On the other hand, many law professors welcome the complete stylistic overhaul that the student editing process permits if unchecked.) My experience indicates, and I commend it to any academic writer seeking control over her own published style, that polite but consistent authorial interest in the editing of a manuscript almost guarantees its appearance in largely the form desired by the professor. Done this way, the editorial suggestions of students may be weighed and discussed between the parties. Improvement can only emerge from such a process.

Academic lawyers otherwise share the writing context, strengths, and weaknesses of their practicing colleagues. Were it not for the anomaly of seeing their work edited by people not yet even in the field (much less senior to them), their approach to writing might be guided by everything else covered in this book. *Caveat:* Academic writers tend to *conclude* documents more systematically and comprehensively than do other legal writers. Thus the lessons of Part IV, particularly §§11.6 and 12.4, might be supplemented by such works as Zinsser, *On Writing Well* 70-74 (*see* Bibliography §1).

§18.6 LAWYERS ABROAD

A contingent of American lawyers embarks every year for assignment abroad. Some work in their firm's foreign bureaus, some practice for corporations with interests abroad, others work for government agencies monitoring foreign programs. Having "done time" in a firm's Paris office, I know that such lawyers probably write less on average than their stateside colleagues but enough to merit a few observations here.

First, I need to separate practice in English-speaking countries abroad from the more frequent situation in which English is not the native tongue. For the American lawyer in Anglophone countries, the linguistic adjustment is present but small. A good British law dictionary may abide the transition (*see* Bibliography §4).

American lawyers practicing elsewhere than in English-speaking countries always would do better to master the *lingua franca*, but their home tongue usually serves them well. Generalizations, of course, do not hold in all the varied contexts of foreign practice, but at the very least, lawyers abroad will be drafting telexes and letters in English. Translations of documents into English may also be part of the job. All of these pursuits require skills discussed throughout the book.

Telex style deserves special attention here. In few other genres does the quest for strong nouns and verbs, so highly recommended for all legal writers in Chapters 4 and 5, pay such dividends. International telexes, perhaps due to their relative costs, seem to bring out an unusual zeal for pithiness among legal draftsmen. In the following example, strong verbs happily abound:

TO   Studio Legale—Rome, Italy Telex No 8572624—Legal 1
FROM   XYZ Paris
Message Date 010986

Attn: AKAFUADEZ10

RE: XYZ Corp. DEF Inc. commenced suit against XYZ and MNO in January in Paris. Smith VP of XYZ also named. This suit pertains to the same transaction involved in the suit you are handling (File #007). It alleges that defendants conspired to defraud DEF into relinquishing possession of the goods to defendants without having a right to same, and that DEF delivered the goods to MNO in reliance upon false representations that goods belonged to MNO. It further states that the B/L was endorsed by Smith after repeat after the delivery was made to DEF. Plaintiff alleges that, as a result of delivering the goods, it was sued in Genoa by MNO and is entitled to be indemnified by defendants based on the false pretenses, false representation, and fraud of defendants. Plaintiff also demands damages for conversion and asks for punitive damages. Copies of summons and complaint will be mailed to you.

Please advise on the status of the Genoa litigation and approximately when we may expect a ruling on *jurisdiction*. Our Paris counsel needs this information as soon as possible before filing responsive pleadings. Also, please advise us as to fiscal aspect.

With regard to requests for admissions nos. 1 through 6, we have no personal knowledge of these matters; therefore, can neither admit nor deny same. With regard to No. 7, Smith does not recall having signed said B/L.

If you have received a copy of the bill of lading bearing Smith's signature, please send me a copy.

Best regards,

Audiberti

The example offers a felicitous mixture of "telegramese" ("after repeat after") and direct, lucid prose ("please advise us" "please send me a copy"). The latter is characterized primarily by the kinds of strong verbs lawyers should also begin to use in noninternational contexts. Audiberti skillfully mustered his linguistic arsenal, employing such verbs as "commenced," "pertains," "alleges," "demands," "advise," "needs," and "send." As I have often stated—and as this telex again proves—lawyers need not employ fancy verbs, only the everyday language that best conveys their thought.

Whether due to a relative paucity of other writing obligations, a need to economize, or a heightened interest in the way language works, lawyers abroad thus offer some lessons to their stateside colleagues.

Judicial Writing

§19.1 REACHING FOR THE CARDOZO WITHIN YOU

The book comes full circle in this concluding substantive chapter, which again conjures its author's favorite judicial writer. Benjamin N. Cardozo, whose style took center stage in Chapter 1 (pages 7-9), returns here to inspire the judicial writer. For those judges who may be reading the book from right to left, a glance at that first chapter now is highly recommended.

Cardozo's style, adulated by many, has not of course won the hearts of all legal analysts. Jerome Frank, using the *nom de plume* Anon Y. Mous, once granted Cardozo's writings "grace. But it is an alien grace."[1] And only recently, Judge Richard A. Posner has described Cardozo as "overtly stylish" yet "somewhat overrated."[2] On the other hand, a legal journal focusing in 1931 on a compendium of Cardozo's opinions, praised in them what it saw as an Anglophile tendency to emphasize "the link between law and lit-

---

[1] Frank, The Speech of Judges: A Dissenting Opinion, 29 Va. L. Rev. 625, 630 (1943).

[2] Posner, Law and Literature: A Relation Reargued, 72 Va. L. Rev. 1351, 1386 (1986).

erature, and between legal writing and good writing."[3] If Frank's phrase "alien grace" thus suggested that only English judges were expected to write elegantly, the preponderance of American commentators roundly disagreed. By now most judges concur with those who eulogized Cardozo as "poetic," and who found that his style was perfectly suited to its judicial function.

I am not endeavoring to impose Cardozo's style on my judicial readers. Quite to the contrary, I am asking each judge to find his own stylistic voice and to recognize that the way the judicial song is sung cannot really be distinguished from its substantive content. Most judges with whom I have worked—trial level as well as appellate—care deeply about their written work. They face the act of judicial writing with some trepidation. No small number of trial-level judges actually avoid submitting opinions for publication until they are sure that a high degree of stylistic and analytical quality has been attained. Appellate judges, constrained to publish, meet the task with varying degrees of fear and trembling. All welcome advice about the particular challenges of judicial writing.

Striking is the refusal of a vast majority of judges to see writing as a merely mechanical means to the end of announcing a judgment. Judges recognize that tone, rhetoric, and structure play a vital role in conveying the substance of their opinions. Here, too, I have already cited Cardozo to good effect (see pages 7 and 41), but he is at his most pragmatic in the following from the essay "Law and Literature."

> The opinion will need persuasive force, or the impressive virtue of sincerity and fire, or the mnemonic power of alliteration and antithesis, or the terseness and tang of the proverb and the maxim. Neglect the help of these allies, and it may never win its way. With traps and obstacles and hazards confronting us on every hand, only blindness or indifference will fail to turn in all humility, for guidance or for warning, to the study of examples.[4]

Cardozo simply states what every judge knows: words are his tools, his "scalpel and insulin."

[3]*See* Book Review, 65 U.S.L. Rev. 347 (1931).
[4]Benjamin N. Cardozo, Law and Literature, Selected Writings 342.

Indeed, Cardozo admits with considerable candor that style sometimes contradicted logical accuracy and completeness (but not rightness!) within his own opinions.

> There is an accuracy that defeats itself by the overemphasis of details. I often say that one must permit oneself, and that quite advisedly and deliberately, a certain margin of misstatement. . . . The picture cannot be painted if the significant and the insignificant are given equal prominence. One must know how to select.[5]

We return, inevitably, to Cardozo's judicial poetics. He knew that words were a disturbingly imperfect medium for the communication of ideas, yet he also understood the power of the medium when structured into an effective formal pattern. Cardozo succeeded, finally, in recognizing that the very contingent quality of language could be an exhilarating and creative element:

> We find a kindred phenomenon in literature, alike in poetry and in prose. The search is for the just word, the happy phrase, that will give expression to the thought, but somehow the thought itself is transfigured by the phrase when found. There is emancipation in our very bonds. The restraints of rhyme or metre, the exigencies of period or balance, liberate at times the thought which they confine, and in imprisoning release.[6]

These words from *The Growth of the Law* typify the place of style and rhetoric in Cardozo's judicial method. Cardozo, although a "word-skeptic," nonetheless grasped the immeasurable "vitalising power" of the judge's medium. We will turn to him again as this chapter develops.

To reach for the Cardozo within, the individual judge does not need to emulate any other judge's unique style. Instead, the judge must recognize the magical power of the process of writing and the central place given to the written opinion within our legal system.

---

[5]*Id.* at 341.
[6]Benjamin N. Cardozo, The Growth of the Law, Selected Writings 225.

§19.2 THE SPECIAL DILEMMA OF THE TRIAL-LEVEL JUDGE

Unlike their appellate-level colleagues at the bench, many trial-level judges face the existential challenge of determining when (as well as how) to publish. Some trial-level judgments can be delivered from the bench. Not all bench opinions are submitted for publication. But most trial-level judges whom I have met are keenly concerned with their written work, whether or not it appears in the reporters.

Aside, once again, from recommending the body of this book, I would stress to the trial-level judge the need to avoid the isolation that often characterizes his task. Several judges have expressed their envy for the ingrained collegiality of the appellate panel, which seems to enforce an immediate and ongoing critique of each panelist's writing. The trial-level judge works alone and, except for the assistance of clerk or secretary, must seek out knowledgeable critics of his writing.

When judges from trial-level courts assemble to discuss writing, as occurs more and more frequently, the isolation of the judge-writer evaporates. Identifying common problems, the group alleviates the sense of isolation and proves to each judge that his problems with writing are hardly unique.

Apart from the issues of when to publish and how to avoid isolation, several problems also preoccupy trial-level judicial writers. Principal among these is the fear of being reversed. The challenge of a written opinion seems to crystallize for the judge the risks—as well as the opportunities—of articulating law and applying it to the case at hand. Sometimes the appellate rule is unclear; often it is complex. Occasionally, the judge finds himself disliking either the law or the outcome that it demands in the case. Writing serves as the legitimate focal point for all these situations, as the act in which the judge's sense of himself emerges fully. Apprehension about reversal does not—and should not—compel an outcome or a rationale.

Tonal considerations can puzzle, but also assist, the judicial writer. If an appellate or statutory rule is clear but dictates an unfortunate result, the judge can use tone to convey his unhappiness at the outcome or, perhaps more rarely, his dissatisfaction with the law itself. Sarcasm, or a host of other rhetorical devices, can be usefully employed to shade the opinion's meaning. Point of view variations permit the judge, alternatively, to personalize (first-person singular) or depersonalize ("The court") each opinion.

Finally, trial-level judges wonder how much latitude they have in *structuring* an opinion. Are they constrained by their court's rules or customs to use one architectonic approach? Must the facts always be recited first, for example? Such questions can be answered only in context, of course. But even if, as occurs rarely, the opinion's organization is dictated from above, there is latitude within each mandated formal section for the creative structuring of paragraphs and sentences. (*See* Part IV.)

Recalling Cardozo's wonderful phrase, "there is emancipation in our very bonds," (*see* page 255), the trial-level judge need not draw back at the thought of committing his decisions to writing and then to publication. One of the highest accolades accorded their colleagues by trial-level judges is "He is the best writer on the bench." Such praise comes from the *practice* of the special art of trial-level writing.

§19.3 THE RHETORICALLY SENSITIVE APPELLATE JUDGE

The Cardozo within the appellate judge dictates the identical consciousness of the power and fickleness of words that should pervade lower court writing. I thus suggest you start with §5 of the Bibliography, which contains a representative sampling of references on general and judicial rhetoric. Judges seeking somehow to "avoid rhetoric" in their writings are disingenuous. Computer-like and mechanical kinds of appellate writing are no less "rhetorical" than the speech of judges fully cognizant of their poetic capabilities. (*See* pages 13 and 259.) Even silence speaks volumes in the appellate opinion. Justice Douglas's single-word dissents in tax cases were just as articulate as the complex rhetorical patterns of some of his brethren.

The essence of it all is *awareness*. Willy-nilly, the appellate judge creates a narrative, not merely a statement of rules. His every word will be judged by the opinion's various audiences, so he must be the first, fully self-conscious judge of his own prose. Throughout this book we have seen examples of mediocre as well as superb appellate writing. In most cases of the former, lack of rhetorical awareness, rather than lack of writing ability, explains the opinion's defects.

As the pinnacle of legal utterance, the judicial opinion achieves authority and endurance through linguistic craftsmanship. To some extent, the dynamism of the Anglo-American legal system derives from the necessity for style in the appellate opinion. Language may be used elegantly or carelessly, but it is the judge's medium. The opinion may be effectively organized or it may be haphazard in its explanation of the facts and issues, but it must have a form, which, as a part of style, contributes to the opinion's present and ultimate meaning.

Appellate judges work, consciously or not, within a linguistic medium that contributes a creative element to their everyday task of decision making. Judges are writers (or at least managers of writers); the way in which they use language will affect future law. A judge need not be a Cardozo, but the bare fact that the judicial medium is language moves that judge's efforts into the domain of narrative and its consequent ambiguities, over which control must be consciously exercised.

Osterlind v. Hill, a 1928 Massachusetts case, serves as an example of insufficient awareness that style and substance always merge. Its rhetoric unwittingly makes it fascinating. It treats the perennial torts issue: Is there in our law an affirmative duty to rescue? The court's answer is no, but its *manner* involuntarily shades the meaning of the negative response and alters the effect that the opinion has had on its legal audience. Hill rented a canoe to Osterlind and another man, both of whom may have been drunk at the time. The vessel overturned; Osterlind clung to it for a half hour screaming for help. Hill noted the incident from the shore, heard the screams, and although neither life nor limb would have been risked, failed to act. Osterlind finally lost his grip on the canoe and drowned. Osterlind's relatives sued Hill on behalf of their intestate, the drowned man. But the Massachusetts Supreme Court affirmed the lower court's dismissal of the tort action. The court used these words:

OSTERLIND v. HILL
160 N.E. 303 (1928)

BRALEY, J., delivered the opinion of the court. The declaration must set forth facts which, if proved, established the breach of a legal duty owed by the defendant to the intestate. The plaintiff relies on *Black v. New York, N.H. & H.R. Co.*, 193 Mass. 448, as establishing such a duty on the part of the defendant. In that case the jury would have been justified in finding that the plaintiff was "so intoxicated as to be incapable of standing or walking or caring for himself in any way." There was testimony to the effect that, "when he fell, he did not seize hold anything, his arms were at his side." The defendant's employees placed a helpless man, a man impotent himself, in a dangerous position.

In the case at bar, however, it is alleged in every count of the original and amended declaration that after the canoe was overturned the intestate clung to the canoe for approximately one-half hour and made loud calls for assistance. On the facts stated in the declaration the intestate was not in a helpless condition. He was able to take steps to protect himself. The defendant violated no legal duty in renting a canoe to a man in the condition of the intestate. The allegation appearing in each count of the amended declaration that the intestate was incapacitated to enter into any valid contract states merely a legal conclusion. The allegations, therefore, in the counts of the amended declaration to the effect that the intestate was incapable of exercising any care for his own safety is controlled by the allegations in the same counts that he hung to the side of the canoe for approximately one-half hour, calling for assistance. . . .

In view of the absence of any duty to refrain from renting a canoe to a person in the condition of the intestate, the allegations of involuntary intoxication relating as they do to the issues of contributory negligence become immaterial. The allegations of willful, wanton or reckless conduct also add nothing to the plaintiff's case.

The failure of the defendant to respond to the intestate's outcries is immaterial. No legal right of the intestate was infringed. [Case dismissed.]

In its rhetoric, there is nothing to distinguish this opinion from many others. Its author, Henry K. Braley, was three years later to be eulogized for "his wide learning, his piercing discernment and . . . his elucidation of the elemental and lasting, rather than the instant or ephemeral issues of any case at bar before him." Yet, for Braley, the human dimensions of Osterlind's case were undeserving of mention; clearly, he did not feel he could find, in Cardozo's phrase, "emancipation in the very bonds" of the legal precedents to which he owed allegiance.

The American legal system, unlike some others, imposes no affirmative duty to rescue upon an otherwise noninvolved bystander. Cardozo spoke of the rule this way:

> For years there has been a dogma of the books that in the absence of a special duty of protection, one may stand by with indifference and see another perish, by drowning, say, or fire, though there would be no peril in a rescue. A rule so divorced from morals was sure to breed misgivings. We need not be surprised to find that in cases of recent date, a tendency is manifest to narrow it or even whittle it away. We cannot say today that the old rule has been supplanted. The rulings are too meagre. Sown, however, are the seeds of scepticism, the precursor often of decay. Some day we may awake to find that the old tissues are dissolved. Then will come a new generalization, and with it a new law.[7]

Judge Braley chose not to dissolve "the old tissues" of the rule. But since his rhetorical options were limitless, as immense as the language itself, he nonetheless moved toward Cardozo's "new generalization" subtly and perhaps unintentionally.

A piece of narrative discourse, this opinion evidences the infinite variety of rhetorical approaches that all judges can take to any situation before them. Instead of a dry rearticulation of the plaintiff's claim, the adjudicator can set forth the facts with a nar-

[7]Benjamin N. Cardozo, Paradoxes of Legal Science, Selected Writings 265-266.

rative sense of their implicit moral and human dimensions. Instead Braley, having first found somewhat strangely that Osterlind's ability to hang on and scream disproved the plaintiff's claim that Osterlind was too drunk to have the canoe rented to him, reached the stylistic pinnacle of his opinion in the blandest of manners, articulated near the end of the opinion: "The failure of the defendant to respond to the intestate's outcries is immaterial." The judge's language reflects not only his unwillingness to change the law, but, more significantly, his apparent approval of that law. His bland style seems least designed to plant Cardozo's "seeds of scepticism." But the starkness of his 13-word phrase has worked to give the opinion a different effect. Subsequent scholars and judges have been struck by the bloodless quality of Braley's response to the human dimension of the facts. Constrained to stylize, as judges in Anglo-American law are, Braley has influenced others to examine and criticize the rule that he himself supported. The case thus establishes an essential point about the appellate opinion: within it, willy-nilly, style serves the function of the law and is inseparable from it.

Therefore, as Harvey Couch declared, "It is no accident that Holmes, Brandeis, Cardozo and Hand are considered the greatest judges as well as the greatest writers of judicial opinions."[8] The often dazzling style of these judges accounts in part for the continuing authority of many of their opinions. Cardozo, in particular, took pains to articulate frequently the place of the "architectonics" of a successful judicial opinion. (*See* §1.2; Chapter 3; §11.3.) Since "right" or "wrong" answers so rarely inhered in the fact situations that arose in his court, Cardozo realized that the framing of the decision, structurally and linguistically, would often decide whether the intended audience would accept his legal reasoning.

When Cardozo speaks of an opinion's ability to "win its way" (*see* page 254), he is referring to its chances of convincing the other judges on the case and of gaining authority within the professional community. (Much the same can be said about any piece of literature or criticism.) In all narrative pursuits, the effective use of style can gain credibility for the idea proposed and lasting accep-

---

[8]Couch, Law and Literature: A Comment, 17 Vand. L. Rev. 911-916 (1964).

tance for its author. Let us not forget that Cicero won the acquittal of a mass murderer of kin with his eloquence.

To this extent, the judge is far more an artist than a logician or technician. Cardozo adds:

> [The judge or advocate] is expounding a science or a body of truth which he seeks to assimilate to a science, but in the process of exposition he is practicing an art. The Muses look at him a bit impatiently and wearily at times. He has done a good deal to alienate them, and sometimes they refuse to listen and are seen to stop their ears. They have a strange capacity, however, for the discernment of strains of harmony and beauty, no matter how diffused and scattered through the ether. So at times when work is finely done, one sees their faces change, and they take the worker by the hand. They know that by the lever of art the subject the most lowly can be lifted to the heights.[9]

Cardozo's method articulates the reality for judges far less conscious of their craft than he. As we observed with Judge Braley, the way in which the adjudicator explains the case determines the ultimate meaning of the decision. As Karl Llewellyn has remarked,[10] "adornment" is inseparable from legal function.

The plea here is not for the adoption of any particular style. The appellate judge needs to accept his role as rhetorician and narrator. Consciousness of the central place of writing will bring its own rewards.

§19.4   COURT ADMINISTRATION AND JUDICIAL WRITING: WHICH WAY TO GO

Efficiency has its limits. Some courts recently, besieged by almost unworkable caseloads, have looked to opinion writing as the primary place to trim down and become more efficient. Some federal

---

[9] Benjamin N. Cardozo, Law and Literature, Selected Writings 355-356.

[10] Llewellyn, On the Good, the True, the Beautiful in Law, 9 U. Chi. L. Rev. 224, *reprinted in* Jurisprudence at 194-195 (1964).

courts of appeal have adopted rules, for example, in which a panel may decide that a case has "no precedential value." If such a determination, combined with several others, can be made, the panel must limit its opinion to the bare statement of its judgment, without any guiding explanation. Other courts have experimented with strict formal limitations on their judges' opinions. Seeking to rid opinions of "adornment," these courts circulate bullet-point instructions on trimmed-down prose. The rule of law alone will emerge, they hope, unencumbered by ambiguities, rhetoric, style.

To such attempts, with all diffidence to the magnitude of the problem of jammed court calendars, I must object. The phrase "no precedential value" has always struck me as complete nonsense, or, at best, as a self-fulfilling prophecy. Under such a rule, Judge Braley's opinion in *Osterlind,* for example, might never have been written. After all, the absence of a duty to rescue was well settled. Yet his opinion, as our last section demonstrated, has had significant "precedential value." No judge can predict the effect his explanatory words will someday have on a court or commentator. Our law grows this way.

As for formal constraints on style, we must recall Professor Llewellyn's *equation* of adornment and law. His own admiration for Cardozo he summed up by identifying the latter's "light-giving answers."[11] The rule makes sense *only* because of the way it is conveyed. Llewellyn, perhaps our greatest esthetician of law, also pointed out how crucial an opinion's reasoning can be for its nonprofessional audience (*see* §3.4.2). The following passage thus reiterates some of this book's central points:

> And still, in regard to the rule of law itself, there remains an esthetic aspect undiscussed. . . . [R]ight law must be intelligible, intellectually accessible, to the people whom that law is to serve, whose law it is, the law-consumers and the citizen "makers" of the law. "Function," conceived purely in terms of the staff of legal technicians, could indeed be achieved by language which would carry no meaning or wrong meaning to such laymen. But as I have tried to develop elsewhere, even the high temporary effectiveness which can be had by skillful black-art language is unsound because it can-

[11]*Id.* at 150.

not be relied on to continue effective. Only the rule which shows its reason on its face has ground to claim maximum chance of continuing effectiveness; so that to satisfy, in this, the lay need of relative accessibility, of friendliness and meaningfulness of the reason, is at the same time to do a functionally more effective job on the side of pure technique. There is thus no need, in widening one's view of what the function of rules of law is, to risk confusion on the marks of beauty. Quite the contrary. For to see the wider function is to find the road back to that rightest and most beautiful type of legal rule, the singing rule with purpose and with reason clear, whose nature, whose very possibility, the Formal Perpendicular has led our legal thinkers to forget—almost to deny.[12]

Llewellyn's wonderful paragraph fittingly ends both this chapter and the substantive book as a whole. Judicial administrators need to attack judicial writing *not* in its formal, traditional patterns but as a species of legal writing generally, with all its virtues and blemishes. The "singing rule" is not the rule unwritten but the rule *well written,* with clarity, directness, and force. Each judge must strive to find his strongest written voice. This he accomplishes neither by administrative censorship nor formal constraint. Instead, as must any lawyer seeking to practice a wonderfully rich craft, the judge must find a voice appropriate to his audiences and to his own unique style.

That challenge faces all of us when lawyers write.

[12]*Id.* at 195.

Twenty-three Rules of Legal Writing

Rule 1. Never apportion less than 25 percent of a project to the piece of writing that culminates it. (*See also,* Rule 20.) (Page 38.)

Rule 2. Never leap into prose. (Page 38.)

Rule 3. Articulate your document's aims before you write it. (Page 46.)

Rule 4. Choose the real, not the passive, subject of your sentence. (Page 51.)

Rule 5. Do not avoid your true subject by lengthening a verb into a noun. (Page 53.)

Rule 6. Having named the true subject of your sentence, keep him, her, it, or them constantly in mind until the sentence is over or a new subject has been named. (Page 54.)

Rule 7. Do not bury the subject, but place it as close to the beginning of the sentence as possible. (Page 56.)

Rule 8. Use forms of the verb "to be" (e.g., is, are, be (+ verb), was, were, etc.) only if other verbs will not work better. (Page 63.)

Rule 9.   Avoid split infinitives. (Page 65.)

Rule 10.   Avoid all lawyerisms and jargon when writing to non-lawyers. (Page 88.)

Rule 11.   When writing for colleagues in house, convey information with the utmost directness and avoid a needlessly complex or impersonal tone. (Page 96.)

Rule 12.   When writing exclusively for fellow specialists or when drafting, use jargon if it is pleasing to you *and* your audience or if it cannot be improved by ordinary English; do not, however, use jargon reflexively or out of habit alone. (Page 100.)

Rule 13.   A lawyer need not sacrifice thoroughness to achieve an effective written presentation. (Page 107.)

Rule 14.   Redundant noun and verb clusters should be excised from the freer flowing forms of legal writing, such as correspondence and legal memoranda. (Page 115.)

Rule 15.   Edit every sentence you write, to spot redundancy and to eliminate verbosity. (Page 117.)

Rule 16.   "Typos" are inexcusable. Re-read your draft with a dictionary at hand before inflicting the document on your audience. (Page 127.)

Rule 17.   A restrictive clause, one that precisely defines a preceding term should begin with "that"; a nonrestrictive clause, which only describes a preceding term, should begin with "which" and be set off by commas. (Page 135.)

Rule 18.   Before writing a single word, consciously grasp, and physically set out, the architectonic system of each document. (Page 151.)

Rule 19.   Unless the letter-writer consciously sees the file perfecting or tonally softening effect of conventional openings as vital, they should be avoided in favor of stronger, information-conveying beginnings. (Page 153.)

Rule 20.   At the beginning of each project, estimate the number of hours needed to complete it. Then mark on your calendar (even if it is for the same day) a date (and time) 75 percent into the estimated time period. Enter the inscription: "Begin writing phase" at that spot. This leaves you at least 25 percent of the time allocated for your project in which to write it up. (Page 191.)

Rule 21.   Always ask questions. (Page 193.)

Rule 22.   Assume, in writing a memorandum, that your audience is virtually ignorant of the factual and legal elements under discussion. (Page 207.)

Rule 23.   No matter how dearly bought, in time and analytical effort, information that is irrelevant to the issue section of a memorandum should be excluded. (Page 209.)

II

Testing What You Know: Some General Exercises on Legal Writing

The exercises that follow are meant to be an overall review of the topics discussed in this book. Some of them, marked with an asterisk (*), have already been analyzed in the text. I have included these previously discussed examples in this review so that you will have a way to check your work and compare your analysis with mine. There are, however, plenty of new exercises for you to grapple with.

A. PRONOUNS (*See* §4.4)

■ **Rewrite the following sentences, making sure that each pronoun's antecedent is easily identified and that the correct verb forms are used.**

*1. Each lawyer is responsible for their own work product.

2. Mr. Jones and the associate had not yet met because he was so busy.

*3. Neither the Fourth Circuit nor the Fifth Circuit recognize that rule.

4. Ms. X told Ms. Y that her writing had improved.

5. The court refused to broaden the rule because it was conservative.

*6. Ellen took Julie to lunch because she wanted to discuss the case.

*7. None of the fasteners sold by Z are manufactured by Y.

B. COMMAS, SEMICOLONS, AND COLONS
(*See* §3.1, Chapter 6)

■ **Correctly punctuate these sentences.**

*1. Assuming that the Board of A has the authority to declare a stock split, there are certain steps the Board must consider in order to distribute the shares of stock in accordance with Ohio law, A's Articles of Incorporation and Code of Regulations and NASD rules.

2. It would appear that the department's proposal is satisfactory to us and the Board will obtain a copy of the legislation when it is introduced.

3. During the reconsideration of the rule the Agency or Court can stay the rule or its approval for a period not to exceed three months.

4. The more recent cases, dealing with the subject were decided in 1979.

5. Although several legal problems are created by the proposed structure; South Dakota does not have a similar mortgage tax.

*6. No policy has been articulated by the courts for this proscription but prudence in bank operations seems to be a primary aim of the National Bank Act.

7. However, the liability that he may limit is that imposed by UCC Article 7-204(1), "failure to exercise such care as a reasonably careful man would exercise under like circumstances".

8. X believes that the vast majority of the non-Czech fasteners entered at New York, but will not be certain until it receives further information from Y.

9. This contract calls for XYZ to prepare the site, install fuel storage tanks, piping systems, auxiliary buildings and the demonstrator and test and operate the demonstrator for a period of 13 months.

270

10. As I stated during a prior conversation our Customer Service Department informed me that the billing problem was not discovered for at least two months after the initial solicitation.

*11. There, as in the case at bar, it was the executive type of secretary, a "Gal Friday" who was served.

*12. X may risk liability, however it continues to produce widgets nonetheless.

13. The firm shall not indicate the possible claims omitted from the inquiry letter, however, the firm should discuss them with the client.

*14. Finally, it seems that the most likely scenario in which the Florida statute would apply to invalidate some or all of the power would be in the case of a Florida forum; Florida land; and a Florida choice of laws rule.

C. SPLIT INFINITIVES (See §5.3)

■ **Eliminate the split infinitives in the following sentences.**

*1. If the Court deems further factual development necessary on the commerce clause claim, for example, it may still be able to finally determine the presumption claim.

*2. There were additional safety features available to further reduce risk.

3. The idea is to completely rid the document of verbiage.

4. No discovery has been conducted to date to amass evidence to support the instant application on behalf of the class and to more importantly assist this Court in reaching its determination.

D. CONFUSING USE OF TENSE (See §9.5)

■ **Rewrite these sentences so that the verb tenses are consistent.**

*1. This was part of the discretion that Mr. X had bestowed on Ms. Y. When Mr. X is out of the office, she would handle many matters.

2. These days, as I wander through the maze of the Law Department, my mind filled with the minutiae of widgets and Ninth Circuit rules, I thought back to the glorious summer just completed.

*3. It was contended that this provision expressed the intention of the testator that X shall not execute the will alone.

E. DANGLING PARTICIPLES (*See* §9.1.3)

■ **Correct the dangling participles in the sentences below.**

1. Preferring not to decide the questions raised by the Order to Show Cause without input from the defendants, the return date of the Order to Show Cause was carried numerous times, and argument was finally heard on the matter on June 1, 1985.

*2. In analyzing the potential liability of XYZ for plaintiff's attorney's fees, it is apparent that similar factors should receive serious consideration.

*3. Walking toward the bench, the argument arose.

*4. Borrowing from the reasoning in the cases and applying the time-worn canons of construction, it may be concluded that the interpretation accorded the predecessor of Section 6511 has been accepted by Congress.

F. RUN-ON AND INCOMPLETE SENTENCES (*See* §§3.1, 9.1.2)

■ **Revise each of the following examples into one or more complete sentences.**

1. Even if the property is considered partnership property, New Jersey law treats such property as personalty only to the extent that it is necessary to pay partnership debts and to the extent that the land exceeds the indebtedness, it is to be considered realty, and thus nontaxable. [Note: Can this run-on be easily cured?]

*2. It must, however, be recognized that the benefits attributable to the allocation of widgets from these projects to the source's residential customers results in a different adjustment charge for this class, it does not produce two separate adjustments for each residential customer.

*3. Since the mechanics of writing will vary enormously with the scope and content of the note and with the style and approach of the authors.

G. SUBJECT-VERB AGREEMENT (*See* §§3.1, 4.2)

■ **Rewrite the following sentences so that subject and verb agree.**

*1. When resolved into plainer English, it is clear to us that all of the quotation preceding the words "I have some very valuable papers," relate to the predicted bad weather, a doubt as to whether decedent will be able to go to Glencoe because of it, and a possible resolution of it in his next letter.

*2. The equitable standards applied by the federal courts in most circuits in determining a motion for relief made under this third provision of clause 5 has been strict—nothing less than a clear showing of grievous wrong.

*3. The City and County of Los Angeles has adopted a Realty Transfer Tax.

*4. After weighing all of the evidence, we find that the reasonableness of licensees' and staff's expressions of risk are not materially affected by the intervenors' criticisms.

5. This third class can be treated in two ways: either the trustee or Bankrupt files proof of claims for them, or no proof of claims are filed for them.

H. THAT VS. WHICH (*See* §10.1)

■ **Correct the use of "that" and "which" (including punctuation) in the following sentences.**

1. The statute which I am analyzing may be compared with the Restatement formulation.

*2. An engineering contractor defaulted under a construction contract which contains a liquidated damages clause limiting the liability of the contract to $1,000,000.

*3. I have attached an excerpt of the report that presents the nine recommendations of the task force and a discussion of each by staff.

*4. The litigation which commenced last year still drags on.

*5. Mr. Peters asked me to send you a copy of the *State Teachers* case which decides four interesting securities laws questions that concern the announcement of corporate information.

I. PARALLELISM (*See* §10.2)

■ **Revise the following sentences by effective use of parallel construction.**

*1. We are authorized and required and intend to pursue and collect this debt through litigation if necessary.

2. These allegations included the failure to estimate fees on a periodic basis, billing based on estimated consumption, billing Mars for widgets used by other contractors at the sites and failure to bill for extended periods.

*3. The court's decision is both intelligent and a necessity.

*4. The allegations included fraud, embezzling, and a charge of malfeasance.

*5. The nature of the study, the risks, inconveniences, discomforts, and other pertinent information about the study are discussed below.

6. These factors include:
    1. whether the legal issues involved were novel and complex or straight-forward
    2. the protracted nature of the type of litigation
    3. the probability of success
    4. the likelihood of settlement

7. A national bank may not only charge the rate allowed its state competitors in the state where it is located but also in

other states, even if the laws of those states would prohibit such a rate.

J. OVERUSE OF JARGON (*See* §§7.3, 8.1)

■ **Eliminate unnecessary jargon in the following sentences.**

*1.   The John Doe Company, heretofore known as The Doe Store, is obligated under said contract to perform such services as are listed in Schedule I, annexed hereto.

*2.   Attached hereto are exhibits A and B, hereinafter referred to as "A" and "B."

*3.   I have also enclosed herewith the original copy of a survey for the above-captioned service station.

*4.   Please acknowledge receipt of the above by signing the enclosed copy of this letter and returning the same to the undersigned.

K. VERBOSITY (*See* Chapters 5, 9)

■ **Reduce these sentences by changing the subject, the verb, or both.**

1.   The ultimate termination of this litigation would be materially advanced by correction, at this stage, of the deprivation of due process resulting from denial to X of access to information at issue.

*2.   In a 1976 amendment to the FEAA, additional remedies were added.

3.   This report is required to include a forecast of nuclear power demands for the next five years.

*4.   The cat was eaten by the dog.

5.   Consequently, Mr. Smith initiated a telephone contact with Mr. Jones, a senior assistant treasurer with Company X.

*6. The duty of payment of the *droit de succession* is upon the beneficiaries.

■ **Reduce the verbiage in the following sentences by *at least 25 percent.***

1. However, it has been recognized by the courts that minority group employees may be validly discharged for violating work rules and regulations if the same rules and regulations are applied to white employees, since an employee's race is not a reason to insulate him from discharge for otherwise valid reasons.

*2. He confessed and acknowledged that the assigned penalty was right and proper.

3. At such time as we ascertain a reasonable response, it is to be hoped that the matter will be finalized.

4. Some of the additional definitions are broad in potential scope and might be deemed to create an obligation for reporting or recordkeeping in situations other than those that one with a casual awareness of the Act would assume were covered thereby.

*5. Moreover, in specific relation to Rule 16-a-6, not only is it required that an insider report the acquisition of a put, call, or straddle (Sec. Exch. Act Rel. No. 9499), but it is also provided that the reporting of the *exercise* of an option is not excused from reporting requirements.

6. Your commission shall be deemed earned only when, as, and if title actually closes upon terms and conditions contained in a signed written contract that is in all respects satisfactory to each party to the contract and each party's counsel.

*7. The notice of default judgment came at a time when our staff was extremely busy.

*8. It is anticipated that this formula will require extensive negotiation.

9. It is arguable that the statute might be applicable to this set of facts.

10. On the basis of the above-stated facts, it appears that our position is correct.

L. ORGANIZATION (*See* Part IV)

■ Choose the sentence that goes better with the topic sentence. Explain briefly the reason for your choice.

1.   A typical night in the delta would begin when the missions of that day were completed.
    a.   Each day the food was cold, but at night we got a hot meal.
    b.   Each day we had cold rations only.

2.   One day I was lying on my bed and was a little confused.
    a.   I decided therefore to go back to sleep.
    b.   I went back to sleep.

3.   It was on November 29, 1970. At five o'clock in the afternoon, I was on a plane going to New York.
    a.   A taxi was waiting.
    b.   By the morning of the 30th, I was in Paris.

4.   I was really anxious to see my brother and his four children.
    a.   Their names were John, Jim, Jane, and Jenny.
    b.   I hadn't seen them in five years.

5.   In a lot of ways, New York City is a great place to live, but in other ways there's a lot of discrimination and abuse.
    a.   The subways are a zoo!
    b.   One experiences these unfortunate aspects while riding the subway.

6.   This is probably one of the most unpublicized but popular American games.
    a.   It just isn't well known.
    b.   It resembles soccer, but it's not quite the same.

7.   Days seem always to differ one from another.
    a.   Sunsets make me sad.
    b.   Yesterday's sunset was special.

8.   Here I am in Madison Square Garden, the home of the New York Knicks.
    a.   When the Dodgers left Brooklyn, I cried.
    b.   They need pro basketball in New Jersey.

9. I was standing at the corner of Church Street and Park Place in Manhattan when I noticed a crowd gathering along Church Street, about two blocks from where I was.
   a. Crowds make me uneasy.
   b. An accident had taken place.
10. June 1975 was the month and the year when a great battle was going on in my mind between getting a job, going to college, or joining the Air Force.
   a. I was graduated from High School that year.
   b. The Pentagon stepped up its manpower drive.

■ **Provide a topic sentence and then reorder the sentence sequence.**

Although it is far from the largest museum in New York, the Cloisters is one of the most interesting for its size in the city, well arranged, and well managed. It provides ready and revealing insight into the Middle Ages. Here, within a few miles of the greatest industrial concentration in the world, is a little bit of the Middle Ages. A thirteenth-century French cloister, with its ancient stonework from corbels to statues, has been taken down stone by stone and re-erected here.

■ **A strong topic sentence does not always guarantee a coherent paragraph. Combine the following two paragraphs into one, so that all sentences clearly support the first one.**

Although XYZ Corp. has vigorously opposed in the past the provision relating to self-weighing of cargo by low-income customers and is gratified at its proposed elimination, it must oppose this bill because of its other provisions.

The bill contains serious ambiguities in draftsmanship and would establish detailed requirements relating to rates without adequate legislative findings. Indeed, the proposal to shift revenue responsibility from small shippers to large shippers is based on erroneous legislative findings. Neither can this proposal be justified on the ground that it will effectively assist low-income customers. Finally, adoption of this proposal would produce seriously adverse customer impacts and would further aggravate the customer confusion and resentment engendered by other differential rate forms.

■ **The following paragraph is poorly organized and choppy in style. To create a coherent and readable unit, supply a topic sentence, reorder the sequence of ideas, and provide transitional words where necessary.**

For one thing, cotton had to be picked by hand in the eighteenth century. The pickers had to spend long hours working with the cotton if they were to get anywhere. Cotton is an example of how the Industrial Revolution developed in the eighteenth century. From the fields the cotton went to the home. Here seeds were removed from the cotton by hand. This job required a considerable amount of time and patience. Then the cotton was spun into thread and woven into cloth. People finally became tired of slow and tedious manual labor, and they began to seek new methods of producing cotton textiles. It was about the middle of the century when a number of inventions appeared that tended to shift the cotton industry from the home to the factory. Hundreds of workers would be replaced by the new machinery. Factories were built in order to house this machinery.

■ **Underline, in the following excerpt from a memorandum of law, the passages that are not clearly linked to the purported aim of the document.**

MEMORANDUM OF LAW

Background. In 1832, the XYZ Company was incorporated under the laws of Anystate. The operative statute then called for a minimum of 50 percent of the directors of a company to be present personally in order legally to transact corporate business. Signed proxies were disallowed under Anystate law unless the company's by-laws specifically permitted them. XYZ, in its 1832 charter, declared its sole corporate aim to be the manufacture and distribution of widgets.

The most recent amendments to the Anystate laws (1956 amendments, cite omitted) permit proxies unless the company's by-laws specifically disallow them and call for 50 percent attendance (including proxies) if there are 10 or fewer directors and attendance of no fewer than 5 directors if there are more than 10. The current XYZ by-laws (effective 1945) permit appearance by proxy and state that a director may call in his/her proxy by telephone. There are now 22 XYZ directors.

On August 3, 1986, the XYZ Board met at their corporate headquarters in Anystate. Four directors were physically present. One phoned in her proxy by telephone. Minutes for the meeting of that day report an allocation of $2.5 million from the treasury to repurchase Company shares.

Issue. 1. Did the Board at its August 3 meeting lawfully do business, including its authorization of the $2.5 million?

Conclusions. 1. Since the Anystate statutes of 1956 continue to speak in terms of written proxies, telephonic appearances are problematical.

2. Although, given the clear-cut language of the XYZ by-laws of 1945 permitting telephonic proxies, the August 3 meeting is likely valid, the Board should re-convene with at least five directors physically present in order to allocate the $2.5 million for re-purchase of Company shares.

■ **What is wrong with the structure of the memorandum above?**

■ **Rewrite the following two-paragraph portion of a brief with an eye toward better structure of the whole.**

Thus it is clear that a playfully induced physical harm can lead to liability for an intentional tort, *Vosburg v. Putney*, 50 N.W. 403 (Wis. 1891). Defendant's claim that plaintiff consented to the touching, since it occurred during a professional football game, is unresponsive to recent cases holding that injuries arising from contact beyond that permitted by the rules is still actionable, *Hackbart v. Cincinnati Bengals*, 601 F.2d 516 (10th Cir. 1979). The football field has been the site of many injuries later resulting in tort liability, *Stevens v. Stone*, supra; *Ingbert v. Smith*, supra; *Leotard v. Sneeks*, supra; *Lambini v. Plotz*, supra.

Consent cannot be inferred from the mere fact that plaintiff chose to play the game. The scope of that consent extended merely to contact occasioned by the game's rules. Defendant may have meant no harm and may not have acted in anger; assuming, arguendo, his mere playfulness, such contact however (if resulting, as here, in injury) amounts to a battery, *Mohr v. Williams,* 104 N.W. 12 (Minn. 1905).

■ **Revise the following paragraph to make it flow better. Specifically, from sentence to sentence, add transitional words that assist the reader to follow the developing sense of the whole. (*See* Chart 3, page 163.)**

*A corporation can be liable for fraud. Plaintiff has to prove defendant corporation possessed an actual intent to deceive him in order to prove fraud. Unless a defendant admits possessing the intent, specific intent can only be inferred from the facts and circumstances surrounding the alleged fraud. The Court has held "It is enough to say, as to this prospectus, that a fraudulent intent on the part of the author and publisher may be inferred from the falsity of the statements therein contained and that alone." [Cite omitted.] To hold a defendant liable for fraud, an intent to deceive must be inferred from the surrounding facts and circumstances. At issue here is the method of establishing the intent of a corporation.

■ **Reorganize each of the following related paragraphs for maximum effectiveness and optimal structure.**

Methods of accounting should clearly reflect income on a continuing basis, and the Internal Revenue Service administers its discretion under sections 446(e) and 481(c) of the Code so that, in general, any distortion of income on an annual basis is minimized. The Service will consider the need for consistency in the accounting when the method of accounting from which the taxpayer is changing clearly reflects income. When there is a change in method of accounting, income for the year preceding the year of change must be determined under the method of accounting that was then employed, and income for the year of change and the following years is determined under the new method of accounting. The section 481(a) adjustment, while necessary to prevent duplications or omissions of income or deductions, by its nature is distortive since it does not reflect the economic income of the year. An adjustment period for the section 481(a) adjustment is provided for in subsections 5.05 and 5.06 of this revenue procedure and is intended to reduce the possibility of change in method of accounting itself creating a material distortion in income in the year of change and to reduce any distortion when it does exist. Also, amounts attributable to changes in methods of accounting are taken into account in determining earnings and profits in a manner consistent with the provisions of this revenue procedure.

When subparagraph (a) of this paragraph 5.06(1) does not apply and 67 percent or more of the net amount of an adjustment is attributable to the 1-tax year period, 2-tax year period, or 3-tax year period immediately preceding the year of change, the highest percent attributable to the 1-, 2-, or 3-tax year period is to be taken into account ratably over a 3-tax year period beginning with the year of change. Any remaining balance is to be taken into account ratably over an additional period equal to the remainder of the number of tax years the taxpayer has used the method of accounting that is being changed. However, the total adjustment period shall not exceed 6 tax years. This subparagraph, 5.06(1)(b), only applied if the taxpayer has used the method being changed for more than 3 tax years. If the method of accounting being changed has been used for no more than 4 tax years, 75 percent shall be substituted for 67 percent. An amount attributable to the 1-, 2-, or 3-tax year period is the difference in the amount of the adjustment determined under 481(a) of the Code for the year of change and the amount that would have been required under section 481(a) if the same change had been made at the beginning of the preceding 1-, 2-, or 3-tax year period. . . .

If the Service receives an application that is not properly completed in accordance with the instruction on the current form, it will notify the taxpayer. In its notification, the Service will allow the taxpayer 45 days from the date of the notification letter to furnish the necessary information. The notification will specify those items that need to be corrected and, when appropriate, transmit a current blank form for the taxpayer's use. If the required information is not submitted to the Service within the 45-day period that form will not be processed. An additional 15 days, however, may be granted to the taxpayer to furnish such information in very unusual and compelling circumstances. If, upon receiving the completed form, the Service finds during its processing that supplemental information is needed, the taxpayer will be required to supply any supplemental information requested by the Service within 45 days. The taxpayer will be subject to the procedures set forth above.

■ No clear principle guides the sequence of paragraphs and sentences in the following "Facts" section of an internal memorandum. Revise into a clear succession of facts and determine how many paragraphs are necessary.

> Anne Smith retired on August 1, 1980, at age 65, pursuant to the Company's retirement plan. She draws a pension and is eligible for certain benefits, but these benefits are less extensive than those available to a current employee.
>
> Her job was quality control supervisor in the customer correspondence section of the Peoria division. She had no policy-making responsibilities and no authority to hire or fire subordinates.
>
> When she retired, her job was filled by a new employee. However, there is now a need for someone else to do the work.
>
> Ms. Smith has approached the Company about returning to work. If she had not asked about returning, the Company would probably hire a new person full time. However, if she comes back part time, schedules could be juggled to accomplish the work without hiring anyone else. It is proposed to hire her part time as an independent contractor, without benefits.

■ Sometimes writers use more paragraphs than their topic requires. Reparagraph the following section from an internal memorandum. How many main ideas are present and, therefore, how many paragraphs? Use any transitional words necessary.

> Waivers of immunity may be explicit or implicit. Explicit waivers can occur by treaty or contractual stipulation. Explicit waivers appear to be the clearest means of subjecting a foreign sovereign to suit in the United States.
>
> However, while a contractual waiver seems to be a prudent course of conduct for the drafter of a contract involving a foreign sovereign or its agency, one problem with explicit waivers must be noted. The party waiving immunity on behalf of the foreign sovereign must unequivocally possess the authority to effect such waiver. For example, a foreign corporate agency may not have the authority to waive sovereign immunity if the laws of the foreign sovereign expressly prohibit waivers of immunity. The waiver may be considered *ultra vires* and an invalid provision of the contract.

XYZ Corp. would encounter this type of problem if it attempted to acquire a waiver from the Ugandan agency, Carbobas, because Ugandan law forbids waivers of sovereign immunity by the government.

Implicit waivers may occur if a foreign state files a responsive pleading in an action without raising immunity as a defense, agrees to arbitration in another country, or agrees that the law of another country should prevail.

■ **Mrs. M. M. Matthews visited the Comstock Lode during the mining boom and wrote a description of the mines. It is jotted down in a disorganized way. Reorganize into one paragraph with a strong topic sentence and an orderly sequence of impressions free of extraneous matter. First, however, prepare an outline.**

In many of the mines the miners cannot strike the pick more than three blows before they have to go to the cooling station and stay double the time they are at work.

The cooling stations are where they have a free circulation of air. These stations are on every level. They have large tanks or reservoirs to hold the water that is pumped from one level to another. These vats are often full of boiling water. In many of the mines the water is so hot that if a person slips into one of these tanks, he is generally scalded to death before he can be rescued.

If he is rescued alive, it is only to linger a few days, suffering the most intense agony, till death relieves him of his sufferings. He is often so completely cooked in the scalding vats that the flesh drops from the bones while taking him out. His suffering and agony are terrible to witness.

The heat of the mines is very great. In some mines it is almost unendurable. In such mines it is almost impossible to work, while in others they can work without such excessive heat.

Miners are brought to the surface almost daily from overheat.

There is scarcely a day in the year that there is not from one to two funerals among the miners; and I have known of there being five in one day.

There are a great many causes of death. Sometimes death is caused by the caving in of rock, or by falling into the scalding tanks, or by a misstep, or by falling hundreds of feet down the shafts or inclines.

■ **Identify at least three ways in which the organization of the following letter loses sight of the audience.**

Letterhead of TTT Tar Co, Inc.

Ms. Portia Lambert, CEO
South East Insurance Co.
800 Main Street
Augusta, Georgia

Dear Ms. Lambert:

It was a pleasure meeting with your staff last Tuesday and Wednesday, at which times we had a chance to discuss the remaining details preventing our two sides from reaching accord on the proper approach to the TUV matter. That meeting, which occurred in our offices here in Phoenix, was attended both by your people and some of our legal staff.

In the TUV matter, Joan Grief is suing the city of Phoenix, and the city impleaded our company. Ms. Grief alleges that, on June 5, 1985, she fell over a defective roadway condition at the intersection of Third Avenue and 12th Streets. Phoenix alleges that we created the condition through the installation of defective tar onto the roadway. However, the only work we did near that intersection was to have been permanently paved by Interstate Paving Co., for whom you are an insurer.

Copies of the pleadings, or work records, and the Certificate of Insurance are being mailed with this letter. Our in-house lawyers have been handling the matter so far, but—as we discussed with your staff last week—we now want you to provide legal representation in this action, as well as indemnification. Please acknowledge receipt of this letter within ten days.

As you may recall, we are also insured by you.

Very truly yours,

Leroy Doe
General Counsel
TTT Tar Co, Inc.

■ Assume you have reached the appellate bench. A law clerk brings you her draft of an opinion you need to write in the *Hollaris* case. Assume that draft to be identical to the actual opinion in the case found on pages 159-160. You agree with the facts as the clerk has stated them and, of course, with the outcome you have asked her to reach. But you wish to reorganize and revise the draft to make your published opinion as effective and authoritative as possible. Take no more than an hour and redraft the opinion to maximal architectonic effect.

FINAL REVIEW

■ Revise the following sentences with an eye toward all errors.

1. There appears to be virtually no case law in New York which adopts a contrary position.

2. XYZ is in the process of negotiating oil contracts with corporate agencies of Venezuela and Brazil. Accordingly, it is essential to determine the Company's rights against these foreign agencies in the event a disagreement occurs subsequent to execution of the proposed contract.

3. The Syrian organization did not have an office in the United States and the contracts with ABC were not executed here.

4. [A title:] Commercial Agreements with Foreign States: Problems Concerning Immunity, Jurisdiction, Service of Process and Execution on Judgment.

5. Applicant completed the following work by February 2, 1986: a new fuel-dispensing facility was built to replace the old facility which interfered with substation construction, the guardhouse was relocated, a new ramp and entry gate were installed and the electrical service to the property was relocated.

6. Our April 9 letter sought HRC consent to an extension of our time to conduct the next full-time exercise until November 30.

7. In times of shortage, this section of the law may give

the Commission authority to approve the Company's tariff provisions as a conservation measure or to avoid hardship to other customers.

8.   The statute could also be read to mean that it is the responsibility of the Commission to determine when weather conditions or the other enumerated problems are sufficient reasons to excuse delay in providing service.

9.   The Age Discrimination in Employment Act broadly prohibits discrimination against an employee or prospective employee on account of age by an employer subject to the authority of Congress under the Commerce Clause.

10.   The evidence presented by plaintiff at trial can be distilled into several fundamental factual allegations.

11.   Neither of such affidavits are annexed to the moving papers.

12.   Parenthetically, the report states that plaintiff was "exposed to leaking refrigerant one week ago."

Suggestions about the Review Exercises

This appendix contains the author's suggestions for a possible revision of each exercise presented earlier in the text at the ends of Parts II, III, and IV. Each represents only one among many potential revisions, and each emphasizes the aspect of the sentence that had just been covered in the textual materials. For example, the sentence, "The appropriate standard by which the existence of a *prima facie* case may be measured in a discharge case is modelled on the test articulated in *McDonnell Douglas v. Green*," is actually revised *twice*. The first time (page 291) the emphasis is on finding a better subject and verb to reduce wordiness; the second (page 292) the emphasis is on reducing verbiage generally while retaining the same subject and verb. These choices reflect each exercise's directions and its place in the materials; these factors should also influence your emphasis in approaching all of the problems.

PART II EXERCISES

■ **Correct punctuation:**

1. In *X v. Y*, a "creeping tender offer" case, the company whose shares were purchased was incorporated in Delaware; how-

ever that was the state's only contact with the transaction in question.

2. Z argued that, as a practical matter, both the conditional sale financing and the chattel lease financing achieved the same net result and that both transactions were regularly entered into as a part of its finance business.

3. The Commission decided that the benefits of normalization exceed the detriments, and it issued the order with changes recommended by staff.

4. Plaintiff had his car towed from the scene of the accident to a repair shop, but he never had the car repaired.

5. With respect to the litigation pending between X Corp. and Y Corp., X Corp. has projected that, if X Corp's motion to stay litigation were granted and an arbitrable award were rendered in Germany, it could not subsequently enforce the award in the federal district courts of the United States, since the arbitration agreement is invalid under German law.

■ **Revisions:**

1. Assuming the Company to be a foreign corporation, we must determine, according to Section 875, whether its subsidiary is engaged in trade or business in the United States.

2. This business and union combination and conspiracy allegedly aimed to engage in a systematic campaign of unlawful and tortious interference with plaintiff's business in the metropolitan area through such acts as business and physical pressure, intimidation, coercion, and obstruction of the plaintiff and the tenants in connection with the move into the building, all designed unlawfully to eliminate plaintiff as a competitor in the metropolitan area.

3. The source of my information and belief is my law office records, which I believe to be true.

4. X told me in our conversation that, if the Company does not take Y back, it will hire a full-time person.

5. X must witness and accept a performance demonstration by Y that evidences completion of payment milestones, but Y's submission of certification or documentation will evidence completion of all other milestones.

■ **Multiple choice:**

1. a
2. b
3. c
4. b
5. c

■ **Verbiage reduced:**

1. *McDonnell Douglas v. Green* articulates the test setting the appropriate standard in a discharge matter by which to measure a *prima facie* case.

2. X will provide a witness to testify as to cost breakdown for the bills that X had previously provided to both defendants.

3. The payroll office manages the distribution of pay checks. (Or even: The payroll office pays checks.)

4. Smith and Smith will accept registration of claims at their offices.

5. Plaintiff must find the hearsay rule exception to have that evidence admitted. (Or: The hearsay rule exception provides plaintiff's only hope of having that evidence admitted. The reader should note that both revisions reduce verbiage by eliminating the gerund as the subject.)

PART III EXERCISES

■ **Revisions (a. for fellow attorney, b. for nonlawyer):**

1. a. (Less than perfect, but no change required.)
   b. In that matter, plaintiff is claiming that defendant must pay these bills because defendant both owns the premises and is plaintiff's customer there.

2. a. Attached are two exhibits, hereinafter referred to as "A" and "B."
   b. I will refer to the two attached exhibits as "A" and "B."

3. a. (Okay.)

b. The John Doe Company, formerly called the Doe Store, must perform various services under this contract, and I list these services in the attached "Schedule I."

4. a. (Okay, except "thereunder" has two possible antecedents—"the latter" and "the rule"—and is thus ambiguous.)

b. We might argue, as a logical use of the latter's rule of just compensation, that we treat *inadequate* liquidated damage provisions as penalty and thus void, the flip-side of the court's treating *excessive* liquidated damage provisions as penalty. (Lesson for the reader: do not hesitate to use colloquialisms and emphasis when writing for the nonlawyer.)

■ Verbiage reduced:

Note: the trick in all the following sentences is to reduce verbiage without (as earlier) altering subject or verb. As I have argued throughout, choosing the best subject reduces wordiness, but here we are concerned with verbosity itself, i.e. needless language.

1. Automobile manufacturers are aware of the risks associated with their plant workers' use of alcohol and drugs and have developed and implemented stringent disciplinary measures should such abuse occur.

2. The appropriate standard to measure a *prima facie* case in a discharge matter is modelled on the test articulated in *McDonnell Douglas v. Green*.

3. The zoning cases, which predominantly permit a purchaser of land to contest the validity of a preexisting ordinance, seem to support the argument that Mr. A may contest the treaty.

4. A filing party failing to produce a privileged document requested by the government will thus be deemed in noncompliance with HSR and precluded by the enforcement agencies from consummating the proposed acquisition.

5. The court is required by Delaware law to apply a fairness standard in determining whether to enforce a contract secured through an officer or director of a corporation having a financial interest in the agreement.

■ Effective use of parallel construction:

1. I submit this statement in support of the cross-motion for an order (1) to dismiss the petition for an order compelling X to remove certain of its facilities or, in the alternative, (2) to grant inverse condemnation of the property where those electrical facilities are located.

2. We need one Grade 11 to assist in light typing and in the investigation required for subpoena compliance. (Note: Place the shorter of your parallel components first.)

3. We are pleased to have you represent us at the forthcoming hearing and actively lobby on our behalf.

4. We shall not be responsible for the accuracy of any particular document or of any other information that we furnish to you in connection with the permits or with this agreement.

■ Syntax rearranged for clarity:

1. In the United States-Iran hostage case, the ICJ distinguished on the facts from the request presented by the U.S. the request for provisional measures that was denied in the *Factory at Chorzow* case.

2. Specifically, under the "sales" method, the average cost of widgets is computed by dividing the quantities of widgets sold to specified customers into the result of multiplying the quantity of widgets purchased during the previous twelve-month period by the supplier rates and charges.

3. U.S. Munitions List "equipment," defined as any article not including technical data, cannot generally be exported from the United States until an export license has been obtained from the Department of State.

4. Therefore, to arrive at [reach!] a conclusion on the issue presented here, resort must be had to cases interpreting the 1924 Code's refund provision.

5. Proper supervision by federal certified applicators of these personnel and by XYZ Corp. employees who monitor their work has proven to be sufficient to insure that the work of these seasonal and temporary employees is conducted in a proper manner, consistent with federal regulations.

■ **That/which usage:**

1. The fact that the defendants appealed the court's prelimi-nary injunction on April 1, which [appeal] deprives the court of jurisdiction "over all matters involved in the appeal" during the appeal perhaps explains why Judge Jones painstakingly avoided using the language "invalid" or "unconstitutional." (But note the ambiguity proved by the following possible revision: The fact that the defendants appealed the court's preliminary injunction on April 1 that [i.e. the injunction] deprives the court of jurisdiction . . .)

2. A preliminary list of work items that contain electrical, mechanical, civil, and insulation work is attached.

3. There are few state court decisions and even fewer federal court decisions [that are] on point.

■ **Bad writing habits:**

1. Typo (liaison)
2. Preposition sandwich
3. Preposition sandwich
4. Redundancy
5. Throat clearing
6. Preposition sandwich
7. Typo (plaintiff's)

PART IV EXERCISES

■ **Outline for the cross-motion:**

I. The claim
    A. Alleged injury
        1. motorcycle accident injuring P
        2. date: 3/12/82
        3. amount claimed: $1m
    B. Origins of lawsuit
        1. received summons and complaint dated 10/27/85
        2. answered 11/13/85

II. Our unsuccessful notices and demands for inspection
    A. Sent two notices, both returnable 11/30/85
    B. Demanded photos in P's possession of accident scene
        1. P's counsel's refusal to give over
        2. P's admission, at EBT of 8/27/86, that he recently used photos
    C. Demanded P's physical exam
        1. have received no info from P's MD
        2. P failed to show at our exam scheduled 6/21/86
        3. our notice called for exam by 6/21/86
            a. giving name of our MD
            b. giving our MD's address
    D. Other demands, all unfulfilled
        1. Notice of Claim
        2. witness's statements
        3. copy of Comptroller's hearing

■ Outline for memo:

I. Injury history
    A. 1978 incident
        1. truck struck P's vehicle
        2. rear brakes on truck failed
    B. Results for P
        1. back injury requiring 2 weeks hospitalization
        2. $4000 in medical expenses
        3. couldn't resume taxi driving job
            a. loss of $25,000 in wages
            b. must wear back brace—our MD says P can't be expected to resume job

II. Litigation history
    A. P commences action
        1. in County Court, Kent County
        2. for $300,000
    B. Mid-trial negotiations
        1. P demand reduced to $100,000
        2. judge recommended $65,000
        3. P now ready to take $50,000

III. My analysis of present situation
    A. Our verdict risk is $150,000
        1. our own MD's findings
        2. no defense as to liability
    B. The jury's potential sympathy for P

IV. Recommendation for settlement

■ **Sample Revision (architectonically improved thanks to the outline):**

In 1978, plaintiff's vehicle was struck by defendant's truck after its rear brakes had failed. Plaintiff's resulting back injury required two weeks of hospitalization; he has incurred over $4,000 in medical expenses. In addition, plaintiff could not resume his job as a taxi driver and therefore lost more than $25,000 in wages. Our doctor found that, because Plaintiff must continue to wear a back brace, resumption of a job as taxi driver is extremely unlikely in the future.

Plaintiff brought suit in County Court, Kent County, for $300,000 in damages. He then reduced this demand to $100,000 soon after trial commenced. The trial judge recommended a settlement of $65,000, but the Plaintiff is now ready to accept $50,000.

In view of our doctor's findings and the absence of any defense on the liability issue, we risk approximately a $150,000 verdict from a potentially sympathetic jury.

We should settle for $50,000.

Bibliography

§1 Selected Works on Style

Austin, J. L. How to Do Things with Words (J. O. Urmson and M. Sbisa 2d ed. 1975).

Barzun, Jacques. Simple and Direct (2d ed. 1984).

_____ . A Word or Two Before You Go . . . (1986).

_____ . On Writing, Editing and Publishing (2d ed. 1986).

Bolton, W. F. A Short History of Literary English (2d ed. 1971).

The Chicago Manual of Style (13th ed. 1982).

Follett, Wilson. Modern American Usage (J. Barzun ed. 1966).

Fowler, H. W. Modern English Usage (E. Gowers 2d ed. 1965).

Lanham, Richard A. Analyzing Prose (1983).

_____ . Style, An Anti-Textbook (1974).

Lewis, C. S. Studies in Words (2d ed. 1967).

Michaels, Leonard and Ricks, Christopher (eds.). The State of the Language (1980).

Mitchell, Richard. Less Than Words Can Say (1979).

_____ . The Graves of Academe (1981).

_____ . The Leaning Tower of Babble (1984).

Myatt, William. Stalking the Wild Semicolon (1976).

Oxford English Dictionary (in 13 volumes) and Supplement (in 4 volumes).

Partridge, Eric. You Have a Point There: Punctuation and Its Allies (1953).

Roget's International Thesaurus (4th ed. 1977).
Strunk, William, Jr. and White, E. B. The Elements of Style (3d ed. 1979).
Williams, J. Style: Ten Lessons in Clarity and Grace (2d ed. 1985).
Zinsser, William, On Writing Well (2d ed. 1980).
_____ . Writing with a Word Processor (1983).

§2 Selected Works on Legal Style

Biskind, E. Writing Right!, 43 N.Y.S.B.J. 185 (1971).
Black's Law Dictionary (5th ed. 1979).
Brand, N. Legal Writing, Reasoning and Research: An Introduction, 44 Alb. L.R. 292 (1980).
Carrick, K. M. and Dunn, D. J. Legal Writing: An Evaluation of the Textbook Literature, 30 N.Y.L. Sch. Rev. 645 (1985).
Chafee, Z. L. The Disorderly Conduct of Words, 41 Col. L. Rev. 381 (1941).
Charrow, Veda R. and Erhardt, Myra. Clear and Effective Legal Writing (1986).
Freeman, Morton S. The Grammatical Lawyer (1979).
Gopen, George D. Writing From a Legal Perspective (1981).
The Guide to American Law (in 12 volumes) (1983).
Hyland, R. A Defense of Legal Writing, 134 U. Pa. L. Rev. 599 (1986).
Kolin, P. C. and Marquardt, R. G. Research on Legal Writing: A Bibliography, 78 Law Lib. J. 493 (1986).
Kunz, Christina L. *et al.* The Process of Legal Research (1986).
Langbein, J. Writing Law Examinations, in West's Study Guide & Law Student Helps Pamphlet (1986).
Mellinkopf, David. The Language of the Law (1963).
_____ . Legal Writing: Sense and Nonsense (1982).
Posner, R. Goodbye to the Bluebook, 53 U. Chi. L.R. 1343 (1986).
Rodell, F. Goodbye to Law Reviews, 23 Va. L. Rev. 38 (1936).
_____ . Goodbye to Law Reviews—Revisited, 48 Va. L. Rev. 279 (1962).
_____ . Woe Unto You, Lawyers! (2d ed. 1957).

Texas Law Review. Manual on Style (3d ed. 1975).
A Uniform System of Citation (13th ed. 1981).
Weihofen, Henry. Legal Writing Style (2d ed. 1980).
Wydick, Richard C. Plain English for Lawyers (2d ed. 1986).

§3   The Special Case of Legal Drafting

ABA Guide to Legislative Research and Drafting (1978).
Dickerson, F. Reed. The Fundamentals of Legal Drafting (2d ed. 1986).
——————— . Professionalizing Legislative Drafting (1973).
Freund, Ernst. Standards of American Legislation (rev. ed. 1965).
Hurst, James Willard. Dealing with Statutes (1982).
Linde, Hans A., et al. Legislative and Administrative Processes (2d ed. 1981).
Nutting, Charles B. and Dickerson, F. Reed. Nutting and Dickerson's Cases and Materials on Legislation (5th ed. 1981).

§4   Some Reliable Guides for American Lawyers in England

Jowitt's Dictionary of English Law (2d ed. 1977).
Oxford Concise Dictionary of English Law (1983).
Stroud's Judicial Dictionary (4th ed. 1971).
Walker, David. Oxford Companion to Law (1980).

§5   Selected Works on Rhetoric

Aristotle. Rhetoric.
Booth, Wayne. Modern Dogma and the Rhetoric of Assent (1974).
——————— . Now Don't Try to Reason with Me (1970).
Burke, Kenneth. A Grammar of Motives (1969).
Cicero. The Orator.
Epictetus. The Power of Speaking.
Foucault, Michel. The Order of Things: An Archaeology of the Human Sciences (R. D. Laing trans. 1970).

Geach, P. T. Reason and Argument (1976).

Howell, Wilbur S. Poetics, Rhetoric and Logic: Studies in the Basic Disciplines of Criticism (1975).

Kennedy, George. Classical Rhetoric and Its Christian and Secular Tradition from Ancient to Modern Times (1980).

Lanham, Richard A. A Handlist of Rhetorical Terms (1968).

Longinus. On the Sublime.

Perelman, Chaim and Olbrechts-Tyteca, L. The New Rhetoric: A Treatise on Argumentation (1969).

Perelman, Chaim. The Realm of Rhetoric (1982).

Plato. Phaedrus.

Quintilian. Institutio Oratoria.

Rhetoric ad Herennium.

Weaver, Richard. The Ethics of Rhetoric (1985).

——————. A Rhetoric and Composition Handbook (2d ed. 1967).

——————. Visions of Order (1964).

§6 Selected Works on Legal Rhetoric

Ball, Milner. The Promise of American Law: A Theological, Humanistic View of the Legal Process (1981).

Cardozo, Benjamin. Selected Legal Writings (M. Hall ed. 1974).

Dahl, R. C. "Soak Your Mind in Cicero": A Bibliographical Essay, 1979 Ariz. St. L.J. 269.

Fuller, L. The Forms and Limits of Adjudication, 92 Harv. L. Rev. 353 (1978).

Fuller, L. Legal Fictions (1967).

Gilmore, Grant. The Ages of American Law (1977).

Hand, Learned. The Spirit of Liberty (I. Dilliard ed. 3d ed. 1960).

Hart, Henry M., Jr. and Sacks, Albert M. The Legal Process: Basic Problems in the Making and Application of Law (Tent. ed. 1958).

Holmes, Oliver Wendell, Jr. Collected Legal Papers (1920).

Leff, A. A. Law and, 87 Yale L.J. 989 (1978).

Levi, E. An Introduction to Legal Reasoning (1949).

Llewellyn, Karl. The Bramble Bush (2d ed. 1950).

_____ . The Common Law Tradition (1960).

Merryman, J. H. The Authority of Authority: What the California Supreme Court Cited in 1950, 6 Stan. L. Rev. 613 (1954).

_____ . Toward a Theory of Citations: An Empirical Study of the Citation Practice of the California Supreme Court in 1950, 1960, and 1970, 50 S. Cal. L. Rev. 381 (1977).

Noonan, John T., Jr. Persons and Masks of the Law (1976).

Simpson, A. W. B. The Rise and Fall of the Legal Treatise: Legal Principles and the Forms of Legal Literature, 48 U. Chi. L. Rev. 632 (1981).

Twining, William and Miers, David. How to Do Things with Rules (2d ed. 1982).

Weisberg, R. How Judges Speak: Some Lessons on Adjudication in *Billy Budd, Sailor* with an Application to Justice Rehnquist, 57 N.Y.U.L. Rev. 1 (1982).

White, J. B. Heracles' Bow: Essays on the Rhetoric and Poetics of Law (1985).

_____ . The Legal Imagination: Studies in the Nature of Legal Thought and Expression (1973).

Wyzanski, Charles. Whereas, A Judge's Premises (1965).

§7 Appropriate Stylistic Models: A List of Legal Novels[1]

Allen, Grant. Miss Cayley's Adventurers

Balzac, Honore de. Cesar Birotteau

_____ . Cousin Pons

_____ . Pere Goriot

_____ . Lucien de Rubempre

_____ . The Lesser Bourgeoisie

_____ . Gobseck

_____ . Colonel Chabert

_____ . A Commission in Lunacy

_____ . The Last Incarnation of Vautrin

_____ . A Start in Life

---

[1] Reprinted from Wigmore, A List of One Hundred Legal Novels, 17 Ill. L. Rev. 26 (1922). A revised list follows.

_____ . The Marriage Contract
Baring-Gould, Sabine. Broom Squire
Becke, Louis, and Jeffrey, Walter. First Fleet Family
Besant, Walter. St. Katherine's by the Tower
_____ . For Faith and Freedom
_____ . Orange Girl
Besant, Walter, and Rice, James. The Chaplain of the Fleet
Blackmore, R. D. Lorna Doone
Burnett, Frances Hodgson. The De Willoughby Claim
Caine, Hall. The Deemster
Collins, Wilkie. The Law and the Lady
Cooper, James Fenimore. The Ways of the Hour
_____ . The Redskins
_____ . Satanstoe
_____ . The Chainbearer
Cox, E. M. The Achievements of John Caruthers
Craddock, Charles Egbert (pseudonym of Mary Murfree). The
    Prophet of the Great Smoky Mountains
Crawford, Francis Marion. Sant Ilario
Crockett, Samuel R. The Gray Man
Dickens, Charles. Barnaby Rudge
_____ . Bleak House
_____ . The Old Curiosity Shop
_____ . Oliver Twist
_____ . The Pickwick Papers
_____ . A Tale of Two Cities
Doyle, Arthur Conan. Micah Clarke
Dumas, Alexandre. The Black Tulip
_____ . The Count of Monte Cristo
_____ . Marguerite de Valois
_____ . Twenty Years After, Part II
Eggleston, Edward. The Mystery of Metropolisville
_____ . The Graysons
Eliot, George (pseudonym of Marian Evans). Adam Bede
_____ . Felix Holt
Erckmann, Emile, and Chatrian, L. G. C. The Polish Jew
Fielding, Henry. Jonathan Wild
_____ . Tom Jones

Fletcher, Joseph S. The Middle Temple Murder
Foote, Mary Hallock. John Bodewin's Testimony
Ford, Paul Leicester. The Honorable Peter Stirling
Franzos, Karl Emil. The Chief Justice
Frederic, Harold. The Damnation of Theron Ware
Gaboriau, Emile. File No. 113
———————— . Monsieur Lecoq
Goldsmith, Oliver. The Vicar of Wakefield
Grant, Charles. Stories of Naples and the Camorra
Grant, Robert. "The Law-Breakers"
———————— . "An Eye for an Eye"
Grey (or Gray), Maxwell (pseudonym of Mary Gleed Tuttiett).
    The Silence of Dean Mariland
Haggard, H. Rider. Mr. Meeson's Will
Hale, Edward Everett. Philip Nolan's Friends
Harte, Francis Bret. Gabriel Conroy
———————— . "An Heiress of Red Dog"
Hawthorne, Nathaniel. The Scarlet Letter
Herrick, Robert. The Common Lot
Hill, Frederick Trevor. Tales Out of Court
Holland, Josiah Gilbert. Sevenoaks
Howells, William Dean. A Modern Instance
Hugo, Victor. Les Miserables
———————— . Ninety-three
———————— . The Man Who Laughed
James, George P. R. Moreley Ernstein
Kingsley, Henry. Austin Elliott
LeSage, Alain R. The Adventures of Gil Blas
Lytton, Edward. Eugene Aram
———————— . Paul Clifford
Mitchell, S. Weir. Constance Trescot
O'Reilly, John Boyle. Moondyne
Ouida (pseudonym of Louise de la Ramée). Under Two Flags
Page, Thomas Nelson. Red Rock
Parker, Gilbert. The Right of Way
Read, Opie. A Tennessee Judge
———————— . The Jucklins
Reade, Charles. Griffith Gaunt

_____ . It Is Never Too Late to Mend

Scott, Walter. Anne of Geierstein

_____ . The Fortunes of Nigel

_____ . Guy Mannering

_____ . The Heart of Midlothian

_____ . The Fair Maid of Perth

_____ . The Antiquary

_____ . Ivanhoe

_____ . Peveril of the Peak

_____ . Quentin Durward

_____ . Redgauntlet

_____ . Rob Roy

Sienkiewicz, Henryk. "A Comedy of Errors"

Stevenson, Robert Louis. Kidnapped (with its sequel)

_____ . David Balfour

_____ . Weir of Hermiston

Stimson, Frederic J. The Residuary Legatee

Stockton, Frank R. The Late Mrs. Null

Thackeray, William Makepeace. Pendennis

Thanet, Octave (pseudonym of Alice French). The Missionary Sheriff

_____ . We All

Tolstoi, Leo N. Resurrection

Train, Arthur. Tutt and Mr. Tutt

_____ . By Advice of Counsel

_____ . As It Was in the Beginning

Trollope, Anthony: Orley Farm

_____ . Mr. Maule's Attempt

_____ . The Vicar of Bullhampton

Twain, Mark (pseudonym of Samuel L. Clemens). Pudd'nhead Wilson

Warren, Samuel. Ten Thousand a Year

Weyman, Stanley. The Story of Francis Cludde

_____ . My Lady Rotha

_____ . The Man in Black

Woolson, Constance Fenimore. Anne

Zangwill, Israel. The Big Bow Mystery

§8 A Revised List of Stylistic Models[2]

Aeschylus. The Eumenides
Anonymous. The Song of Roland
——————. Nibelungenlied
——————. Njal's Saga
——————. The Old Testament
——————. Poema de mio Cid ("The Cid")
——————. Le Roman de Renart
——————. Le Roman de Thebes
Ashford, Jeffrey. Burden of Proof
Auchincloss, Louis. "Arnold and Degener, One Chase Manhattan
    Plaza" (in Tales of Manhattan)
——————. A Law for the Lion
——————. The Great World and Timothy Colt
——————. I Come As a Thief
——————. "The Legends of Henry Everett" (in The Romantic
    Egoists)
——————. The Partners
——————. Powers of Attorney
Balzac, Honore de. An Historical Mystery
——————. The Gallery of Antiquities
——————. Lost Illusions
——————. Scenes from a Courtesan's Life
——————. Ursule Mirouet
Barth, John. The Floating Opera
Basso, Hamilton. View From Pompey's Head
Becker, Stephen. A Covenant With Death
Beroul. Le Roman de Tristan
Betti, Ugo. Landslide (in Three Plays on Justice)
Bok, Curtis. Backbone of the Herring
——————. I, Too, Nicodemus

---

[2] Reprinted from Weisberg, Wigmore's "Legal Novels" Revisited: New Resources for the Expansive Lawyer, 71 Nw.U.L. Rev. 17 (1976) and from Weisberg & Kretschman, Wigmore's "Legal Novels" Expanded, 7 Md. L.F. 94 (1977), *reprinted in* 50 N.Y.S.B.J. 122 (1978).

_____ . Star Wormwood

Boll, Heinrich. End of a Mission

_____ . The Lost Honor of Katharina Blum

Borden, Mary. Action for Slander

_____ . You, the Jury

Botein, Bernard. The Prosecutor

Boulle, Pierre. The Executioner

_____ . Face of a Hero

Burgess, Anthony. A Clockwork Orange

Busch, Niven. The San Franciscans

Camus, Albert. The Fall

_____ . The Rebel

_____ . The Stranger

Carlisle, Henry. Voyage to the First of December

Cecil, Henry. According to the Evidence

_____ . Alibi For a Judge

_____ . Brief to Counsel

_____ . Brothers in Law

_____ . Daughters in Law

_____ . Friends at Court

_____ . Full Circle

_____ . Independent Witness

_____ . Long Arm

_____ . Natural Causes

_____ . No Bail for the Judge

_____ . Settled Out of Court

_____ . Tipping the Scales

_____ . Ways and Means

Chaucer, Geoffrey. "The Man of Law's Tale" (in The Canterbury Tales)

Chretien de Troyes. Yvain

_____ . Lancelot

Churchill, Winston. Mr. Crewe's Career

Clark, Walter van Tilburg. The Ox-Bow Incident

Cozzens, James G. By Love Possessed

_____ . The Just and the Unjust

Deal, Borden. The Advocate

Dewlen, Al. Twilight of Honor

Dickens, Charles. Great Expectations

Doctorow, E. L. The Book of Daniel
Dostoevski, Fyodor. The Brothers Karamazov
_____ . Crime and Punishment
_____ . The Idiot
Dreiser, Theodore. An American Tragedy
Drury, Allen. Advise and Consent
_____ . Capable of Honor
_____ . Preserve and Protect
_____ . A Shade of Difference
Dürrenmatt, Fredrich. A Dangerous Game ("Die Panne")
_____ . The Marriage of Mr. Mississippi
Eliot, George (pseudonym of Marian Evans). Middlemarch
_____ . Mill on the Floss
Faulkner, William. Intruder in the Dust
_____ . Light in August
_____ . Sanctuary
_____ . Snopes Trilogy
Frisch, Max. I'm Not Stiller
Gaither, Frances Ormond. Double Muscadine
Gardner, John. The Sunlight Dialogues
Garfield, Brian Wynne. Death Sentence
Gerber, Albert. The Lawyers
Gilbert, Michael. Flash Point
Gogol, Nokolai. Dead Souls
Gottfried von Strassburg. Tristan
Gregor, Manfred. Town Without Pity
Hamilton, Bruce. The Hanging Judge
Hawley, C. Cash McCall
Herbert, Alan Patrick. Holy Deadlock
Hugo, Victor. The Last Day of A Condemned Man
Hunter, Evan. The Paper Dragon
Kafka, Franz. "In the Penal Colony"
_____ . "The Judgment"
_____ . "The New Advocate"
_____ . The Trial
Kazan, Elia. The Assassins
Kleist, Heinrich von. Michael Kohlhaas
Koestler, Arthur. Darkness at Noon
Lebowitz, Albert. Laban's Will

Lee, Harper. To Kill a Mockingbird
Lewis, Sinclair. Cass Timberlane
Lipsky, Eleazer. Lincoln McKeever
_____ . Malpractice
_____ . The Scientists
Lothar, Ernst. Loom of Justice
Lytton, Edward. Night and Morning
Malamud, Bernard. The Fixer
Mankiewicz, Don M. Trial
Marie de France. Lanval
Masur, Harold. The Attorney
Melville, Herman. "Bartleby, the Scrivener"
_____ . Billy Budd, Sailor
_____ . White Jacket
Mills, James. One Just Man
Motley, Willard. Knock on Any Door
Oates, Joyce Carol. Do With Me What You Will
O'Hara, John. Ten North Frederick
Oleck, Howard. A Singular Fury
Osborn, J. J. The Paper Chase
Ovid. "The Argument Between Ajax and Ulysses for the Armor of
     Achilles" (Metamorphoses, Book XIII).
Pangborn, Edgar. The Trial of Callista Blake
Pearson, William. Trial of Honor
Porter, Katherine Anne. "Noon Wine"
Porter, Monica E. The Mercy of the Court
Powell, Richard. The Philadelphian
Prescot, Julian. Case for the Accused
Reywall, John. Trial of Alvin Boaker
Rosmond, Babette. The Lawyers
Rylee, Robert. Deep Dark River
Sartre, Jean-Paul. No Exit
Schweitzer, Gertrude. Born
Shakespeare, William. Hamlet
_____ . King Lear
_____ . Measure for Measure
_____ . The Merchant of Venice
_____ . Othello

Bibliography

——————— . Richard II
——————— . A Winter's Tale
Smith, Edgar. Reasonable Doubt
Snow, C. P. The Affair
——————— . Corridors of Power
——————— . In Their Wisdom
——————— . Strangers and Brothers
Solmssen, Arthur R. G. Alexander's Feast
——————— . The Comfort Letter
——————— . Rittenhouse Square
Solzhenitsyn, Aleksandr. The First Circle
——————— . The Gulag Archipelago I, II
Sophocles. Antigone
——————— . Oedipus Rex
Stein, Sol. The Magician
Strindberg, August. The Scapegoat
Tolstoi, Leo N. "The Death of Ivan Ilych"
Train, Arthur. Ambition
——————— . McAllister and His Double
——————— . Mr. Tutt at His Best
——————— . Mr. Tutt Comes Home
——————— . Mr. Tutt Finds A Way
——————— . Page Mr. Tutt
——————— . Tut, Tut, Mr. Tutt
Uris, Leon. QB VII
Vidal, Gore. Burr
Villon, Francois. Le Testament
Voelker, John D. Anatomy of a Murder
Warren, Robert Penn. All The King's Men
——————— . Meet Me in the Breen Glen
Warren, Samuel. Confessions of an Attorney
——————— . Experiences of a Barrister
West, Jessamyn. The Massacre at Fall Creek
West, Morris L. Daughter of Silence
Williams, Ben Ames. Leave Her to Heaven
Woolfolk, William. Opinion of the Court
Wouk, Herman. The Caine Mutiny
Wright, Richard. Native Son

§9 The Special Relationship of Law and Literature: Some Critical Perspectives[3]

Abraham, K. S. Statutory Interpretation and Literary Theory: Some Common Concerns of an Unlikely Pair, 32 Rutgers L. Rev. 676 (1979).

_____ . Three Fallacies of Interpretation: A Comment on Precedent and Judicial Decision, 23 Ariz. L. Rev. 771 (1981).

Alford, J. A. Literature in Medieval England, 92 PMLA 941 (1977).

Alford, John A. and Seniff, D. Literature and Law in the Middle Ages: A Bibliography of Scholarship (1983).

Andrews, Mark E. Law Versus Equity in The Merchant of Venice (1965).

Axelrod, A. Law and the Humanities: Notes from the Underground, 29 Rutgers L. Rev. 228 (1976).

Ball, M. The Play's the Thing: An Unscientific Reflection on Courts under the Rubric of Theater, 28 Stan. L. Rev. 81 (1975).

Band, A. J. Kafka and the Beiliss Affair, 22 Hasifrut 38 (1976).

Barricelli, J. Jurisprudence in the XVIIth Century from Manzoni's Viewpoint, 9 University of Hartford Studies in Literature, 141 (1977).

Barricelli, J. and Weisberg, R. Chapter on "Law and Literature" in Interrelations of Literature (1982).

Baughman, R. Dickens and His Lawyers, 6 ALSA F. 168 (1982).

Berg, T. Text and Meaning in *The Trial*, 93 PMLA 292 (1978).

Bergmann, J. D. "Bartleby" and the Lawyer's Story, 47 American Literature 432 (1975).

Bloch, Howard R. Medieval French Literature and the Law (1978).

Bloomfield, M. The Man of Law's Tale: A Tragedy of Victimization and a Christian Comedy, 87 PMLA 384 (1972).

Blotner, J. William Faulkner: Author at Law, 4 Miss. C.L. Rev. 275 (1984).

Braithwaite, W. T. Poetry and the Criminal Law: The Idea of

---

[3] Reprinted in part from R. Weisberg & J. Barricelli, Literature and the Law, in The Interrelations of Literature (Publications of Modern Language Association (PMLA); 1982).

Punishment in Shakespeare's *Measure for Measure,* 13 Loy. (Chi.) U.L.J. 791 (1982).

Brest, P. Interpretation and Interest, 34 Stan. L. Rev. 765 (1982).

Carbonneau, T. Balzacian Legality, 32 Rutgers L. Rev. 719 (1979).

Cardozo, Benjamin. "Law and Literature," in Selected Writings of Benjamin Nathan Cardozo, M. Hall ed. (1947).

Chafee, Z. The Disorderly Conduct of Words, 41 Colum. L. Rev. 381 (1941).

Christie, G. C. Vagueness and Legal Language, 48 Minn. L. Rev. 885 (1964).

Collins, P. A. W. Dickens and Crime (1965).

Comment. Clear and Convincing Libel: Fiction and the Law of Defamation, 92 Yale L.J. 520 (1983).

——————— . Defamation by Fiction, 22 Md. L. Rev. 387 (1983).

——————— . Defamation by Fiction: With Malice Toward None and Punitive Damages for All, 16 Loy. L.A.L. Rev. 99 (1983).

——————— . Hey, That's Me!—The Conundrum of Identification in Libel and Fiction, 18 Cal. W.L. Rev. 442 (1982).

——————— . Toward a New Standard of Liability for Defamation in Fiction, 58 N.Y.U.L. Rev. 1115 (1983).

Couch, H. Law and Literature: A Comment, 17 Vand. L. Rev. 911 (1964).

Countryman, Vern. The Douglas Opinions (1977).

Cover, R. Forward: Nomos and Narrative, 97 Harv. L. Rev. 4 (1983).

Cowan, T. The Law at Finnegan's Wake, 29 Rutgers L. Rev. 259 (1976).

Danzig, R. & Weisberg, R. Reading List on Law and Literature, 7 Humanities 6 (1977).

Davenport, W. H. Law and Literature Once Again, 50 Law Libr. J. 396 (1957).

Davis, C. K. The Law in Shakespeare (1883).

Davis, T. M. Crying in the Wilderness: Legal, Racial, and Moral Codes in *Go Down Moses,* 4 Miss. C.L. Rev. 299 (1984).

Dunlop, C. R. B. Human Law and Natural Law in the Novels of Theodore Dreiser, 9 Am. J. Jurisprudence 61 (1974).

——————— . Law and Justice in Dreiser's *An American Tragedy,* 6 U. Brit. Colum. L. Rev. 379 (1971).

Dworkin, Ronald. Law As Interpretation, 60 Tex. L. Rev. 527 (1982).

_____ . My Reply to Stanley Fish (and Walter Benn Michaels): Please Don't Talk about Objectivity Anymore, in The Politics of Interpretation (W. Mitchell ed. 1983).

Elkins, J. R. The Paradox of Life in Law, 40 U. Pitt. L. Rev. 129 (1979).

Fallon, P. P. The Relation between Analysis and Style in American Legal Prose, 28 Neb. L. Rev. 80 (1949).

Ferguson, Robert A. Law and Letters in American Culture (1984).

Frese, J. Swift's Houyhnhms and Utopian Law, 9 U. Hart. Stud. in Literature 187 (1977).

Friedman, D. Private Creation and Enforcement of Law: A Historical Case, 8 J. Legal Stud. 399 (1979).

Fish, S. Interpretation and the Pluralist Vision, 60 Tex. L. Rev. 495 (1982).

_____ . Wrong Again, 62 Tex. L. Rev. 229 (1983).

Fiss, Owen. Objectivity and Interpretation, 34 Stan. L. Rev. 739 (1982).

Fried, Elsie. The Law in Literature, 1981 Nassau Lawyer 150.

Frye, N. Literature and the Law, 4 Law Soc. Gazette 70 (1970).

Fuller, L. L. The Case of the Speluncean Explorers, 62 Harv. L. Rev. 616 (1949).

Gadamer, Hans-Georg. Truth and Method (1960).

Gates, H. L. Race, Writing, and Difference, 4 Miss. C.L. Rev. 287 (1984).

Gest, John Marshall. The Lawyer in Literature (1913).

Gibson, W. Literary Minds and Judicial Style, 915 N.Y.U.L. Rev. 928 (1961).

Glaser, R. & Roth, S. In the Matter of Heep, Jaggers, Tulkinghorn & Fogg: An Unjarndyced View of the Dickensian Bar, 29 Rutgers L. Rev. 278 (1976).

Grenander, M. E. The Heritage of Cain: Crime in American Fiction, Annals 423 (January 1970).

_____ . Criminal Responsibility in *Native Son* and *Knock on Any Door*, 49 Am. Literature 221 (1977).

_____ . *Benito Cereno* and Legal Oppression: A Szaszian Interpretation, 2 J. Libertarian Stud. 337 (1978).

Grey, T. The Constitution as Scripture, 37 Stan. L. Rev. 1 (1984).

Hirsch, Eric. Validity in Interpretation (1967).

Holdheim, Wolfgang. Der Justizirrtum als literarische Problematik (1969). Discussed in Law and Humanities Institute (LHI) "Mediator," III #1.

Holdsworth, William S. Charles Dickens as a Legal Historian, (1929).

Ives, C. B. Billy Budd and the Articles of War, 34 Am. Literature 31 (1962).

Jacobson, R. Law, Ritual, Absence: Towards A Semiology of Law, 9 U. Hart. Stud. in Literature 164 (1977).

_____ . Satanic Semiotics, Jobian Jurisprudence, Semeia 63 (1981).

Jolly, E. G. Feelings for Flem, Faulkner and Federalism, 4 Miss. C.L. Rev. 217 (1984).

Knight, W. Nicholas. Shakespeare's Hidden Life: Shakespeare at the Law 1585-1595 (1973).

_____ . Equity in Shakespeare and His Contemporaries, 56 Iowa S. J. Research 67 (1981).

Koffler, Judith S. Capital in Hell: Dante's Lesson of Usury, 32 Rutgers L. Rev. 608 (1979).

_____ . Fleurs du Mal: Literary Stultification in Law, 5 ALSA F. (1981).

_____ . Terror and Mutilation in the Golden Age, 5 Hum. Rts. Q. 116 (1983).

Levinson, S. Law and Literature, 60 Tex. L. Rev. 373 (1982).

Llewellyn, K. On the Good, the True, the Beautiful in Law, 9 U. Chi. L. Rev. 224 (1942).

London, Ephraim. The World of Law: The Law as Literature; The Law in Literature (2 vols. 1960).

Lucifredi, L. A. Manzone e il diritto (1933).

Mahlendorf, U. R. & Tobin, F. J. Legality and Formality in the *Niebelungenlied*, 66 Monatshefte 225 (1974).

Manheim, L. The Law as "Father": An Aspect of the Dickens Pattern, 9 U. Hart. Stud. in Literature 100 (1977).

McIntosh, S. Legal Hermeneutics: A Philosophical Critique, 35 Okla. L. Rev. 1 (1982).

McKeithan, D. M. The Trial of Luigi Capello in *Pudd'nhead Wilson,* in Mark Twain and Other Essays (1958).

Michaels, W. Against Formalism: The Autonomous Text in Legal and Literary Interpretation, 1 Poetics Today 23 (1979).

Papke, D. Law and Literature: A Comment and Bibliography of Secondary Works, 73 Law Libr. J. 421 (1980).

Parker, M. D. H. The Slave of Life: A Study of Shakespeare and the Idea of Justice (1955).

Phillips, Owen Hood. Shakespeare and the Lawyers (1972).

Politzer, H. The Puzzle of Kafka's Prosecuting Attorney, 75 PMLA 432 (1960).

Polk, N. Law in Faulkner's *Sanctuary,* 4 Miss. C.L. Rev. 227 (1984).

Posner, R. A. The Homeric Version of the Minimal State, 90 Ethics 27 (1979).

————————. Law and Literature: A Relation Reargued, 72 Va. L. Rev. 1351 (1986).

Rabinowitz, P. J. The Click of the Spring: The Detective Story as Parallel Structure in Dostoevsky and Faulkner, 76 Modern Philology 355 (1979).

Reinhard, J. R. Setting Adrift in Medieval Law and Literature, 56 PMLA 33 (1941).

Riedel, Frederick Carl. Crime and Punishment in the Old French Romances (1938).

Robinson, M. The Law of the State in Kafka's *The Trial,* 6 ALSA F. 127 (1982).

Saint Germes, Madeleine. Balzac Considere Comme Historien du Droit (1936).

Schoeck, D. and McConica, D. (eds.). A Finding-List of Renaissance Legal Works to 1700, 4 Renaissance and Reformation 2-28, 33-85, 97-126 (1967-1968).

Smith, J. A. Job and the Anguish of the Legal Profession: An Example of the Relationship of Literature, Law and Justice, 32 Rutgers L. Rev. 661 (1979).

————————. The Coming Renaissance in Law and Literature, 7 Md. L.F. 84 (1977).

Smolla, R. Let the Author Beware: The Rejuvenation of the American Law of Libel, 132 U. Pa. L.R. 1-94 (1983).

Snell, S. Phil Stone and William Faulkner: The Lawyer and The Poet, 4 Miss. C.L. Rev. 169 (1982).

Soifer, A. Listening and the Voiceless, 4 Miss. C.L. Rev. 319 (1984).

Stern, J. P. The Law of *The Trial*, in Kuna, On Kafka: A Semi-Centenary Perspective 22-41 (1976).

Staves, S. British Seduced Maidens, 14 Eighteenth-Century Stud. 109 (1980/81).

——————— . Players' Scepters: Fictions of Authority in the Restoration (1979).

Steele, T. The Structure of the Detective Story: Classical or Modern?, 27 Modern Fiction Studies (Winter 1981-1982).

Suretsky, H. Search for a Theory: An Annotated Bibliography of Writing on the Relation of Law to Literature and the Relation of Law to Literature and the Humanities, 32 Rutgers L. Rev. 272 (1979).

Sussman, H. The Court as Text: Inversion, Supplanting, and Derangement in Kafka's *Der Prozess*, 92 PMLA 41 (1977).

Tick, S. Toward Jaggers, 5 Dickens Stud. Ann. 133 (1976).

Touster, S. Law at the Bar of Literature: Some Aspects of Dostoevski and Brecht, 5 ALSA F. 13 (1981).

Weisberg, Richard. The Failure of the Word: The Protagonist as Lawyer in Modern Fiction (1984).

——————— . Law, Literature and Cardozo's Judicial Poetics, 1 Cardozo L. Rev. 283 (1979).

——————— . How Judges Speak: Some Lessons on Adjudication in *Billy Budd, Sailor*, with an Application to Justice Rehnquist, 57 N.Y.U.L. Rev. 1 (1982).

——————— . The Quest for Silence: Faulkner's Lawyer in a Comparative Setting, 4 Miss. C.L. Rev. 193 (1984).

——————— . Text Into Theory: A Literary Approach to the Constitution, 20 Ga. L. Rev. 939 (1986).

Weisberg, R. & Kretschman, K. Wigmore's "Legal Novels" Expanded: A Collaborative Effort, 7 Md. L.F. 94 (1977), *reprinted in* 50 N.Y.S.B.J. 122 (1978).

White, J. B. The Legal Imagination (1973).

——————— . When Words Lose Their Meaning (1984).

——————— . Heracles' Bow (1985).

Wigmore, John H. A List of One Hundred Legal Novels, 17 Ill. L. Rev. 26 (1922).

Wilson, Vivian. "The Law of Libel and the Art of Fiction," 44 Law and Contemp. Prob. 27 (1981).

Wolff, Morris. The Legal Background of Cozzens' The Just and the Unjust, 7 J. Mod. Literature 505 (1979).

——————. Faulkner's Knowledge of the Law, 32 Miss. C.L. Rev. 245 (1984).

Younger, I. On Judicial Opinions Considered as One of the Fine Arts, 51 U. Colo. L. Rev. 341 (1980).

Yunck, J. The Venal Tongue: Lawyers and the Medieval Satirists, 46 Am. B. Assoc. J. 267 (1960).

§10 Symposia on Law and Literature

20 Georgia Law Review (1986). The Constitution and Human Values: the Unfinished Agenda.

4 Mississippi College Law Review (1984). The Law and Southern Literature. Articles by Susan Snell, Richard Weisberg, Robert Ferguson, Joseph Blotner, Henry Louis Gates, Stanley Fish, J. B. White, and others, principally on Faulkner.

5 Human Rights Quarterly (May 1983). Includes essays on "Terror in the Modern World" by Terrence Des Pres, George Gibian, Geoffrey Hartman, Judith Koffler, David Richards, Richard Weisberg, Robert Szulkin, and their respondents.

60 Texas Law Review (March 1982). Includes essays on interpretation by Ronald Dworkin, Stanley Fish, Sanford Levinson, J. B. White, and others.

9 Critical Inquiry (Fall 1982). Includes essays by Ronald Dworkin and Stanley Fish.

6 ALSA Forum (1982). Includes essays on the law in Chaucer, Dickens, Kafka, and so on.

32 Rutgers Law Review (1979). Includes a bibliographical piece, essays on interpretation and on the law in Balzac, Camus, Dante, and the Book of Job.

9 University of Hartford Studies in Literature (1977). Includes essays on semiotics and on the law in Dickens, Manzoni, Solzhenitsyn, and so on.

7 University of Maryland Law Forum (1977). Includes a bibliographical essay, a piece on the law in *Othello* and J. Allen
Smith's "The Coming Renaissance in Law and Literature."
29 Rutgers Law Review (1976). Includes poems by Charles Black,
essays on the law in Camus, Dostoevski, and Joyce, and essays
by J. Allen Smith and Allan Axelrod on the uses of literature
for legal education.

Index